# Nasty Work

# Nasty Work

## Resist Systems, Explore Desire, and Liberate Yourself

ERICKA HART

CROWN
NEW YORK

CROWN

An imprint of the Crown Publishing Group
A division of Penguin Random House LLC
1745 Broadway
New York, NY 10019
crownpublishing.com
penguinrandomhouse.com



Library of Congress Cataloging-in-Publication Data is on file with the publisher.

Hardcover ISBN 978-0-593-49797-5

Ebook ISBN 978-0-593-49798-2

Editor: Chelcee Johns
Editorial assistant: Isabela Alcantara
Production editor: Serena Wang
Text designer: Aubrey Khan
Production manager: Jessica Heim
Copy editor: Carol Burrell
Proofreaders: Andrea Peabbles and Katy Miller

Manufactured in the United States of America

1st Printing

First Edition

The authorized representative in the EU for product safety and compliance is Penguin Random House Ireland, Morrison Chambers, 32 Nassau Street, Dublin D02 YH68, Ireland, https://eu-contact.penguin.ie.

To my first love,
my mother, Patti L. Hart

•

To my first teacher,
my father, Ricky R. Hart

•

To my heartbeats,
East Francis and Ebony

•

To the ancestors,
known and unknown

# Contents

# Introduction

> "Most of all, I do not see how men, women and children can grow and live healthy, productive lives in a world where—even if all other forms of racism and Jim Crow have disappeared—the racism of sex still prevails to plague, to distort, and to deprave the human conscience of blacks and whites alike."
>
> —Calvin C. Hernton, *Sex and Racism in America*

> "No one is going to give you the education you need to overthrow them. Nobody is going to teach you your true history, teach you your true heroes, if they know that knowledge will help set you free."
>
> —Assata Shakur

As a descendant of stolen people on stolen land, I'd like to open this book by acknowledging that most of it was written while on Turtle Island (which white settler colonialists renamed North America), specifically on the unceded territory of the Lenni Lenape peoples in what is now called New York City.

I open this book with a land acknowledgment to center the Indigenous peoples of Turtle Island who were forcibly removed from their sacred land via faux treaties, heinous violence, and forced assimilation. This land acknowledgment also includes the Indigenous Africans who were removed from everything that is familiar, involuntarily enslaved, and subjected to unimaginable violence for two hundred fifty years to build what is now known as the United States. As a descendant of chattel slavery and a queer, nonbinary femme, first-time consensual parent, and sex educator, it is of the utmost importance that I begin this book with a land acknowledgment, as I am clear that without the repatriation of the land to Indigenous Americans and reparations to the descendants of chattel slavery, the patterns of violence that subjugate Black and Indigenous peoples in order to "pedestalize" whiteness will continue. Our relationship with our and other people's bodies is inextricably linked to the continued terror of colonialism.

In Western societies, our relationship with sex and sexuality has been fundamentally shaped by historical beliefs that devalued certain people's humanity, justifying their displacement and dispossession of their lands. The Ghanaian concept of Sankofa—"to go back and get it"—teaches us that we cannot create a meaningful future without acknowledging the past. America has a history of cutting off Indigenous ancestral memory through genocide, spiritual warfare, book burnings, and whitewashing history to maintain a dominant narrative. The study of sex and sexuality has not existed outside of a history of colonialism; it has been used as a vehicle for continued colonial violence. The gender binary, sexual violence, homophobia, anti-Black racism, transmisogynoir, and patriarchy function as instruments of colonial power—not only dispossessing people from their lands but also severing their connections to culture, language, and ancestral lineage and forcing us into limited descriptors that serve no one but the dominant class.

Acknowledging stolen land honors the rightful owners of said land and the Indigenous American ancestors who were forcibly removed and who also fought back. Land acknowledgments should incite resistance, not stagnancy. As Assata Shakur says in her book *Assata: An Autobiography*, "theory without practice is just as incomplete as practice without theory. The two have to go together." If I steal something from you and, instead of giving it back, keep it and just agree to tell everyone that I will acknowledge that I stole it, I am now just a gaslighting thief.

To be clear, it is not the labor of Black and other marginalized groups to return the land to Indigenous Americans; that work rests on white people's shoulders. It is our job, however, to not halt or uphold systems that would impede those efforts. I know that may be hard for white people to grasp, and I won't be holding their hand through it. Our society is organized around white people's feelings; their guilt, anger, or otherwise is situated above the harm their impulse for domination has caused. If simply acknowledging stolen land makes you uncomfortable, consider how your comfort is hinged upon theft, sexual violence, and erasure. My hope is that this land acknowledgment propels the reader to take actions to have the land returned and to consider the ways in which bodily autonomy is removed and justified, especially in a country where colonialism is celebrated in many ways, rather than condemned.

Over the last fifteen years as a sex educator, I have talked to thousands of people about sexuality, gender, sex, relationships, body image, fatphobia, and more. What I've consistently discovered is genuine shock when highlighting how colonialism directly permeates all these topics. In many ways, discussions about sex will present how the world demands our identities remain fixed, follow predictable linear paths, and conform to narrow, prescribed appearances, but rarely is it linked back to the source.

Sex is discussed as if it should be a reprieve from having to think about systems of oppression. But that couldn't be further from the truth, not if we want to experience true freedom in how we love, show intimacy, and explore desire. Radical movements have been diluted with slogans like "love is love." Yet love is never just love under a white supremacist capitalist transmisogynistic police state (thank you, bell hooks!). It is not possible to talk about love, sex, desire, gender, sexuality, and relationships without investigating how structures of oppression are present in them. That's a bit of the work we'll do here.

*Nasty Work* deliberately exposes how structures of oppression are in bed with (pun intended) our interpretations and understandings of love, sex, desire, relationships, sexuality, and body image. The title is a play on words, using African American English (AAE) or Ebonics. Due to the proliferation and melding of various Black American subcultures, who are becoming ever more aware of subregional dialect and lexicon given AAE's widespread use (and co-optation) on the internet, especially social media, it is hard to pinpoint the exact origins of the term within the Black community (likely the Northeast, and New York more specifically). Calling something "nasty" or "mean" to denote it being good, skilled, positive, etc. likely can be attributed to Black ballroom communities, but as we will discuss more in depth in this text, with Black queerness being so intrinsic to Black culture as a whole and Black queer and trans people often being major progenitors of said culture, it is difficult to trace the etymologies of this term (luckily, this is not a linguistics text, so forgive any oversight!). The phrase "nasty work" is an adjective that describes the intricacies of a situation, moment in time, or an individual's actions being deplorable without being detailed; two words reveal the world of the issue. Here, *Nasty Work* is a double entendre: "nasty" being a placeholder for the realm of sex or pleasure; the "work" in question being done by state/systems of oppression in keeping us bound to inherited parochial beliefs about sex, even the belief that some people are, indeed, "nasty" (morally, pejoratively, etc.); and at the same time, the "work" we as people will all have to undertake regarding our and others' bodies, what we think of them, what we do to them. *Nasty Work* is as much of an interrogation as it is an exposé on the ways white supremacy shows up in our most intimate capacities. This book rages against the idea that anti-Blackness is a footnote or afterthought to our discussions about everything under the sex and sexuality sun but instead highlights its leading role. As you read, take heed to the words of Audre Lorde, Black lesbian poet activist and writer—"The personal is political"—and situate your own stories and experiences throughout the chapters. You'll begin, or continue, your own interrogation of how these various systems show up in your personal lives and how that work brings us toward a more equitable world.

Less "orgasms are liberation," and more "we can have *better* orgasms (if that is what we want) in a world that is not grounded in anti-Blackness, capitalistic greed, houselessness and food insecurity." *Nasty Work* is an inquiry. How do Black people and other marginalized groups relate to their bodies when everything that is familiar to their culture and objectively theirs has been taken? What is the impact on our relationships when we are taught that conflict should be handled with carcerality? How are desire and attraction informed by white supremacy? What is pleasure like if you have been living in a place that has been intentionally stripped of hospitals, grocery stores, clean air, and transportation? What has been the impact on pleasure in neighborhoods that are systemically neglected and overpoliced? What has been the impact on Indigenous peoples and their relationship to their bodies considering whole communities, languages, and histories have had to survive extermination? What is the relationship to consent for the colonized?

Typically, my students will ask me, "Okay, so, what is the answer or the solution to these questions?" The question is asked in good faith, but our reluctance to *sit* with our feelings, which can oftentimes be uncomfortable, is also an impact of white supremacy. Capitalism demands that we be constantly producing; rarely is the *process* valued. My hope in writing this book is that you take time to process as an act against the state. The stories and experiences shared here happened to real people—so, rather than rushing to a solution, how can you be a witness or center your feelings? You might certainly come to a level of resolve to decolonize your love life, but furthermore, if you truly do the interrogation and listening here, I believe you'll move through the world with more empathy, more awareness, and more freedom.

In *Nasty Work*, we examine society's anti-Black, capitalistic, transmisogynistic, and ableist views on sex and pleasure throughout history and offer a candid and intersectional inquiry as to how we must reclaim our pleasure.

So often, books exploring sex and sexuality speak first to a white, cisgender, and heterosexual audience as a way to reinforce these identities as the norm, but sex and sexuality have always been expansive and experienced by so many beyond cis heterosexuality; and not enough books center trans, disabled, queer, and Black people's experiences of sex and sexuality.

As a disabled Black queer nonbinary femme, my life has been a testament to this work. Using my own story, cultural history, and observations from my classrooms, we'll pull back the layers to reveal how systems of oppression, such as gentrification, white supremacy, transphobia, and capitalism, limit overall access, and understanding, of pleasure.

In each chapter, we'll explore an aspect of sexuality and pleasure, such as what is considered normal and who controls that narrative; how and why we pedestalize romantic relationships; America's history of consent or the lack thereof; the de-sexualization of disabled and chronically ill bodies; how reality TV dating shows inform the anti-Black roots and realities of desirability; and the detrimental role that transphobia, specifically transmisogynoir, plays on how we view gender and sexuality.

Our ideas of pleasure and attraction are not rooted in our free will but in millennia of programming. Sexual liberation is inextricably linked to the freedom of all oppressed peoples and an active deconditioning/unlearning of sexuality, gender, and relationships as breeding grounds for anti-Blackness and, more broadly, as sources of hegemonic power over others—but instead, seeing these as a clearer means of empowering yourself and community against hegemonic power.

Throughout this book, you will notice that I only make distinctions between trans and cisgender if necessary to clarify. If I am talking about women, that means anyone who identifies as a woman and those who are perceived as such. I do not constantly make a distinction between the two, because trans women are women, I do this intentionally so that our usage of the very limited English language can attempt to reflect the varied and vast expansiveness of gender identity and expression. It is important to note that some people do not identify as women but are nonetheless perceived as women, so as to not erase the injustices that people of various marginalized genders (including agender folks) experience; throughout this book you will see me use "perceived as" to account for the innumerable ways people can identify their gender or eschew gender altogether despite public (often binary) perception.

• • •

If you're wondering, "No shade, but when will we get to the sex part?"—well, this *is* the sex part, the part to which the mainstream, white-led discipline of human sexuality has devoted little regard, research, or funding. Lots of folks would agree we live in a sex-obsessed society, yet people do not readily connect sex and sexuality to matters of sociopolitical import. Conventional histories of sex education typically begin with ancient Greece and crescendo with the sexual revolution of the 1960s–1970s, rarely acknowledging how early explorations of the clitoris, masturbation, and sexually transmitted infections developed alongside racist assumptions about Black bodies.

In *Becoming Human: Matter and Meaning in an Antiblack World*, Zakiyyah Iman Jackson writes, "Gendered and sexual discourses on 'the African' are inextricable from those pertaining to reason, historicity and civilization, as purported observations of gender and sexuality were frequently used to provide 'evidence' of the inherent abject quality of black people's human animality from the earliest days of the invention of 'the human.'"

For example, sex education was first implemented at the federal level during World War II to encourage family planning and to prevent the spread of disease among white cisgender men, after an influx of servicemembers returned from active duty with sexually transmitted infections. Paradoxically at this same time, the Tuskegee Syphilis Experiment (1932–1972) conducted by the United States Public Health Service, the Center for Disease Control and Prevention (CDC), and Tuskegee University, intentionally left three hundred Black poor sharecroppers in Macon County, Georgia, with untreated syphilis, resulting in permanent neurological changes, blindness, and the spread of the disease to their children and sexual partners within the community. Although studies had determined that penicillin was effective in the treatment of syphilis, Black people were still kept from necessary treatment for forty years.

A professor in my graduate course on the history of sex once informed the class that "there is not much history about sex in Africa," prompting me to dedicate my life's work to honoring the individuals, both named and unnamed, who have made significant contributions to the field of sex education, consensually and nonconsensually. This class would have been the perfect opportunity to honor the life of Saartjie Baartman or to highlight the fact that Indigenous Africans did not practice the gender binary, but rather had it imposed through colonization. Most discourse around sex history begins in the 1800s, when white doctors diagnosed upper-class white women with hysteria if they had no interest in having children.

This history is further oversimplified by discussing the history of the Magic Wand, one of the first (and greatest, might I add) vibrators. Doctors would use early versions of a Magic Wand to stimulate orgasm as a cure for hysteria. But what is rarely talked about is the fact that this was not just seen as a disease because white women did not want to have children, but also because they were seen to be contributing to the age-old concern that white people would be replaced, according to Laura Briggs's book *The Race of Hysteria*. Upper-class white women who did not want to have children were seen as "overcivilized"; their access to education was seen as a barrier to convincing them that they should have no bodily autonomy. Black women, and those gendered as such, were not diagnosed with hysteria, as they were seen as subhuman; their access to bodily autonomy was not even remotely considered, as their bodies were used like cattle for the purposes of maintaining slavery.

By not including this history as a part of sex education and thus not giving the people whose bodies nonconsensually contributed to this field their credit and acknowledgment, sex ed normalizes the mistreatment and degradation of Black and non-Black communities of color. There is a distorted worldview that makes white people and Europe the center, the starting place for civilization. Society today often treats the descendants of conquests as a community undeserving of love and care. How do privileged classes view sex and sexuality? What is the sexual psyche of those deemed powerful in dominator culture? The next time you see a white person being named as sexually liberated, consider who never gets that title, whose sexual expression is supposed to be consumed.

As Ruth Wilson Gilmore, racial capitalism scholar and activist, states, "race is a space-based concept." Black people were preyed upon by the pseudoscientific progenitors of race that used sex and gender to make Black people appear deviant to perpetuate purity for white people. White colonizers created imaginary lines of separation before the physical lines that would lead to slicing up the continent of Africa into pie pieces that they would pilfer from, leaving Indigenous Africans with crumbs.

White people's presumptions, assumptions, and cultural attitudes about Black bodies were there from the inception of sexuality education; the field stood little chance of being a stalwart against racism but rather proved to be a powerful tool in reinforcing it. Furthermore, it is deeply telling that in the study of sexuality, Tuskegee's forty years of harm toward Black people is hardly discussed.

People will go into the field of sex and sexuality thinking that they are revolutionaries simply because they feel free discussing a taboo topic. Sex ed has become yet another space for white people to pathologize Black people, to nervously laugh at how incestuous Sigmund Freud's theories were or how Michael Foucault shouldn't be "canceled" for his alleged sexual abuse of Tunisian children, while revering the work of Masters and Johnson, Kinsey, Betty Dodson, and Dr. Ruth. Only recently has there been a push to politicize a white-dominated field.

• • •

Many have been perfectly content making assertions about sex and sexuality in the absence of race, gender expansiveness, and class analysis. A complete departure, this book will delve into how our personal and political ideals from the dominant mainstream society inform our viewpoints around sex and sexuality, touching each living person in this world and in, as the focus of this book, the so-called United States—from the metropolitan centers and the coastal cities of the South and to the farthest reaches of Appalachia.

How have our desires been, in large part, preselected by the society under which we live, are molded by, and are forced to contend with? Whether we know it or not, or agree with it or not, we are using 400-year-old inherited thoughts and belief systems to determine how we treat ourselves and one another in the twenty-first century. We don't drive the same cars we used to in the 1940s, so why are we still carrying forth these ancient parochial values that have never served the vast majority of their adherents? Well, how we relate to our and others' bodies is a product of being brought up in a white supremacist capitalist patriarchal police state; a state that is the intentional product of colonization has bred a culturally accepted or almost naturalized othering that undergirds most social interactions inside and outside of the bedroom. We must see white supremacy as the only unnatural, nonnormative aspect in all our lives, not our inherent diversity that exists naturally among all living beings.

Sex strikes people as ancillary to the larger, seemingly more numerous societal ills and issues facing humanity today. Land and bodies alike have been colonized, and that control is built on the desired dominance of white, cisgender, heterosexual, able-bodied people. In this book, I assert that sex is not a separate consideration relegated to the remote annals of our private lives behind closed doors or this hot-button social media pop-cultural cabaret—all whips, floggers, dildos, and Magic Wands (a few of my favorite things)—but an exploration of how we name intimacy for ourselves free of systems that inherently keep us *from* intimacy. There's a tendency to think that sex education is a space of levity, naturally radical because we yell "penis" and "vagina." That we don't need to talk about race, because we're talking about fucking—and that couldn't be further from the truth. Race, gender, class, and ability are in everything, especially your love and sex life.

# 1

# Resist Normalcy

"Whiteness is not really a color at all, but a set of power relations."

—Charles W. Mills,
*The Racial Contract*

"Early twentieth-century sex education existed to convince students of the natural, apolitical connection between sexual self-restraint, an erotic ethic of monogamy in marriage, and the strength of white civilization."

—Julian B. Carter, *The Heart of Whiteness: Normal Sexuality and Race in America, 1880–1940*

As a sex educator, I often hesitate to divulge my profession to new people, as every time I do, someone is ready to share their most intimate concerns with me on some Janet Jackson "Anytime, Anywhere" tip: at home with the plumber, in the middle of the grocery store, and the security line at the airport after the TSA agent searched my carry-on only to come upon a treasure trove of essential "adult novelties." In over a decade of teaching sex ed at the elementary, secondary, and collegiate levels, the questions I field range from the rather innocuous but wondered earnestly by the darndest third graders among us, "How did people even come up with sex?" to the high school students who ask, "How do lesbians have sex?" or the young adult who's nervous to try anal for the first time, "What if I poop during anal?" or the political, "As a white person, if I am attracted to Black people, does that mean I am fetishizing them?" The common theme seems to be an overwhelming hope that I will affirm their concerns as "normal." The yearning for normalcy is so pervasive that the question will usually begin with, "Is it normal to . . . ?" Is it normal if I do not orgasm? Is it normal if I am attracted to the same gender if I'm straight? Is it normal if I don't want to have sex at all? Is it normal to masturbate every day? Is it normal to not be interested in penetration? Is it normal to watch porn every day? These questions reveal to me a profound insecurity that seems to be at the root of all of them: Am I normal?

Adults and children alike are forced to subscribe to this fake notion of normalcy rooted in what bell hooks coined "white supremacist capitalist patriarchy," a complex of Western power relations that all work to reify the domination of white cisgender heterosexual men's domination. Such a system has us all believing that there is only one type of person we should desire (or desire to be) and only one way to engage in sex/pleasure. It enforces the belief that our genders and sexualities are congruent and that our bodies should all look and function the same. This conditioning emphasizes obedience and inhibits self-expression in favor of mechanized thinking and being which may bode well for a socially conservative political agenda to control the masses by the ruling class but is inconsistent with how humans actually behave.

Our desires and fantasies are often shaped not by our own imagination but rather by millenia of continued colonial violence which has created mores that privilege the colonizer as the standard bearer of "normalcy" within sex and sexuality and the colonized as perpetually transgressive of it, reinforcing a complex of power structures that keeps us from forming our own identities. As author Siobhan B. Somerville points out in *Queering the Color*

*Line*, citing Nancy Stepan, Londa Schiebinger, and Sander Gilman, "any attempt to establish that the races were inherently different rested to no little extent on the sexual difference of the Black." Somerville takes this a step further, asserting that these differences were emphasized through gender. Scientists went as far to suggest that Black people with vaginas had larger clitorises and as such were inherently sexually promiscuous as a result. Although these particular falsehoods were blatantly promulgated from the early 1800s to the mid-1920s and plenty of evidence has been formed to the contrary, Black women and those gendered as such across the diaspora continue to find themselves in the crosshairs of the white sexual imagination, seen as hypersexual regardless of what they are wearing or how they present.

Prior to college, I certainly did not understand the implications of how people related to my body, but the absence of such knowledge would not keep me from being swept up by its wrath. Indoctrination into white colonial thought begins young, and even toys are employed toward this aim. Mattel intentionally taught me whose body, hair, skin, and eye and lip shape were superior. I used my Barbies to perform what I thought adults did—they'd drive to the beach, go for walks, and when nobody was watching, I'd strip Ken and Barbie and smack their plastic bodies together to mimic sex, or at least what I imagined sex to be. My parents were constantly managing what media I consumed, constantly in an uphill battle to keep me from seeing sexual content. My Dad would even try to protect me from the messaging Mattel delivered via Barbie. "That's not the texture of Black people's hair. That Barbie is just a white doll that they slapped Black paint on." I'd get defensive, not wanting my pipe dreams of matching Barbie's hair texture and features to be thwarted.

My parents could put their hands over my eyes whenever a sexually explicit scene came on TV, but that did not prevent me from eventually seeing all that they were trying to shield me from. At a very young age, we start to receive messaging around what is normal, and we begin to walk a tightrope to stay within its arbitrary confines—"normal" being synonymous with anything that is in proximity to a white, cisgender, heterosexual, wealthy, thin, able-bodied identity.

Believing that there is a normal and thus a right way to experience desire and pleasure, view our bodies, and express gender or sexuality can be incredibly detrimental to the development of our own individual sexuality, free from the white colonial imaginary. With very little input, I had built enough context clues to simulate what I imagined sex to be with Barbie and Ken: a man smacking his body against a woman, while the woman just lies there and receives whatever the man is doing. A main objective for many sex educators is to undo the inherited notions of normalcy formed long before we even know what sex really is, but while talking about the intersection of sex and colonialism is usually reserved for a collegiate level course, that still does not lessen the impact of not being able to see the connection or its erasure in everyday life, including our most formative years.

I have talked to countless people and have been listening to my friends' concerns that all circle around the same issue of using their body in service to someone else's needs when that isn't necessarily what they want at the moment. How do I tell my husband no to sex; shouldn't we just be having it anyway? Is there something wrong with me if I have not healed from sexual trauma? Or I'm unhappy at my job, am overworked, underpaid, but don't feel I can leave—what do I do? These questions not only challenge and push up against embedded notions of normalcy but are also rooted in race and gender. If we each look back on our origin stories, we may uncover how some of this early processing began.

• • •

My family and I lived in the middle of a cul-de-sac in Severn, Maryland, a neighborhood full of white middle-class folks that fled Baltimore to create a whites-only haven forty-five minutes away. White flight is rooted in an impulse to flee from the potential of having to interact with a Black person; or worse in their eyes, a poor Black person. Their isolation was disrupted by a growing Black middle class who also moved to the suburbs, Toni Braxton's family included. However, we were the only Black family on Clearfield Circle. I was forbidden to wander beyond my street as a kid, so it wouldn't be until I got older that I learned other Black families also lived in the neighborhood, just a street over.

So many wildlife habitats were destroyed to erect a swath of three-bedroom, two-bath houses for these families to maintain the illusion of a middle class, grinding nine to five (and sometimes like my parents, an additional part-time job) in various fields to afford aboveground pools, two cars, the latest game systems, and ever-increasing electricity bills. Our backyard was full of massive pine trees, American holly, and eastern cedar trees that seemed to go on forever. Those trees witnessed many performances of SWV's "Weak" and Salt-N-Pepa's "Shoop" starring one Black kid and her two white neighbors, and solo covers of Tevin Campbell and Whitney Houston. I would spend hours in the woods, picking pokeweed berries that would bleed all over my hands as I pulled them from their vine, wearing flowy outfits my mom bought from Burlington Coat Factory (intended for church, not the woods), transported to some other world in my imagination.

I didn't realize this as a kid, but that freedom I had to frolic in the woods was healing ancestral wounds, a place where my ancestors bravely fled captivity, where their blood permanently became a part of the soil when their bodies were the strange fruit hanging from the trees. I felt held in the woods, surrounded by trees that were larger than life, protected from the sun's rays by branches, listening to chipmunks scatter the leaves or a flock of birds flying freely; my presence wasn't questioned or unwelcome. I didn't have the language for this as a kid, so I created playful worlds in my head, in which my home was the woods. My imagination would be my salvation and balm, buoying me within the moments of life that required escape. White supremacy is threatened by imagination; staying connected to imagination is always troubling to a system whose modus operandi is control. The feeling of safety and comfort I felt alone in the woods would quickly dissipate when I left.

"You are never going to be able to wear skirts." My mother fussed at my ten-year-old self, speaking directly to the cut on my leg. The blood dripped down my leg, forming its own path, outlining the other scabs and bruises. I stood there quietly, knowing that if I engaged, it would take longer to get back outside to beat the "mean boys" to the top of the tree we were about to climb. "And how'd you get this one?" I shrugged my shoulders, and she shook her head in dissatisfaction.

I have to be honest: I come from vain people. My mother was a Leo, need I say more? She was the epitome of Black femininity. Black women are in fact the blueprint for femininity, although in the creation of gender they were used as the basis for what not to be. Contradictions of the gender binary lie in femininity being reserved for white women, but white women consuming everything Black women do. (More on that in Chapter 6.) She'd spend hours in the hair salon, even though she sported a low-maintenance pixie cut. She smelled like cocoa butter, vanilla, and Nag Champa incense. Even when chemotherapy took all of her hair, she wore scarves around her neck in fear that, without it, she would be mistaken for a man. I don't think I ever saw my mother wear pants or jeans outside of the house; she was always in a skirt or a dress. Everywhere we went, she was complimented. My legs are just like my mom's: a mix of clearly defined muscles, fat, and small ankles. At my Uncle Marty's wedding, she wore a dress that showed her legs, and as she walked down the aisle, guests affectionately yelled, "Come on, legs!" In this society, there is a high premium placed on girls/women being seen as desirable. I would argue femininity has not only been reserved for white women but also proximity to Eurocentric beauty standards. I think subconsciously—or even consciously—she wanted me to be seen as attractive, too, and did not want anything to tamper with that.

The "mean boys" were a group of prepubescent white boys that would have been considered a gang if they were Black. They were a bit older than the rest of us, and although we all lived on the same block, they only hung out with each other. Their main goal was to terrorize the rest of the neighborhood, mainly the girls of the neighborhood. We called them the "mean boys" so often that I cannot recall their names. They lived in the round part of the cul-de-sac, and their lives seemed separate from those of the families at the mouth. On walks, my family spoke to everyone leading up to the circle. When we got to that part, I could hear the suburban hum, lawnmowers, airplanes slowly flying overhead, and the breeze kicking freshly raked leaves across the pavement. "I don't want you playing over here," my mother would say. Because those parents barely came outside to speak to us, she worried that they could be anti-Black. White racist people are rarely holding pitchforks and Confederate flags. As Black people, we have had to identify context clues to decipher who is safe and who is not. My parents, especially my mom, erred on the side of caution, believing that if a white person spoke to us it meant that they were "safe" still keeping her guard up as far too often "niceness" is also used as a cover up to impending racism.

Her intuition was not leading her the wrong way. We were divided like the Mason-Dixon Line separates the North from the South. I was operating under the naive premise that these "mean boys" wanted to beat me at climbing a tree or a bike race; instead, they were out to prove that they were better than me any way they could; their whole sense of self, or that they even had a "self," depended on it. As if they could not (or would not want to be) a person if I was one too.

My mom placed the Band-Aid on my leg, and before she could get the adhesive to attach to my skin, I was out the door, running down the street so as not to miss a thing. A Sagittarius's FOMO begins early. Everyone was waiting for me at the bottom of the tree, and when they saw me running in the distance, I could hear them say, "Okay, she's back."

This tree was situated between two transmission utility lines in an open field. You could see marks on its trunk from the years of sneakers. I had memorized this tree's branches. Having climbed it so many times, I knew which branches were sturdy and which to avoid. I held my breath as I climbed to the top, the new Band-Aid stretching to its limit. "I win," I shouted, nearly out of breath as I looked down on the "mean boys" still trying to make their way up. They looked up at me with disappointment and shifted their bodies to climb down, their feet hitting the dried-up grass likely damaged by the volts of electricity surging between the power lines. "You cheated, nigger," one of the boys said under his breath, head down as if he knew it was wrong but still wanted me to hear it.

I had only recently learned about the n-slur. My family had watched a movie about Ruby Bridges, and I had heard this word among the insults that were hurled at her, the nooses white adults put around their necks and threatened her with, all as she walked into school, the first Black child to desegregate not just her New Orleans elementary school but all US schools. It made my skin crawl with rage. Protestors held signs created from pure evil, displaying images such as a Black doll in a coffin, images that Bridges has said haunted her for most of her life. The movie was in black and white to lend the impression that racism was a thing of the past, but I was learning firsthand that was a fallacy. "I didn't cheat, you loser!" I shouted, fighting back tears. Tears are always the first thing that comes up for me, my nervous system exactly as it should, but emotions are seen as weakness under white supremacy. Even now, writing this down, my impulse is to critique my response to his violence: "Loser" is the best you could come up with? Society has gaslit me to believe that my response to harm is what needs fixing, not the harm itself.

"Come on, Ericka, don't fight; they aren't worth it," said my best friend, Leah, as I made my way down the tree; Leah was my first friend, nextdoor neighbor, a white girl who shares my birthday. My mom affectionately called her my "soul sister." Black and non-Black people of color (NBPOC) have mastered making nice with white people, a fear-based tactic. Leah would slide into my DMs on Instagram some twenty years later to apologize for not having my back and making fun of me when we were growing up. It didn't matter that I was her soul sister, I was still Black.

I would be called a nigger while living on this cul-de-sac more times than I could count, both directly and indirectly; a white person knows how to treat you like a nigger without needing to say the word. Can I pinpoint these instances of being called the n-slur as the precise moments when my molecules began to rearrange, when I started to see myself as "other," as not "normal"? It's not that easy. Leah would often ask me why my hair stood up on my head rather than cascading down into thin, bouncy blond curls like hers, why my nose was big, why my lips were full, and why my belly button was an outie. A belly button is not racialized, but it is a part of my body, and she was keen on pointing out every way in which I was different from her. By the age of ten, my bathroom mirror collected my most vulnerable questions: What's wrong with me? Why doesn't my hair move like theirs? Why do they call me a nigger?

I put tape over my belly button and prayed that it would become an innie. "Look, Leah! It's normal now." I lifted my Winnie-the-Pooh T-shirt to show her, hoping for her approval. I'd go on to spend so much of my life searching for white people's approval, searching for my own sense of normalcy.

Having been taught that racism was a thing of the past, at the time I could not see how it was also showing up in the open fields of my cul-de-sac.

And on my body.

I hear many people say, "You have to love yourself before you love anyone else." But what does that really mean? An assumption that a person does not love themselves is often automatically applied to those who are not seen as conventionally attractive.

Changing your body to fit more in line with conventional beauty standards—can be perceived as loving yourself, even when that behavior can reveal the exact opposite.

The quest for "normalcy" as it relates to sex and sexuality is deeply rooted in anti-Black, transphobic, classist, and ableist structures. This might be hard for some readers to swallow, given that the ubiquitous notion of "normalcy" haunts us across age, gender, class, and racial lines. Its definitions are subjective, broad, and evasive. It is difficult to even determine precisely what "normal" is, and yet we are all squeezed beneath this ever-present peer pressure of "everyone's doing it" or "everyone looks this way so I should too." Its definition unwritten, the specter of "normal" is almost made more powerful by the insecurity of not knowing. For those of us who fall short of meeting this nebulous but incredibly influential standard, there is no shortage of adherents—true believers who will torment us with their enforcement of it.

For this reason, sex and sexuality are perfect avenues of control, which is why religious institutions, media, educational and political systems all have a vested interest in how we fuck (or not), love, express our gender, and wield our bodies. You don't need a course on what is "normal" sexually, it is embedded in the fabric of our society by the privileging of certain identities and behaviors over others. Said another way, you don't question how many partners you have had, your sexuality, the color of your skin, or use of an assisted mobility device until you see it made fun of in a popular film or never mentioned even in a rudimentary sex ed class. More significantly, how far or near we fall to the white European beauty metric, as in how "hot" we are according to it, determines not only how we live (or die) but whether or not we are valuable enough to be seen at all, this reserved only for those deemed the "hottest" while the societal desexualization of disabled bodies or folks living with chronic illness continues to pose state-sanctioned barriers to pleasure, especially for Black and non-Black people of color living with chronic illness/disability, navigating medical racism, and lacking of focus on sexuality and intimacy in treatment options for various conditions. After all, it's no coincidence that in almost unbelievable yet pointedly colloquial fashion, the White House official government website, quoting President Donald Trump in a speech disavowing "wokeness" and a perceived historical overemphasis on "how bad slavery was," declares America as, "the HOTTEST country anywhere in the world."

The field of sex education relates to racism insidiously, like the auntie you only speak to occasionally so you don't feel guilty for ignoring their comments on all your Facebook posts. In the classroom, a cursory (but solemn) land acknowledgment here and there, a footnote in a book or presentation apprising, "Experiences may differ based on race and gender." This may be where the conversation about racism begins and ends, no different from many other fields of study in the United States school system. Sex education is often viewed as a safer space to discuss your deepest, darkest fantasies and fetishes—just not race, that's not included in the steamy details. As a Black, queer, nonbinary femme professor in overwhelmingly white academic spaces, regardless of what I am talking about, the "angry Black woman" trope/presumption lurks in the ether before I even open my mouth. I could be delivering a speech on the vulva (recall that pseudoscientists falsely linked large clitoral sizes solely to Black people) and, inevitably, someone will be peeved at me that their anatomy lesson contained the mere mention of race; peeved at me, and not Aristotle, whose proto-racist defenses of slavery in antiquity would pave the way for a slew of white cisgender men who literally made race (and the rest is history—literally!).

Yet, everything *is* about race. And not because I said so, but precisely because people like W. H. Flower, Johann Friedrich Blumenbach—racist pseudoscientists and researchers—along with countless slave traders who lined their pockets with the blood money extracted from unfree labor centuries to come said so. And they went to great lengths (i.e., nonconsensual experimentation on non-white bodies; the largest commercial maritime trade in human flesh in human history; the creation of an entire system of categorization based on eyeballing people's physical features and passing it off as "science" to further legitimize their enterprise, etc.) to prove it. Racism has a massive impact on sex and sexuality. Many people of all races feel less attractive because they lack white skin, blond hair, blue eyes, and a thin, abled body. And this is no coincidence. Still, there will be readers who immediately claim that they never judge themselves or others against the white supremacist, Eurocentric confines of beauty. But there is no way to escape its clutches.

The nomenclature itself, "white," synonymous with/invoking the words clean, blank, pure, unsullied, signifies an un-deviated. A sex education textbook filled with images of only white penises and vulvas sends the message that white people are the normative race, the standard. White people seldom point out when Black, Indigenous, or NBPOC are missing from a given text or lesson. In my teaching experience, unless I bring up the words "race" or "culture," only then will white students question who might be missing from the pages.

In secondary school, conversations about Blackness were reserved for the shortest month of the year. It was in graduate school that I began to see courses on White Studies. As white people sit in various positions of power, they get to dictate the narrative about themselves and everyone else. In mainstream media, white people are conveniently cast as harbingers of civilization, "pioneers" of industry, smarter, better looking, stronger, beneficent despite a historical proclivity toward violence and greed. But the prevailing narrative about Black and non-Black people of color is that we are inherently violent, unintelligent, and ugly. This paradigm serves to maintain white people's power, but it's also a trap. White people are impacted by racism, not to the same extent as Black and non-Black people of color, but racism perpetuates the supremacy of a white person who is able-bodied, neurotypical, thin, cisgender, heterosexual, and wealthy, and being held to this impossible and unrealistic standard is harmful to white people as well. It's ironic that white people's creations failed to work for all of them.

. . .

As I grew up, my landscape changed. Tree climbing turned into movie nights, attempting to watch softcore porn through the static blur, and being discreetly dry humped by Delante while our mothers talked upstairs. In middle school, I had all racially Black friends. We'd sit together at round plywood lunch tables eating and laughing. When the bell rang, like clockwork we pulled out our black lip liner and clear gloss and reapplied like we wouldn't be admitted to the next class without it. We would lie and say that we were mixed with Indian or Puerto Rican. We'd all been sold the same lie, that to be attractive you had to be anything but Black. I'd lay my baby hairs, combing every follicle with a damp toothbrush, Blue Magic hair grease, and Ampro Pro

Styling gel. Every product promised that I, too, could achieve the bouncy curls the white girls had or the "good hair" that was guaranteed with a white and Black parent. By the strength of my ancestors, my curls coiled tighter, more formidable than my anti-Black hopes and dreams.

"I want my babies to be mixed," my friends and I would say to each other. We didn't want our kids to hope that they were something other than Black; we just wanted them to be so. Being seen as pretty was (still is) thought of as our biggest currency. Life would be easier if people thought we were pretty, and we would stop at nothing for that. We were Black, and *they* were pretty. So, what could I do to make myself pretty? Discarding my Blackness always seemed like the best option to achieve the standard.

"You have DSLs," Dionne muttered to me. I had asked her what a nearby circle of boys was chuckling about as I passed them in the hallway.

"What are DSLs?" It was actually terrifying to have a large group of teenagers say your name followed by deep belly laughter, the kind of laughter that makes fun of you without any words.

"Dick-sucking lips," she said quickly, like it was a foregone conclusion, like she agreed with them.

My best friend Dionne was a redheaded, thin, light-skinned Black girl. From my middle school vantage point, she had it all. High schoolers wanted to be with her. Everywhere we went, there was someone trying to date her. Most of the time, I acted as her wingperson, managing a roster of suitors. Dionne was phenotypically Black, but some of her features indicated a distant white ancestor. Her dad was light-skinned and had a red beard, so that's how she got her hair coloring.

No one was talking about colorism, texturism, or featurism when we were in middle school, so I looked at everything but skin tone to figure out why I wasn't considered as attractive as her. Her forehead was bigger than mine; maybe that was it? Pretty privilege is normalized to create another binary—pretty vs ugly—to solidify whose body is worthy of love, care, and in many instances, life. Folks who are deemed ugly are encouraged from every direction to fix aspects of themselves to fit the standard that has been normalized by dead racist white men, rather than critique that we have a standard in the first place. Dionne seemed oblivious to her effect on people. Whenever I told her about yet another boy who liked her, she'd always respond the same way: "Really?!" followed by a giddy, self-assured laugh. She never left the house without her hair straightened via a box of relaxer and a flat iron. Her lips were full, but they weren't as big as mine. I'd always wished mine were smaller, ideally to look more like hers. No one talked about Dionne the way they talked about me; she was never made fun of or even teased; people just loved her.

I was twelve years old, forcibly growing out of my tomboy phase (a term only applied to girls who are not acting how the world expects them to act that is always seen as a phase). I conceded to the belief that once I got my period, I needed to dress feminine, wear makeup, and learn how to walk in heels. I was no longer dressing for me, but rather for the male gaze. I knew that people were doing things in the woods in front of our middle school, but I never imagined people were giving head or that I was somehow a candidate to do the same because of how my lips were shaped. This did not make me feel desired or wanted. My Nickelodeon-and-Lifetime education did not depict crushes playing out in this way. In those shows and movies, a note got passed secretly around the classroom that asked if you liked the recipient and to answer by circling yes or no. I had not received a secret note; instead, I got a conversation about my lips sucking dick. A public discourse for everyone to join in on. Being objectified made me feel even more unwanted. I wanted to be seen for more than just my full lips. I'd argue that being seen as one part of our face or bodies is hardly being seen at all. I wanted someone to want all of me. It seemed as though my lips could have been on anyone.

There was focus on my body without any consideration as to how I would feel. The insinuation that my body was only worthy if it produced labor for someone with a penis made me want to downplay those parts of my body. I sought to avoid having anyone ever think about me in this way again. I stopped lining my lips and wouldn't dare wear lipstick for fear that it made my lips appear bigger and drew more attention to them. I carried around confusion as to why people looked at me differently than they looked at Dionne. I thought because Dionne—and every other light-skinned person I knew—had a big forehead, that was why they were seen as prettier than me. My Black features were objectified and hypersexualized; I was made to feel inherently ugly. I was nothing more than an object from which others could extract their own pleasure. I felt like a zoo animal, put in a cage for everyone to gawk and point at.

Today when I reflect on that time in my youth, it's hard not to think about Saartjie Baartman. Baartman was born in South Africa to the Khoikhoi tribe. Scholarly and popular sources differ regarding her birth year, which was likely sometime between the 1770s and 1789. Tragically, when she was fifteen years old, she was sex-trafficked by British Naval Surgeon Alexander Dunlop and lured to London under false promises that she would become wealthy.

She was put on stages for white Europeans' entertainment. They gawked, stared, and threw objects at her. If a spectator had the extra money, they could pay to rape her. During the Victorian era, it was a sign of beauty among white cisgender women to have large butts—dresses were even padded to give the appearance of a larger bottom. On an African person, though, it was a cause for exhibition. In *Fearing the Black Body: The Anti-Black Origins of Fatphobia*, Sabrina Strings writes of Baartman, "her figure was deemed 'very different from the feminine standards of London and its ladies' long, slender, lines' (93). You may have heard her referred to by the now-famous moniker 'Hottentot Venus,' and it's important to note that Samuel Morton, a racist pseudoscientist who drew unsubstantiated and erroneous connections between brain size and intelligence to justify the enslavement of Black people, said that the term 'hottentot' was the nearest approximation to the lower animals." Baartman was kept in cages and forced to perform until she died of alcoholism (allegedly) in 1815.

Even in death, her body was disgraced, ripped apart, with her brain, vulva, and anus preserved, put on display in glass jars by celebrated zoologist Baron Georges Cuvier for the Musée de l'Homme, a museum known for showcasing what at the time would have been referred to as "primitive" art (Picasso studied their collections often). Her body would remain on display in France until, following years of advocacy by her family and with the support of Nelson Mandela, it was returned to South Africa in 2002 (yes, you read that correctly).

The hypersexualization and proverbial pulling apart of Black women's bodies has not ended. Literary critic and scholar Hortense Spillers writes that "Black women are the beached whales of the sexual universe, unvoiced, mis-seen, not doing, awaiting their verb." In middle school, I was just a child but already felt like a sort of orca calf clinging to life along the vast shore of the inherited, often outdated mores, discourse, and attitudes of the sexual universe Spillers describes, wondering what was to be my body's fate. Spillers notes that Black femmes are "awaiting their verb." My lips were not being complimented for their shape or how full they were; they were relegated to what they could do for someone else, how they could verb.

The hypersexualization of Black women does not begin during adulthood. Those who experience Black girlhood (regardless of sex assignment at birth) are subjected to all imaginable assertions about their bodies, including what they should and should not do with them, before they even develop the language to rebuke said assertions. I learned early that my body did not belong to me; it was a spectacle for the world's scrutiny. Who I was as a person did not matter: I needed to use my dick-sucking lips in service of the well-formed racialized fantasies of teenage boys, who were likely taught that their self-worth was dependent on an imagined masculinity that required them to conform to a white male standard of power—a power over people who looked like me, in the face of powerlessness in a white-dominated world they themselves could not exist in safely. If that sentence was exhausting to read, imagine how exhausting it is to live through.

When colorism, featurism, and texturism entered my lexicon in undergrad, my understanding of these systems was that they only impact those who were seen as conventionally attractive. Only later did I understand more deeply; they impact how people are treated, what rights we have access to, and who is punished more harshly for crimes. This is more than a like or dislike of dark-skinned individuals; it is a global, thousands-year-old structure that can be seen across the diaspora. As a brown-skinned person with phenotypically Black features, I do not have the same disadvantages of those who are darker than me, nor the advantages of those who are lighter than me. I sit in the in-between of a harmful binary that requires me to acknowledge my privilege, to not take up space in an experience that is not my own, and also to speak out against the structures that have all of us picking ourselves apart.

When I started reading a deeper analysis of Black history, rarely discussed in schools, I began to see that my experience was not unique to me but rooted in a long history of linking Blackness and hypersexuality. I did not make these connections immediately—history is often told in a way that cements it to the past, so it took me some time to understand that colorism, featurism, and texturism were integral factors during chattel slavery and are still integral to society today. One's role on the plantation depended on looks; those with features and complexions that held proximity to whiteness were given the illusion of more power.

. . .

A century after her death, white researchers W. H. Flower and James Murie would compound Cuvier's theft of Saartjie Baartman's body, using it to build more pseudoscientific evidence that the African bodies with uteri and vulvas were biologically different from those of white Europeans. The racial difference of the African body, implied Flower and Murie, was located in its literal excess, a specifically sexual excess that placed her body outside the boundaries of the "normal female." Flower and Murie were only adding further evidence for what slave traders were doing to the genitals of Indigenous Africans to determine their value. As Jessica Marie Johnson explains in *Wicked Flesh: Black Women, Intimacy, and Freedom in the Atlantic World*, "they measured the reproductive capacity of captives, regardless of sex, by weighing breasts, measuring penises, and inspecting vaginas. Slave traders studied enslaved Africans to predict fertility, health, productivity, and fitness for Atlantic passage."

Further studies would continue by many other sexologists and gynecologists (which were subsequently added to medical journals), studies of elongated and large clitorises, arguing that they were associated with lesbians and Black women and therefore were not "normal." These "findings" suggested a promiscuity that was presumed to be natural to Black women. Johnson continues, "and while seeming to affirm gender, these invasive evaluations actually rejected the human metrics that gender required—intimacy, rites of passage, community and sociality." These studies of genitalia were not only building evidence for legitimizing the gender binary but also asserting an inherent difference between Black and white people.

The United States has not stopped being obsessed with genitals; the zeitgeist is filled with countless magazine articles and media that make jokes about penis size or if someone with a vagina has had any arbitrary number of sexual partners, the belief is that the person is now "loose," although that is not how the vaginal canal works and gives the five inches of an average-size penis entirely too much credit. There is an obsession with asserting who is a woman or a man based on how your genitals look. We have not stopped using the eighteenth-century pseudoscience used to maintain the slave trade as a way to view genitals. As Oyèrónkẹ́ Oyěwùmí notes in *The Invention of Women*, "The idea that biology is destiny—or, better still, destiny is biology has been a staple of Western thought for centuries. Whether the issue is who is who in Aristotle's polis or who is poor in the late twentieth-century United States, the notion that difference and hierarchy in society are biologically determined continues to enjoy credence even among social scientists who purport to explain human society in other genetic terms." The obsession with biology as destiny has informed everything from invasive gender tests to determine who can play sports in the Olympics or on a high school football field to intersex children being mutilated by doctors who were taught to be more concerned about instituting the gender binary than the health and well-being of people. These illogical connections between genitals and identity have been a distraction from the complexity of genitalia. For example, in my classrooms, students are often shocked to learn that the only part of the clitoris that is visible on a vulva is the hood, there is an entire structure that is internal. The first sonogram of the internal clitoris was done in 2008! How much sooner could we have had a sonogram of the cute wishbone-like structure if white cis men were not hitting us over the head with a biological essentialist agenda. The often most shocking revelation is that all of us are anatomically female up until six and half weeks gestation. The clitoris and penis are homologous. Pseudoscientists studied the labia but never thought to look at scrotums that are formed simply from the labia fusing together and forming a sac. The clitoris just like the penis fills with blood and becomes erect. Just like humans, genitals are more alike than they are different, it is socialization and propaganda that perpetuate harmful notions that they are inherently different.

The idea of normalcy has been carefully crafted to center white people, making everyone else a case for experimentation to deduce how they are abnormal because they are not white. We will never know Baartman's gender, favorite color, happy memories, sexuality, crushes, or dreams. All of her complexity was reduced to a pendulum swing between obsolescence and moral outrage, all that mattered was how she was in service to the white gaze.

As long as systems of oppression exist to convince us that we should hate our bodies and strive to be "normal," we will be caught in a web of anti-Blackness. This is not the book that's going to tell you to look in the mirror and say "I love my body" ten times and then all will be well with the world. This is also not a book that's going to pathologize not believing that you are beautiful, when all of us are being bombarded with messaging that directly betrays a belief in our own beauty. I do not have the answers on how to release yourself from the hold anti-Blackness has on all of us or delete the colonizer in your head, but what I do know is that white supremacy does not like to be questioned. So, below are a few questions that I'd like you to ruminate on whenever you find yourself hating the very thing our society says you should hate.

The various ways I have been taught to hate my body were intentionally designed to fill mostly white cisgender heterosexual men's pockets and to ensure their dominance via a multibillion-dollar "beauty" industry. We are so much more than who or what we attract; being desired does not need to be our currency. Acknowledging this has always brought me back to myself. Collectively, we must resist the notions that make us believe that our bodies have failed us because they do not follow the stagnant confines of false dominant narratives, else we end up replicating them.

- What are you hating about your body that is directly linked to anti-Blackness?

- What lies have you been told about your body/genitals that are tied to the conventions of normalcy?
- How can divorcing yourself from hating that part of you be an act of resistance?
- How have you (consciously or subconsciously) colonized your body?
- How can your intention to honor your body on your own terms be supported by your community?

# 2

# "I Got a Text!"

## *Explorations on an Island Without Love*

"Not my type on paper."

—every single *Love Island* contestant

"If I were a man and it was between you and Cindy Crawford, I wouldn't make a stop at you."

—Joan Rivers to Whoopi Goldberg in an early 1990s interview

People love to ask me what I do for self-care, and my answer is always the same: watching either true crime or reality TV dating shows. My acupuncturist suggested I stop watching so much true crime when I told her I was losing sleep due to the constant fear of break-ins. Every night, I would push my very light rattan hamper up against the locked bedroom door to ease my anxiety. Surely if someone tried to open the door, I would be alerted by the hamper moving. Only when I explained this out loud did I see how my love of true crime was disrupting my nervous system. It's not just fear that keeps me up, though; it's also the thrill of watching any kind of reality TV, dating shows in particular. I am not afraid to admit that *Love Island*, *Love Is Blind*, *Married at First Sight*, and *90 Day Fiancé* have been my consistent trash TV go-tos for years.

When my "explore" pages on social media begin repopulating my plant, home decor, and political-organizing content with hot takes about the new set of contestants (also known as Islanders), I know a new season of *Love Island* has begun. If you are unfamiliar, *Love Island* is a reality TV dating show that began in the UK, but there are now twenty-two different versions, including South Africa and the US. The UK version is a classic, and it is one of the UK's most watched shows. The first episode begins with Islanders choosing who they want to "couple up with," a scene which feels reminiscent of white slave owners at the auction block, choosing the most fit enslaved Black person to nonconsensually advance their wealth by expanding and caring for their families. The main difference here is that these people are on this show of their free will, and they are not being tasked with doing labor for someone else. And yet, the measurement of who is most fit is rooted in the same historical desires. The Islanders walk in one by one, greeting each other with excited screams and comments on each other's appearances. As a viewer, you can almost see the contestants' wheels turning as each new person walks in. Women are edited to look nervous and/or envious of the other women, and commentary on each other's looks is meant to be congratulatory with an air of envy. The men are edited to appear to be in competition for the one or two women they have all agreed upon as the most attractive.

Season eleven of *Love Island UK* started at the same time as season six of *Love Island USA*. When I saw the first batch of Islanders in both productions, I was excited to see more than one Black person. The bar for Black people represented in the media is so low, it's practically in hell. Although ITV, the parent company of *Love Island UK*, has received countless requests to diversify the show, they have only taken baby steps toward that effort.

Mimi Ngulube, a tall, dark-skinned, thin Black woman, walked into *Love Island UK* season eleven on the first day. She immediately coupled up with a tall, dark-skinned Black man named Ayo Odukoya. As someone who is inclined to root for everybody Black (thank you, Issa Rae), I am already fully invested. They had the same surface-level, fluffy "getting to know you" type of conversations (or "banter," as they say on the show) as everyone else, but to see two phenotypically Black and dark-skinned people choose each other made me feel hopeful for the season, and perhaps even for a change in our beauty standards. My private thought, which I will now admit publicly, is that I place entirely too much hope (and pressure) on Black contestants on *Love Island* to single-handedly uproot fetishization, texturism, and colorism. My consistent disappointment has not stopped me from watching anyway.

Roughly three or four episodes into the season, a racially ambiguous light-skinned contestant named Uma Jammeh entered the villa. Ayo's head—as they say on *Love Island*—began to "turn." He went on one date with her and decided that he wanted to "stay open." Staying open meant that he wanted to explore things with Uma even though he had been in a couple with Mimi. I watched Mimi's energy shift; she wore sunglasses more often, as though trying to hide her emotions, but she never vocalized or expressed upset about Ayo getting to know Uma. Mimi not expressing herself could be chalked up to being shy, but it also seemed like a strategic way to mask her feelings to not be marked as angry for expressing disappointment or frustration.

Uma began sharing with other contestants that she believed Ayo would choose her over Mimi. During "recouplings," the contestants get to . . . well, recouple, or stay with their original mate. They recite corny speeches as tributes to those they've chosen and melodramatically pause before saying the person's name. During the recoupling where Uma got to choose who she wanted to be with before Mimi had a chance, she chose to be with Ayo, rendering Mimi single. When it was Mimi's turn to choose, seeing a dark-skinned Black person have to pick from a sea of white people who never expressed any interest in her unveiled *Love Island*'s role in perpetuating the harmful trope that Black women are undesirable. I thought this was the end of Mimi's time on the show. I'd seen this same trajectory play out time and again: Black women quickly discarded because they didn't meet the impossible standards of desire inherently stacked against them. But Mimi coupled up with a white contestant and remained on the show. Ayo continued to flirt with Uma and Mimi, claiming that his focus would mostly be on Uma. Uma, on the other hand, told Ayo that he wasn't her usual type but that he had shown the most interest in her. She dodged his attempts at a kiss and recoiled from affection. While absolutely well within her rights, her resistance seemed to reinforce that she had chosen him just because he was interested in her. Uma treated Ayo like a stepping-stone, a means for her to stay on the show and find someone she was genuinely interested in. The dynamic of a contestant using a dark-skinned Black person as a placeholder until they get what they really want is far too familiar.

Ahead of the next recoupling, the focus was on the triangle of Uma, Mimi, and Ayo. When Mimi chose Ayo, Uma was in complete shock. She did not hide her emotions or quietly accept the defeat as Mimi had done before. Instead, she expressed upset in a way that revealed she was likely used to getting her way based on her looks. When Uma found out that Mimi and Ayo kissed in bed after the recoupling, she was furious, interrogating Mimi and Ayo for hiding how they really felt about each other. Uma stated plainly during the exchange that Ayo was "more interested in her" which felt more like a refrain that she was used to hearing from dark-skinned Black cisgender men than the reality of how Ayo felt. Uma being a light-skinned, racially ambiguous Black person, expecting to be chosen over a dark-skinned unambiguous Black woman, is the result of colorism—a form of prejudice that places light-skinned Black people on a pedestal.

Take fifteen seconds. Run through a roster, in your mind, of all the most famous contemporary Black singers: Most of the legends, those once-in-a-generation unimaginable talents, were darker-skinned. The highly commercially successful talents tend to be light-skinned. Jasmine Sullivan is one of my favorite artists of all time, and to me there is no legitimate reason why she is not more popular—other than colorism. Colorism dictates who is seen as violent and thus punished more often, versus who is given more grace, opportunities, and access. Even the legacy of Rosa Parks is *colored* by colorism. Parks is venerated as the tipping point in the Montgomery Bus Boycott, when she refused to move to the back of the bus. However, Claudette Colvin, a dark-skinned fifteen-year-old girl, actually refused to move to the back of the bus in Montgomery and was arrested nine months before Parks, but her activism was overshadowed. Parks, as a lighter-skinned Black person, was placed on a pedestal, and was seen as a more palatable face of the boycott.

People often assume that physical attraction, desire, and appearance don't influence dynamics in social justice and organizing spaces—but these factors shape everything we do. Angela Davis is one of the most well-known Black Panthers. She was formerly incarcerated and still went on to work in prestigious universities as a professor, write several books, and facilitate speaking tours all over the world. Assata Shakur was also a Black Panther, also formerly incarcerated, and although she has an autobiography, she has received no royalties, no speaking tours, no fancy appointments. But she was the first woman to appear on the FBI Most Wanted List. Although the Panthers represented a threat to white dominance, and were shut down by the US government, Davis was able to reinvent her image to be palatable enough for white consumption. A tweet written by "rhymes with balang" tells the story of attending one of Davis's speeches and asking her if she understood that colorism played a role in her being the most visible Black Panther, more than Afeni Shakur and Paula Hill. Davis agreed and said that "no light-skin person is ever doing enough while colorism is a functioning system." In place of the work of undoing colorism, I mostly encounter resistance and denial that colorism exists. Simply telling people with darker skin to "be confident" shifts responsibility away from addressing systemic colorism. Rather than dismantling the structures that link skin tone to professional opportunities, respect, and perceived character, this approach wrongly suggests that individual self-esteem is the solution to deeply rooted discrimination.

Uma ended the drama on *Love Island* by "removing" herself from the triangle, emphasizing that she just wanted to be with someone who knew what he wanted. Ayo seemed upset when Uma removed herself from the narrative, revealing that perhaps he was more interested in her than Mimi. But, since Uma had taken herself out of the equation, Ayo focused on Mimi. They continued getting to know each other, but the question always lingered in the background: Was Ayo really interested in Mimi, or was she just a fallback option for him?

Like most Black contestants on the show, their storyline began to fade into the background, intentionally edited out or not given any screentime as opposed to the storylines of their mediocre white counterparts. Two such paragons of mediocrity were Joey Essex, a well-known UK TV personality, and Sean Stone, a self-identified candy salesman whose cheesiness constantly relegated him to the friend zone. Joey and Sean struggled to maintain their "coupled up" statuses throughout most of the season, and their main functions seemed to be to chastise the Black contestants. ITV received thousands of complaints and accusations of racism after the season ended but dismissed them as normal viewer discord—everyone has their own favorite and least favorite contestants—once again allowing white men to avoid accountability for their harmful actions. Stone's and Essex's fixation on targeting the only dark-skinned Black couple, Mimi and Josh, seemed driven by a need to diminish them in order to validate their own dwindling strategic partnerships in trying to trick the UK into handing them $66,500.

Before filming *Love Island*, producers ask contestants to describe their ideal partner—both in looks and personality—and then they cast other cast members who match these "types." The show functions like a real-life dating app, with contestants constantly discussing and filtering potential matches based on their stated preferences. The question "What's your type?" becomes central to the show's engine, with contestants anxiously hoping someone will arrive who fits their (often quite narrow) criteria.

White contestants often use coded language to describe their "type" without explicitly saying "white"—phrases like "dark and handsome" are meant to indicate Mediterranean features (olive skin, dark hair, brown eyes), not Black people. They've even created an informal hierarchy based on hair color, debating "blondes versus brunettes" as if these are meaningful categories of attraction. Meanwhile, Black contestants appear to be cast as an afterthought, tossed into the villa with limited romantic prospects since the show's implicit assumption is that white contestants will ultimately pair with other white contestants. In all the seasons I have watched, I have never heard anyone describe their "type" as a Black person. When Samira Mighty, *Love Island UK*'s first Black woman contestant, said that her type was "blond hair, blue eyes," social media was in an uproar. The show had finally taken a minuscule step to diversify, but they had cast someone whose romantic interests still centered on whiteness.

People often treat beauty standards as if they're natural or divinely ordained—"beauty is in the eye of the beholder"—invoking Christian ideas of God-given preferences rather than acknowledging them as constructed ideals shaped by historical white male dominance. This isn't divine or arbitrary; it's deeply political. Between 1512 and 1515, German artist Albrecht Dürer helped codify these Eurocentric beauty standards, explicitly writing that "Negro faces are seldom beautiful because of their very flat noses and thick lips." So, while beauty may indeed be "in the eye of the beholder," that beholder has historically been white European men, not a diverse range of cultural or spiritual perspectives. Attractiveness is not casual; it has been used for centuries as yet another form of racial superiority. Reality TV dating shows are acting as adult analogs to Disney movies. As children we watched *Snow White*, *The Little Mermaid*, *Beauty and the Beast*, and *Cinderella*, and all the female protagonists looked similar; even the aesthetics of *Pocahantas* and *Mulan* were crafted within racialized beauty standards. *Love Island* follows the same script.

What the viewer does not see is the rigorous application process before contestants are selected. Weight, age, height, and social media accounts are all evaluated. Casting has noted that they are looking for contestants with large followings and a social media narrative in which they can clearly deduce that the person is single, confident (which is just code for conventionally attractive), and not afraid to wear a bikini or be shirtless on camera. Almost all contestants are conventionally attractive, white or light-skinned, blond hair, blue eyes, thin, thin nose, full lips, high cheekbones, white and straight teeth, young (contestants that are twenty-seven are described as "old"), long hair for women and muscular and tall for men. Every episode contains scenes in which the women are doing their makeup together and montages of the male contestants taking showers with their trunks on—no washcloths, just suds. I always find myself hoping that they eventually take real showers off camera. These scenes reinforce the gender binary in the least subtle of ways: Women wear makeup and do their hair, while men only need a shower. Although contestants wear bathing suits (note: women also wear heels with their bathing suits) during the day, they are expected to get dressed up at night in what Black people have colloquially named "freakum dresses and heels," not much of a departure from the daytime bikinis in terms of coverage.

The beauty industry is worth $625 billion globally, proving that marketing has been effective in having us believe that we need certain products to enhance or hide features. Capitalism and desire go hand in hand: If you can afford to look conventionally attractive with makeup, plastic surgery, and veneers, then you have a shot at being desired. If you cannot afford these things, then you should just be confident and hope for the best. It's not a far stretch from that to the message that poor people should not be desired and having money makes you inherently more attractive. Billionaire white cisgender men will be married to women who are conventionally attractive while they look like the grim reaper. I do not write this as an assault on cosmetics—makeup has allowed gender-expansive folks to exist in the ways that are most affirming to them, and it is also a beautiful art form that is dismissed as frivolous by the patriarchy. I myself can spend hours in a makeup aisle. But I am clear-eyed about the fact that I have given these companies money because they have convinced me that dark spots, pimples, and discoloration should be hidden.

. . .

The lack of Black contestants on *Love Island* isn't simply due to a shortage of applicants—it's calculated casting that perpetuates the message that Black people are undeserving of love, pleasure, and romance. The show systematically sets up white couples for success with multiple compatible dating options and clear paths to the £50,000 prize, while Black contestants are often eliminated after finding no interested partners. This reflects capitalism's fundamental need to create a hierarchy where one group must be diminished for another to be elevated. There's a dark irony in how *Love Island* has commodified "love" itself, attaching a cash prize to relationships that overwhelmingly reward those who conform to European beauty standards and fall in line to colonial scripts of cis-heteronormative relationships.

On dating apps, Black women are often fetishized by users, receiving messages that hypersexualize their bodies and relay an expectation of sexual labor. Dating apps often fail their users in two ways: matching them with people who don't fit their stated preferences or failing to protect them from harassment due to inadequate screening. On apps like Grindr, primarily used by queer men, users frequently express their biases through exclusionary language in their bios—explicitly stating who they don't want ("no fats, no femmes") rather than describing who they *do* want. Fatima Jamal, a trans femme artist and archivist, produced a documentary on these very common descriptors, exposing, yet again, the fatphobic, anti-Black, and patriarchal notions of attraction that are not absent even in queer spaces.

Fat people are completely left out of reality TV dating shows. In all the seasons of *Love Island* that I have watched, there has maybe been one person of size, and I believe they were a US size 12 at most. By not including fat people on any dating show, this plays into the belief that fat bodies are temporary and should always be in a moment of change. Fat bodies have existed since the beginning of time, and everyone is not intended to be thin. As much as I say that in my classrooms, I have so many institutions stacked against me, upholding the belief that fat is wrong. Medical institutions will spend more time judging and assessing someone's body size than running labs. There are more reality shows dedicated to fat people losing weight than dating shows that include fat people, speaking volumes to who society believes is worthy of love and who needs to change in order to receive love.

The idea that thinness is linked to health is a strongly held fallacy directly harming fat folks and perpetuating the notion that everyone should look the same. Between 2022 and 2024, diabetes patients have struggled to access their vital medication, Ozempic, as it's been repurposed and aggressively marketed as a weight-loss drug. Ads and billboards promise "get thin with just one shot." Despite serious side effects like constant nausea and loss of appetite, these health risks are dismissed in pursuit of the ideal body, because the desire to be thin outweighs concerns about physical well-being. I cannot blame individuals for wanting to be thin—fatphobia is a systemic issue, and the rewards for thinness are tangible and compelling. Finding plus-size clothes in most stores is next to impossible, airplane seats are getting smaller, some airlines are requesting people who need seatbelt extenders to bring their own, and the constant media depictions of fat people as lazy and undesirable only further motivate people to be on this constant hamster wheel of grasping for thinness as if it will bring them happiness and joy. Rarely do people consider what they are missing out on when they spend their time looking down at a number on the scale.

Although it is painful to witness, I lose sleep rooting for the Black people who dare to go on these shows, especially the Black women; though their fate is essentially sealed before they even appear on-screen, I still want them to win and find love. The public has opportunities throughout the season to vote for their favorite couple; and this also reflects who people in the UK, the ground zero for colonization, view as worthy of the £50,000 prize. You can take one wild guess who the UK tends to vote for on these shows as the favorable couples: They don't need to do much other than be white. There are many instances when votes will be cast for the "favorite Islander" and Black people consistently rank lower, but they've also been given less screen time. The season 10 winners of *Love Island*, Sammy Root and Jess Harding, hardly displayed much interest in each other until the very end, conveniently when no other options were available. The runners-up were a dark-skinned Nigerian Black woman, Whitney Adebayo, and Lochan Nowacki, who is mixed white and Asian. Whitney and Lochan displayed more affection throughout the season than the winners. When Root and Harding won, there was an overwhelming sentiment of defeat among Black and non-Black people of color viewers. Their tweets and posts lamented a familiarity with the situation, how it reflected reality-outside-TV that the blond-haired woman and "dark"-featured white man were chosen over the couple that included a Black person.

The mistreatment of Black contestants extends beyond audience voting into direct interactions. Yewande Biala, a Black woman on *Love Island UK* season 5, detailed in an article how contestants repeatedly mispronounced her name and dismissed her frustration when she corrected them. After her love interest chose a white contestant following weeks of leading her on, Biala's understandable upset was twisted by the media, casting her in the "angry Black woman" stereotype. While reality TV offers entertainment, it holds a mirror to real-world injustices. These shows perpetuate societal biases around race, colorism, features, body type, and class—especially in dating. Notably, Biala has phenotypically Black features (wide nose, dark skin, full lips, curvy hips)—and in an era of Blackfishing, where Black features are selectively praised on lighter/white skin, these same features are often devalued on Black women. Instead, Black women are typically only considered conventionally attractive when they possess more European features. This preference has deep historical roots. François Bernier, a French race scientist born in 1625, wrote that Black women were only beautiful when they had an "aquiline nose, small mouth, coral lips, ivory teeth, large bright eyes, gentle features." Black contestants with similar features to Biala's have reported comparable experiences of discrimination. This pattern of blatant racism continued unchallenged until the summer of 2024, when the show finally crowned its first Black winners.

Even though a couple is formed, that does not mean that they have to stay together for the entirety of the season. All contestants are encouraged to talk to other people (or as the Brits say, "have a chat!"). This gets sticky the longer they are on the show, or the longer they are coupled up. *Love Island* is designed to test couples' loyalties by putting them through a series of challenges, some of which are simulations of real-world temptations. Midway through every season, the contestants are separated by gender and brought to a place called Casa Amor. During Casa Amor, a new crop of Islanders, who are distinguished as bombshells, are brought in to shoot their shots with the existing Islanders, some of whom have established connections and some of whom are still looking. At this point, Mimi had two potential matches, though she struggled to focus on them while thinking about Ayo. He, on the other hand, was pursuing Jessica Spencer—a light-skinned, petite, racially ambiguous woman. At the Casa Amor recoupling (the season's peak moment), contestants choose whether to stay with their original partner or couple with someone new. This dramatic moment captivates viewers, who know everything that happened while couples were separated, though the contestants themselves remain in the dark.

During season 11's recoupling, all the committed women stayed loyal to their partners, and their men reciprocated—except Ayo. When he announced Jess as his choice, the contestants who had witnessed Mimi's loyalty in Casa Amor audibly gasped. Even the host struggled to maintain composure as Mimi walked in alone, having chosen to stay with Ayo only to find that he hadn't done the same. The villa fell silent; contestants exchanged concerned glances, eyes darting and tearing up on Mimi's behalf.

As an avid *Love Island* fan, watching Mimi walk back alone was deeply upsetting but painfully familiar. I wanted to reach through the screen to comfort her and confront Ayo. She maintained a smile and when asked how she felt, simply said, "It is what it is." Her face revealed she was dumbfounded, disappointed, yet unsurprised. Social media exploded: "I hate Ayo so much after tonight!" and "Ayo is so manipulative wtf" and "Mimi walking alone is heartbreaking. She deserves SO much better than how Ayo has treated her."

I personally felt *done* with season 11 at that moment—my stomach and heart could not take watching another Black woman cruelly discarded. But then the show did something that they rarely do. They brought in another Black male contestant, who was interested in Black women. When Josh Oyinsan entered the villa, unlike Ayo, he made it clear that he was interested in Mimi. He spent time getting to know her and even grew jealous of the connection that she had with Ayo. Like most contestants, Mimi went back and forth deliberating over who she really wanted, Ayo or Josh. In the meantime, a blond, blue-eyed, and white contestant named Grace Jackson made her interest in Josh clear. After speaking with him a few times, *she* told other contestants that he was more into *her* than Mimi. At the recoupling where Josh had to choose who he wanted to couple up with, he chose Mimi, and all the other contestants were shocked. Again, I bore witness to the preconception that there is no way that a dark-skinned Black man would elect to be with a dark-skinned Black woman over a white woman. This stoked confusion among the white contestants and further harassment from Joey Essex and Sean Stone. Stone even went as far as to express disbelief, in front of all of the contestants, and insisted that Josh was more into Grace than Mimi.

You might be wondering at this point, "Okay, Ericka, so why do you watch this trash?" As someone who understands the beauty-industrial complex, is media literate, and understands how certain bodies are valued while the rest of us are devalued for not living up to narrow beauty standards, I know I am not the show's target audience. Beyond the regional UK accents, which are fantastic, I watch as a sex educator curious about all the ways we have been indoctrinated into this cult of beauty; how we have adopted this view of who is deserving of love and relationships. It has been formulated throughout history in some of the most heinous ways. Even while I root for the few Black contestants who make it onto the show, I am critiquing the toxic cis-heterocentric ableist romantic culture that, by design, excludes us.

I grew up in predominantly white neighborhoods and schools—in a way, my own prepubescent version of *Love Island*, during an era when people believed that Jennifer Aniston was the most beautiful person to ever walk the earth. I never understood what made someone who looks like every other middle-aged white woman so special, so elevated above everyone else. A question I would contend with often: If Jennifer Aniston is the most beautiful person, then what am I? Maybe you are reading this and thinking, "I never thought she was all that attractive, but yeah, I remember that era"; or maybe you are one of my younger readers, in which case, go Google Jennifer Aniston. I wanted to figure out why Aniston was seen as beautiful so I, too, could be seen that way. I was willing to do pretty much anything to be seen as attractive. I bought all the makeup. Covergirl, Maybelline, L'Oréal—I had something from each brand. Saucony sneakers were very popular when I was younger, and I cried when I couldn't buy a fourth color to match a new outfit. I'd spend hours in the kitchen or bathroom, my grandmother or mom fussing over whether the Just for Me chemical relaxer would finally make my 4C hair soft, bouncy, long curls that they could be proud of. I relished getting my hair braided, swinging my head from side to side and seeing my locks follow the motion. I thought distancing myself from Blackness would guarantee me beauty and a boyfriend. The line between being attractive or not was thick and stark, an ever-changing goalpost, and although I had grown accustomed to being overlooked and called ugly, I still held on to hope that if I just added *this* feature or *that* product, I'd finally crack the code, cross that line. According to writer, speaker, and activist Vanessa Rochelle Lewis in her book *Reclaiming Ugly*, "uglification is used to indoctrinate and propagandize. Uglification is used to convince oppressed, exploited and violated people that the violence and neglect they experience is just the way things are or their fault altogether. It coerces people to be complicit in, and complacent with, their own oppression—and to glorify, respect, and aspire to emulate the people who steward and benefit from their oppression." I believed that I was ugly, and Jennifer Anniston must be attractive considering all the agreement that existed about her. So, I did everything in my power to emulate.

In a society rooted in anti-Black racism, we learn early that how we look matters more than how we understand the world or understand ourselves. Reality television—including dating shows like *Love Island*, and even true crime programs—are a microcosm of whose bodies are valued and whose are not. True crime media overwhelmingly features white, middle-class or wealthy, able-bodied, heterosexual, cisgender victims. In the early 2000s, Elizabeth Smart's kidnapping dominated international headlines while thousands of Black and Indigenous girls vanish annually without attention or press coverage. Reality TV producers exploit these same anti-Black beauty standards to attract viewers, perpetuating the age-old spectacle of Black people being inherently undesirable while white people are the standard.

I almost had to stop watching Samira Mighty on season 4, the first Black woman to be cast on the show, rejected by most of the boys, ostracized by the girls. Producers played a blatant role in creating angry Black woman tropes to villainize her, naming episodes "Samira Kicks Off Out of Nowhere"; meanwhile she looked like she was burying her anger, actively resisting showing it for fear of being labeled angry, only for the label to have been preloaded. Mighty questioned, out loud, why no one was interested in her, often on the verge of tears, and her white castmates attempted to console her with compliments on her personality. The rejection of Black people feels deeply familiar, so much so that many Black femmes tell me they can't watch dating reality shows. The poor treatment of Black women feels retraumatizing, reopening old wounds and reflecting our daily experiences. From my position in a queer bubble, I can view cis-hetero culture as entertainment, something I'm thankfully removed from. But then I remember queer dating shows like *I Kissed a Girl*, *The Queer Ultimatum*, and *Are You the One?*—all of which perpetuate the same exalted Eurocentric beauty standards and discarding of Black women. Even queer-coded shows still find a way to perpetuate the anti-Black stereotypes rather than bravely reject them.

When Mighty finally got chosen for a couple, my deep sigh of relief was cut short—her partner clearly saw her as a placeholder until a white contestant could "rescue" him from being paired with the only Black girl. There is a tweet by "Nadisugly" that says, "Ok but when did you realize you weren't ugly, you were just a POC around too many white people." White supremacy has done such a number on desire that many people actually walk around convinced that their desires are preferences devised uniquely in their hearts and minds, separate from the biases and conditioning the rest of the world constantly feeds them, the same such conditioning that suggests that producers and showrunners likely have motives beyond just entertainment. If there is an agenda to promote white cis-hetero supremacy, ironically this mission appears to be backfiring as viewers witness these superficial relationships built on nothing, but "vibes" inevitably fall apart.

This not-so-hidden agenda is not new. We learn about our ancestors, but we rarely hear the stories of enslaved Indigenous Africans who burned plantations, poisoned their kidnappers, and escaped to freedom. White supremacy has not only carved out who is seen as attractive, but how Black history is written about and even what a Black historical figure looks like. The Black people who are pedestalized in these narratives are either the ones who in their pursuit of freedom are most palatable and nonthreatening and/or the ones who are conventionally attractive; and by that, I mean, according to questionable observations by the authors of some of the earliest hagiographic accounts of the peculiar institution itself, in the eye of the slaveholder. The veracity of the messages themselves is less significant than the whiteness that designates the messengers as more apt authorities on Black life than living Black people themselves. After all, Pulitzer Prize–winning historian C. Vann Woodward, who was white, was reported to have declared, "Negro history is too important to be left entirely to Negro historians." Carter G. Woodson, the creator of Black History Week in 1926, which would eventually become Black History Month some decades later, was granted no distinction in his lifetime. Even history has a look, including those privileged to tell it and be believed.

In *Delectable Negro: Human Consumption and Homoeroticism within US Slave Culture*, Vincent Woodard writes of Nat Turner, a revolutionary hero who murdered roughly 40 white kidnappers on his plantation, an event commonly known as Nat Turner's Rebellion. As punishment for his attempt to liberate himself and others across Southampton County, Virginia, Turner was publicly lynched, and "after he was executed his body was delivered to doctors, who skinned it and made grease of the flesh. Mr. R. S. Barham's father owned a money purse of his hide." For over one hundred years, Turner's skull had been in the possession of a white family, passed down like a precious heirloom. Both slave rebellions and cannibalism are notably absent from secondary and college-level courses on slavery. This selective history serves to deradicalize Black people—when you don't know your ancestors fought back, compliance and "resilience" seem like the only options. The erasure of cannibalism helps white people maintain control of the slavery narrative while preserving their image as "civilized" and "benevolent." This history of consumption remains relevant to discussions of desire—while physically eating people is now taboo, Black people continue to be metaphorically consumed.

Lip injections, Brazilian butt lifts, tanning, long nail extensions, small waists, and wide hips. The Kardashian-Jenner family is a perfect example of the ways in which Black people are still being consumed. Plastic surgeons have documented that the Kardashian-Jenner family single-handedly made lip injections, small waists, and large butts among the most popular requests in their practices. In 2014, Kim Kardashian was on the cover of *Paper Magazine*, in an issue called "Break the Internet: Kim Kardashian"; she was naked, posing with her back to the camera, holding a black-sequined bolt of fabric below her butt. The images were reminiscent of the ways Black women and those gendered as such had been photographed for human zoos in the 1800s, where their bodies were nonconsensually put on display and abused by white people. The number of people (Kim included) who had to sign off on this photoshoot . . . without any consideration as to how race played a role in the composition. This insidious obliviousness exacerbates the ways in which Black bodies are relegated to just that: bodies. Bodies that can be taken, pulled apart, essentialized to their most appealing features. The Kardashian-Jenner family have been criticized for their appropriation of Black culture, mostly by Black women whose voices seem to fade to the background of the discourse, with the Kardashians' rising fame and ubiquity in the foreground. In the same ways enslaved Indigenous Africans amassed large quantities of wealth for white people, our bodies are still sites of commodification for white people's benefit.

The exaltation of certain bodies over others is deeply rooted in anti-Blackness and ableism. From 1867 to 1974, US "ugly laws" banned people who were "maimed, unsightly or disabled" from public spaces, forcing many to remain permanently homebound. These laws, lasting over a century, clearly signaled whose bodies were deemed worthy of public visibility.

Only recently has the media begun showing people with disabilities in romantic relationships. *Love Island* featured just one contestant with a visible disability—Tasha Amber Ghouri, who had a cochlear implant. Though conventionally attractive (thin, blond, white, blue-eyed), producers focused entirely on her disability storyline, highlighting moments where she insisted on her being seen as "normal." Rather than challenging the narrative that only able-bodied people deserve love, they exploited her disability for ratings.

While ugly laws were abolished in 1976, their spirit persists through inaccessible public spaces. Simply eliminating these laws wasn't enough—society found new ways to signal that disabled people shouldn't be seen or desired. The "marriage tax" exemplifies this: Disabled people receiving government benefits lose them upon marriage, as the state considers them their spouse's "burden." This policy actively discourages disabled people from marrying and potentially procreating—a direct continuation of eugenic ideology.

Given this, it should follow that the prevailing oversimplification of desirability politics meted out in the public square of the internet or in popular culture to a discussion of "pretty privilege" is reductive. This framing ignores how white supremacy, featurism, texturism, capitalism, fatphobia, and ableism operate together to determine who is deemed desirable. Desire was the driving force behind the eugenics movement, which I would argue never ended: the racist belief that the genetic makeup of a human population can be improved. The United States' methods of genocide—forced sterilization and dispossession of those deemed to be "destroying the white race"—became a model for Nazi Germany. Hitler didn't even live up to his own standard of blond hair and blue eyes, but upholding the standard was sufficient enough to shield him from being seen as a hypocrite; besides, the blueprint had already been created as to who was an "undesirable" long before the rise of Nazi Germany. Being seen as pretty or desirable isn't just about receiving compliments from random people, it's about access, being free from harm as opposed to being seen as deserving of harm. It is a matter of who lives and who deserves to die.

Following the invasion of Ukraine by Russia in 2022, the prosecutor general of Ukraine was interviewed by the BBC, stating, "It's very emotional for me because I see European people with blue eyes and blond hair . . . being killed every day." He was not alone in his sentiments that blond-haired, blue-eyed, white Europeans should be sheltered from harm; many other racist statements revealing the detrimental implications of desirability politics were made during that time, revealing yet again the belief that people who do not fit those standards should just expect violence as part of their reality. The United States still actively participates in eugenics by nonconsensually sterilizing incarcerated people, supplying weapons to places like Israel to commit genocide, and the mass disabling of the Palestinian peoples. The justification for murdering people or permanently disabling them through violence earns strength and support from the weight that Eurocentric beauty standards hold. You may have thought a chapter about desire was just going to discuss people's "types," but it must be explicitly stated that what informs our type is a violent history rooted in eugenics.

In 2024, *Love Island USA* and *Love Island UK* saw their first all-Black (and dark-skinned) couples win the $100,000/$50,000 prize. The internet was overtaken with photos and clips of the couples, mostly expressing congratulations and excitement, but what curtailed the excitement were murmurs from other fans, disputing that the white or non-Black contestants should have taken home the prize. Mitch Taylor from *Love Island UK* season 10 took to Instagram recording his reaction to the finale, where he watched in disbelief, stating, "they shouldn't have won" and turning to another white former contestant from his season asking for agreement. Arguably, Mitch's opinion means very little in the grand scheme of things, but his reaction spoke volumes about the long-standing anti-Blackness that has sent most Black contestants home; and that would not magically disappear when the first Black winners were crowned. When Serena Page and Kordell Beckham won *Love Island USA*, Leah Kateb, a light-skinned Persian woman, and her partner Miguel Harichi, a light-skinned Black man, were second runners-ups and had earned a devoted following, so much so that their popularity overshadowed the winners'. Before taping ended, Leah's quips had gone viral, and she had amassed one million followers before the winners (or even the runner-up couple that included a dark-skinned Black woman, Jana Craig, and her Dominican partner, Kenny Rodriguez) had gotten their phones back. *Love Island* and other reality dating shows reveal a host of societal hierarchies linked to desirability and love. Although Leah did not win, people were still determined to show, albeit parasocially, that she was more desirable than the all-Black couple who won.

• • •

We live in a society that actively bulldozes our relationship to ourselves to convince us that our main goal should be to be seen as worthy in the eyes of someone else, a romantic partner. But in order to be seen as worthy, you will have to meet x, y, and z standards that are either impossible to achieve or inaccessible without wealth.

Reality dating shows aren't the core problem, though their mistreatment of Black women leads some to question whether they should even apply to appear on those shows anymore. The real issue lies in how viewership and participation are driven by our warped, preformed views of who deserves adoration and by toxic romanticism disguised as authentic connection. When we celebrate a Black couple winning these shows, we're operating within the same problematic structure rather than disrupting it—expressing hope that Black people might receive the same respect white people automatically get, rather than demanding that respect as a given. Our collective agreement about who is and isn't attractive has been force-fed to us and runs deep, but it's not impossible to uproot.

Without an in-depth interrogation of who we are attracted to and why, we are just regurgitating who the state has deemed worthy of life. Decolonization of desire does not happen solely between our ears and behind our eyes; the uprooting of white supremacy at the root of our desire must be done in community. When I lived in Miami, I would go to clubs on South Beach, which are notorious for their velvet-rope entries. I never needed an ID to go out; my cleavage and thin frame were my access. When my friends and I approached the velvet rope, allowing the bouncer to evaluate us, the bouncer would often exclude me or my friend who was fat. "You can go in, but not you." If one of us was excluded, all of my friends and I would leave and go home or go to another spot. Before we left, I would make sure to lay into the bouncer. Resisting the shallow bouncers might sound inconsequential, but imagine if all of us pushed up against systems wherever they reared their head? If none of us said anything, we would have fallen right into the trap of pedestalizing certain bodies over others, for our benefit at the expense of our friend (and for what, a mediocre night out?). Disrupting desirability politics is going to require more than just shouting at bouncers on Miami Beach. It's going to require many actions, some of which may include calling out dating apps and social media for not uprooting anti-Blackness, fatphobia, transphobia, and ableism; calling out media outlets who convince us that everyone on-screen should look a certain way; questioning our friends making statements like "I am just not attracted to fat people";

advocating for the houseless, disabled, neurodivergent folks who are often cast away and seen as undesirable. And we need to stop blaming our own bodies for being seen as unlovable, rather than blaming the structures that situate them that way. If you are attracted to thin, muscular, blond people with Eurocentric features, you might consider that your type has been inherited as a relic of both Nazi Germany and chattel slavery.

I want to caution people away from dating people for the sake of decolonization, a quick and fast route to fetishization. Instead, consider how desirability prevents you from acknowledging someone asking for money on the street; causes you to follow or support a white person talking about racism before a Black person; finds you giving your undivided attention to someone who is light-skinned with ambiguously Black features but ignoring those who are unambiguously Black and dark-skinned; or grants you a willingness to fight for Ukrainian and not Palestinian liberation or for Palestine and not Haiti, Sudan, or the Congo. Liberation starts with recognizing colonial frameworks as inherited beliefs, not natural truths. True freedom comes through working daily in community to uproot these views, holding each other accountable while building lasting partnerships.

- How do desirability politics show up in your friendships, family life, and organizing spaces?
- Were/are you or a sibling doted upon based on your looks? How did/does that impact your family dynamic?
- Is the porn you watch, the social media accounts and celebrities you idolize a match for who you express your attraction to out loud? If not, why?

- What do the leaders of the organizing spaces of which you have been a part look like? Has this ever been discussed?
- Is there a disconnect between your understanding of systemic oppression and your desirability politics?

# 3

# Whose Body Is Worthy of Love?

## *The De-Sexualization of Chronically Ill, Disabled, and Fat Bodies*

"If I cannot air this pain and alter it, I will surely die of it. That's the beginning of social protest."

—Audre Lorde

CONTENT WARNING:
*Fatphobia, ableism and mentions of EDs*

I sat on a cold cement bench in the center of the Wall Street neighborhood and listened to my doctor on the phone, speaking to be heard above the finance bros self-importantly speedwalking to their next exploitative ventures, the UPS trucks honking at pedestrians, the bicyclists yelling at cars double-parked in the bike lane, the tourists trying to get the perfect shot of the buildings that sit on top of an African burial ground and former slave auction block. "Ericka, you have breast cancer in both breasts."

My anticipatory nerves had me sitting up straight and holding my breath, but as soon as I heard the news, I sank into the cement bench, my nervous system no longer able to bear the weight of my anxiety. I physically hunched over and tried to catch my breath. The quiet part slipped from my lips before I could catch it. "Am I going to die?"

"No, you will not die, but you do have to have a double mastectomy," he responded. All of a sudden, I could barely hear him over the waterfall of tears falling from my face.

After ten hours in surgery, two weeks spent between the couch and the corner of the bed, daytime television in the background of my Percocet dreams, measuring and then dumping the blood that filled my four drains every other hour, and the sweetest West Indian nurse who came to change my bandages daily, it was time for me to go back to work. Yes, you read that correctly: I went back to work two weeks after my double mastectomy. I was diagnosed in May of 2014 at twenty-eight years old. I conducted a self-exam after my then-wife noticed something different while being intimate. I could feel the lump sitting right under the surface of my breast but felt stumped as to what to do next. I was working part-time and did not have health insurance. Two days before I was diagnosed, I had accepted a full-time position which had health insurance benefits but would not kick in until after a ninety-day trial period. I begged the Affordable Care Act representative to make an exception for me, as I had missed the deadline for applying. In order to make an appointment with my breast cancer surgeon, get a mammogram, do a needle biopsy, and eventually see an oncologist, I needed health insurance. "Health care" in the United States is the antithesis of care: No one should need a full-time job or have to pay exorbitant costs just to receive lifesaving medical treatment.

"If you cannot work, you will lose your job," the HR director sternly told me after I shakily revealed my diagnosis and told them that I would need time off for surgery and recovery. I had to make a special request that I receive health insurance before the end of the three months. My life was in jeopardy, but my employer prioritized my ability to work. My body was only valuable if it could produce labor for someone else. Capitalism is deadly. The HR director made it clear that she would have to "pull strings" to get my two weeks off approved. Although my job served the Lower East Side, a predominantly Black and Puerto Rican community, my health and well-being as a Black staff member were not of their utmost concern. When the last drain was removed, and I no longer had silicone-grade tubes hanging from my body, I asked the doctor for reassurance that it was safe to return to work. She was concerned that I didn't have more time to rest but said it was safe, emphasizing that I couldn't do heavy lifting or be in large crowds. I nodded in agreement, knowing I would be on a packed rush hour train the next day. I spiraled the morning before my first day at work: What are you supposed to wear after weeks of living in oversize button-down shirts or pajamas from the Target men's section? I tried on a yellow formfitting Zara dress, and although I liked the vibrant color and how it hugged my curves, I hated how my breasts looked. It looked like I had two square Tupperware containers on my chest, and the Zara dress only accented them. In between frustrated wardrobe changes, I would step away from the mirror whenever I was naked. For the first time in my adult life, I was avoiding the sight of my naked body. When I finally mustered up the courage to just stand and look at myself, it was disorienting. I felt dysmorphic.

I had historically always felt comfortable being naked. Right before I had my double mastectomy, I had a topless beach party. I had sought out nude beaches and prided myself on honoring all bodies, but those fiercely held beliefs were challenged by my ableist views. I was filled with guilt. Although the cancer had been removed from my body, my disappointment with my appearance overshadowed everything I had endured. I told myself I needed to look presentable for work, but this was a reflection of something deeper. I was experiencing firsthand how capitalism devalues bodies that don't meet its standards of productivity. The state marks disabled and chronically ill bodies as disposable, creating a binary between able-bodied and disabled people based on their perceived ability to produce. This classification often has little to do with actual capabilities, yet it shapes how society views and values our bodies. My cancer diagnosis was disruptive to my job with an organization that claimed to care about Black and Latinx communities because it revealed what they really cared about: making a profit.

My inability to look at myself in the mirror was the by-product of living in a world that portrays disabled and chronically ill people as ugly and distorted, implying we are unworthy of pleasure and love. I was perfectly content honoring bodies that did not look like mine as long as they were not mine. I have had what may be described as an athletic build for most of my life. "Big boned" as my below the Mason-Dixon Line Baltimore family described. Even at six years old, I had thighs that made me look like a baby bodybuilder. As I got older, I had a thin frame, but my thick thighs remained. When I was thirteen, my family took a small seaplane on a Key West vacation, and we all had to either be weighed or report our weights. I didn't want to go on the scale, so my dad said, "Ericka, you are about 160, right?" One hundred sixty pounds felt astounding to me. I howled in disbelief that he would assume such a thing. Faced with concerns that the plane could crash if we had inaccurate data, he responded, "You are a big girl, and these weights need to be right." I wanted to just go down with the plane.

Despite my thin frame, I was still perceived as large—not just because of my 5'7" height or thick thighs I inherited from my mother, but because my Blackness made me inherently "fat" in society's eyes. I knew, rationally, that 160 pounds wasn't fat, but I had internalized the belief that the numbers on a scale determined my worth. I worked out incessantly; drank cayenne, lemon, and honey water for meals as popularized by Beyoncé, which made it an acceptable eating disorder; counted calories; had food diaries; and removed carbs from my diet entirely. I did everything to distance myself from fatness. However, I did not realize my resistance to being fat was fatphobia. I believed that I just wanted to be healthy.

Capitalism creates the conditions to focus on the superficial; how someone looks determines their worth; this is profoundly how healthism operates. While on chemotherapy, I could not keep food down; I ate only white rice for months and began to lose weight. I can confidently say that I received more compliments on my looks than any other time in my life. Fatphobia is so pervasive that we have been indoctrinated into the fallacy that the worst possible fate for our bodies is to be born fat and remain fat, or to become fat. Fatness is only supposed to be temporary: acceptable while pregnant but not after, fat breasts and butts but nothing else. Everyone is supposed to be working to avoid fatness and, if not, your body is seen as a threat to the flimsy foundation of the thin ideal.

Fatphobia disables fat people in an attempt to limit their mobility and visibility in public space; from tiny airplane seats, to lazy medical practitioners who pressure patients into losing weight to cure every ailment, to the lack of size-inclusive clothing in the market, there is a deeply ingrained resistance to fatness. Our society has framed disability and fatness as temporary problems to be "fixed" or "overcome"—as if self-love can only exist on the other side of becoming thin or able-bodied. This perspective stems from a false narrative that we all naturally begin life able-bodied, grow up to be fit and thin, and remain that way until death. Most homes, schools, stores, and public buildings are not designed for people who are disabled, further ratifying the assumption that everyone is (or *should* be) able-bodied. The truth is, most of us will become disabled in our lifetime. Is it possible to consider that we are all disabled? Why is able-bodied the standard? Who determined that? On whose body are we basing able-bodied-ness? I will give you one guess. Clinging to the belief that our bodies will remain able-bodied, or that able-bodied-ness is the standard, creates a never-ending cycle of killing ourselves to be thin out of fear of the repercussions of fatphobia and ableism.

My reactions to my newly disabled body were funneled through my inherited bias about whose body is a good body, a body worthy of being seen in public space, a body worthy of life. Racial capitalism structures us to value marginalized bodies based solely on their capacity for labor. In Western society, fat bodies are associated with assumed lower-class standing, while thin bodies are automatically linked to wealth. This perspective stems from a long, racist history that determines whose body is deemed worthy of life by casting aside fat and disabled bodies.

People often ask me: How has my relationship with my body changed post-cancer? This question seems laced with the assumption that I must have loved my pre-cancer body and hated my post-mastectomy body, rooted in a belief that nonnormative bodies are wrong. My pre-cancer body was privileged in its size and weight but not free from fatphobia or anti-Blackness. Although I felt comfortable being naked around others, I still fell prey to the calorie counting, the food diaries, and every diet trend out there. I was relatively thin, but I wouldn't describe my body as skinny, being size 8–12 for most of my college years and twenties; I had hips, a butt, breasts, and sturdy thighs. I was what African American Vernacular English (AAVE) would describe as thick. The maintenance required to stave off a fat stomach, flabby arms, or a double chin consumed most of my mental capacity.

Although I strived for thinness, I still wanted to have big breasts. Growing up, I did not think too much about my breasts until puberty. I noticed that everyone else was getting attention from their growing breasts, so I'd come to school with toilet paper filling up the gaps in my training bras. By the time I went to college, my breasts were a 36C, but attending college in Miami, where plastic surgery was practically an extracurricular sport, I dreamed of much bigger breasts. I moved on from toilet paper to overpriced Victoria's Secret push-up bras and V-neck tops that showed just enough cleavage.

The first guy that I hooked up with in college seemed to love my breasts. "You have great boobs; they are not too big and don't sag," he'd say. Our time together centered around hooking up only. He never took me on a date or asked me to be his girlfriend; I was solely his occasional titty fuck. My breasts seemed to exist only for others' enjoyment, whether I was showing cleavage to get into clubs or attracting people who valued me solely for them. The rest of my body must have been a disappointment to those willing to hook up with me at night but who pretended not to know me during the day. I was again being hypersexualized, my body dissected into parts that could pleasure others, with little regard for my feelings. My perceived confidence likely stemmed from others' hope that it would translate into sexual availability but never anything deeper. I'd emphasized what I thought gave me value, my sense of worth dependent entirely on others' desire or lack thereof.

In college, I had a huge crush on a tall, fat, light-skinned, dreadlocked man who worked with me at a coffee shop. We often worked the same shift, and sometimes we were joined by our other colleague, a fat Cuban young woman. He clearly flirted with us both, but she didn't seem as interested in his advances as I was. One night, I invited him to my apartment, and we sat on the couch talking for hours. At some point, he asked to see my nipples, I obliged, and he played with them like they were the buttons on his game controller. I sat there, aroused by the thought that he was finally making a clear advance toward me, but shortly after, he made a joke about it being past his bedtime, pulled down my bra, fixed my shirt and patted my chest like I had done him a favor, gave me a cousin side hug, and left. He never flirted with me again, and shortly after this night he made the Cuban girl his girlfriend.

My breasts felt like they were on their own island, detached from the rest of my body. They were the part of me that was seen as attractive and desired, while the rest of me was ignored. I don't think this is an unusual feeling in a world that has made breasts into solely sexual artifacts designated for a man's pleasure, so much so that public breast/chest-feeding is controversial. Imagine a child eating being up for debate. When I was diagnosed with bilateral breast cancer, I was hit with a whole host of emotions, none of which included mourning my breasts. They felt like extensions of exploitation, tools that only worked in favor of other people's fantasies. What difference would it make if this set was gone?

When my breast cancer surgeon told me that I would have to

have both breasts removed, he seemed to be anticipating a reaction of sadness. I simply responded that if they had to go, then that's what needed to happen. I'd grown so used to other people quantifying the value of my breasts that this was the first time someone was considering how I felt about them. He continued to explain that I would not be able to breast/chest-feed. I shrugged—having a child was the last thing on my mind. Most of the literature and advocacy around breast cancer centers on the assumption that it is a chronic illness that impacts cisgender women and that survivors feel less like women after their breasts are removed. While that feeling is valid, I do think it is important for folks who feel like their gender identity is bound up in a body part to investigate why that is the case. Breasts are given a great deal of importance, but for whom? It is completely fine to mourn your breasts, and breasts do not have to be sexualized or an expression of gender; they are body parts. Femininity is not automatically attached to breasts; you get to define what femininity is for you.

I personally never felt that my breasts helped me be in touch with womanhood, as I never felt like a woman. As a queer person on the cusp of naming my gender identity, my cancer diagnosis changed my relationship with my body. I was forced to confront the ways I had stumbled into cis-heteronormativity, anti-Blackness, fatphobia, and ableism. How my relationship to my breasts was more of a performance of what and who I was supposed to be, not my authentic self. When I was diagnosed, I spiraled. How could this happen to me? I was eating all the "right" things and practicing yoga four times a week. I was doing all the things deemed as "healthy" but was still diagnosed with cancer. I placed the blame squarely on my body.

Searching for an explanation of how my body caused this, I

started to further speculate on why Black people die from cancer at higher rates than white people. My stress-induced spiral concluded that this must have been due to how much chicken we eat. Yes, chicken. My internalized anti-Blackness and outright fear of what was occurring had me blaming myself and other Black cancer patients for eating chicken. I was tested for the BRCA gene due to my family history, and I was negative, which only further solidified my very little empirical data that chicken was the culprit. As a society we are inundated with anti-Blackness that has successfully stopped us from seeing the forest for the trees. My internalized anti-Blackness led me to blame myself and cast assumptions about Black people's diets as the sole reason why we die at higher rates than white people.

The thought never crossed my mind to consider the stress from having to constantly navigate anti-Blackness or the systemic violence that upholds it, such as contaminated water, exposure to pollution, racist medical institutions, and machines to detect cancer only being made for white skin—none of these determinants crossed my mind as a reason. I was solely to blame, and no one was telling me off that hill either. Unlike the cultlike following of the book *The Body Keeps the Score*, which also controversially blames our bodies for holding stress rather than focusing on the stressor itself. Author, speaker, and breast cancer survivor Audre Lorde writes in *The Cancer Journals* of the possible culprits that could cause cancer and how we should not gaslight ourselves into thinking our disposition will protect us:

"The happiest person in this country cannot help breathing in smokers' cigarette fumes, auto exhaust, and airborne chemical dust, nor avoid drinking the water, and eating the food. The idea that happiness can insulate us against the results of our environmental madness is a rumor circulated by our enemies to destroy us."

Trying to figure out how I got cancer was causing more stress in my body than that which had already been passed down generationally due to anti-Black racism, misogynoir, fatphobia, and ableism; but testing to determine how much your body has weathered or is in fact susceptible to illness due to stress is rarely used by medical institutions to support patients.

While I was on chemotherapy, I noticed that people would look at me like they were staring death in the face. Doctors, nurses, friends, and colleagues would address me with their brows scrunched up and tears in their eyes. Regardless of how I felt, I found myself comforting them. To this day, anytime I share that I am a cancer survivor, I am inundated with stories about how someone's auntie or grandma died from cancer too. Everyone seemed to be following a similar script: their relationship to cancer, followed by words of sympathy, revealing that no one really knows what to say to cancer survivors or those living with chronic illness. For the record, a cancer survivor rarely wants to hear about someone who has died from cancer when death is likely something they already think about often. I went from people never talking to me about death to having a death sentence stamped on my body, people treating me as though I could die tomorrow—and as if they couldn't. Most of the messaging surrounding cancer involves death. Have you ever seen a movie with a cancer survivor that had amazing sex scenes and flourishing relationships, or even a storyline that did not focus on their cancer?

I finished chemotherapy one year after my double mastectomy. I was newly divorced (having been married for a year and a half identifying as nonbinary and feeling reconnected to my Blackness). I had spent a good chunk of my twenties in a romantic relationship with a white lesbian. Dating a white person (albeit not for the first time), not to mention entering into a marriage with one, was not healthy for me. Similar to the ideas I had inherited about my breasts being outlets for men's pleasure, I'd thought being desired by a white person meant that I was beautiful. Whiteness is the standard for beauty, and I was beautiful by association.

*Loving v. Virginia* is one of the most referenced legislations related to marriage equality, even being cited as a precursor to the legalization of gay marriage. Black and white romantic relationships in a racialized country require intentional conversations about race and racism; they can't rest on the assumption that sharing a bed has marked the end of racism as we know it. While I felt that I was beautiful in proximity to a white person, my ex-wife felt that her proximity to my Blackness solidified her status as a woke, cultured white person, and that meant more to her than caring about me ever did. I sat at most chemotherapy appointments alone and spent a good chunk of my time out of hospitals arguing. I realized that she wasn't very different from the men who had played with my breasts, as she also didn't value all of me. Sitting alone at those chemotherapy appointments, I had time to reflect on what I deserved, not yet realizing that my new disabled body would render me devalued in similar ways my Blackness had.

At thirty years old, I moved into a windowless room that had likely been a closet in Williamsburg, Brooklyn. I was sleeping in my own bed for the first time in eight years, and rather than keeping it empty, I joined some dating apps. I jumped in headfirst. A particular woman caught my eye, and we began flirting, thinking that it could lead to a date or a late-night hookup. After talking for most of the night, she asked me to send her a nude. I told her to go first, and she obliged. I positioned my phone camera to get the best angle, lifted my shirt, and snapped the photo.

At this point, my scars had fully healed, stitches had melted away, and although I wished my scars would run under my breasts, the fact that they ran across made me feel like I had an extension of a nipple. I chose the best photo and hit send. After ten minutes had gone by with no response, I reached back out, "I guess I should have mentioned that I am a breast cancer survivor." She never responded. The breasts that had once garnered me exploitative attention had gone into a medical waste receptacle in the Bronx, never to be seen again. I was now seeing firsthand how people nonconsensually render disabled folks asexual. I know what you are thinking: I dodged a bullet. And yes, I agree. But I will still have to do the complicated work of reconciling how fat and disabled people are told over and over that our bodies are not enough.

A popular assignment I give in my grad school courses is for students to create a poster composed of images of people that they find attractive. They can use photos from whatever source they like; they can even draw. Nine times out of ten, I have posters that depict white, thin, acceptably curvy bodies (small waist and large butt), thin or muscular frames, and if a dark-skinned person appears, they are often a man, rarely a woman. If they are a dark-skinned woman, then they are thin, with a thin nose and thin lips. The presence of Eurocentric beauty standards is still evident even among students who are actively striving to demonstrate some distance from that indoctrination. In my eight years of teaching grad school, I've never had a student express attraction to someone who uses a wheelchair or to someone who is deaf, blind, or neurodivergent. While this might raise questions about fetishization, it's worth noting that even who gets fetishized and who doesn't is socially normalized. Fetishization itself represents an absence of true desire, treating people as objects by fixating on one aspect while neglecting the whole person.

As a disabled/chronically ill person, when I first shared my double mastectomy scars online, people asked, "How did you come to love your body?" This question carries undertones of fatphobia, ableism, and anti-Blackness. What they're really asking is: "How dare you stand naked where people can see you without shame?" Or "How can you be topless, looking the way you do, and still not hate yourself?" Or they offer backhanded comfort: "You make me feel better about my body because yours is so damaged!"

The concept of "loving your body" is primarily demanded of those whose bodies society refuses to love—it's capitalist, apolitical body-positivity nonsense that puts the onus on the individual and not the systems that would have one hating their body in the first place. Love alone won't cure the years of internalized fatphobia, ableism, and anti-Blackness. Real healing comes from calling myself out, addressing the root causes, and refusing to be constrained by standards implemented by privileged white cis men. This goes beyond my students' indoctrination; it exposes how media machinery controls which bodies are deemed attractive.

I would love to see a disabled person in a rom-com-type film. Throughout all the seasons of *Love Island* that I have watched, there has been one disabled cast member. Even in porn, I have yet to see someone in a wheelchair getting head or someone with a mastectomy sitting on someone's face. The late speaker and disability activist Stella Young coined the term "inspiration porn" to describe the compliments that people living with disabilities and chronic illnesses receive for doing nothing. In her TED Talk, she refers to posters depicting someone with a physical disability with the quote, "There are no excuses," messaging clearly intended for able-bodied people who are supposed to have it "easier" and thus not make excuses. As soon as someone is known to be disabled or chronically ill, there seems to be this switch that flips, rendering us sites of inspiration only, unworthy of pleasure and being desired. Our bodies do not exist to make able-bodied people feel better that they are not disabled. Yet there are instances where chronic illness is used as a means to get closer to a thin ideal.

In 2017, *Cosmopolitan* received criticism for publishing an article titled "How This Woman Lost 44 Pounds Without ANY Exercise." The article detailed the experiences of Simone Harbinson, a mother of two who had recently been diagnosed with a rare cancer. After an onslaught of various surgeries to remove the cancer, she was too weak to work out and, as a result of emotional eating, gained thirty-five pounds. She was later diagnosed with post-traumatic stress disorder due to her cancer diagnosis and was put on medication. After some time, Harbinson learned that her cancer had metastasized and that she would have to undergo chemotherapy.

The article then pivots to sharing how, in an Instagram twelve-week weight-loss program, she was able to lose forty-four pounds, quoting her saying, "It's not just a physical transformation, but the mental transformation within has been incredible. I love my body, flaws and all . . . I am so proud of all that I have accomplished after everything I have been through." Social media users called out the article. Dr. Jen Gunter tweeted, "She had cancer, change this headline. This is despicable." And another social media user tweeted, "Get cancer and lose weight WITHOUT exercise! Wtf, really, *Cosmo*?"

A few days after the article was posted, *Cosmopolitan* eventually changed the title to "A Serious Health Scare Helped Me Love My Body More Than Ever." Changing the title of the article did not contend with the fact that the magazine felt it appropriate to publish an article about someone whose weight loss seemed to provide solace and comfort in the midst of navigating cancer. The article does not share what happened to Harbinson as it relates to her cancer diagnosis, just that she is happy mentally and physically with her body now that it is thin and that it's possible to attain thinness without the gym, showcasing that even when faced with a life-threatening illness, thinness is still the priority in a fatphobic world.

*Cosmopolitan* magazine has been touting the message that thinness is the ideal since the late 1800s. In 1890, Elizabeth Bisland, *Cosmopolitan*'s assistant editor, wrote an article titled "Famous Beauties" in which she expressed admiration for white women with a mixed Northern European heritage. At the time, racial hierarchies were being cemented, using fatness as the key measurement. These classifications placed Black people at the bottom, as Blackness was deemed to make them inherently "fat," while positioning Northern European people at the top as inherently "thin." This rhetoric was constructing evidence for a white American beauty ideal rooted in thinness. Bisland's article was to further hone in who was the most desirable white people, Nordic peoples, even if they had mixed heritage, stating, "while the women's racial makeup is the foundation of their attractiveness, the physical features that made them beautiful were their elongated, svelte physiques." The issue of *Cosmopolitan* from 2017 presents an unsettling mirror to this origin story, tracing a centuries-long mission to make thinness the center of someone's universe at the expense of everything—even chronic illness.

Medical institutions have been the primary proponents of thinness, asserting that arbitrary numbers on a scale make you overweight and thus unhealthy, with little to no concern for the diversity of bodies (or for the dangerous ways some people become or remain thin). Many of us became familiar with BMI

(Body Mass Index) in a middle or high school gym class, where a teacher pinched our arm fat with a measuring tool or had us stand on a scale that determined our body fat, a tool still used by medical institutions to this day even though it was never intended to measure fat. The BMI that is used today was created by Adolphe Quetelet in the 1830s; originally named the Quetelet Index, it was devised to measure weights across a population—European populations specifically, as it was designed with white people as the foundation.

In the 1930s, men pivoted from relying on a tide of fatphobic information from women's magazines like *Cosmopolitan* and *Harper's Bazaar* and began using medicine to convince women that they needed to be thin. According to author and educator Sabrina Strings in *Fearing the Black Body*, "In 1934, *The Washington Post* ran the headline 'Weight Shortens Life of Women: Results of Studies is Published.'" These articles used medical-speak and the backing of insurance companies to stoke a fear of fatness. In the 1960s, biologist and doctor Ancil Keys renamed the Quetelet Index as BMI, though the original scale was never designed to measure body fat. BMI would later be adopted as a medical scale to address obesity—not for biological or health purposes, but because Keys harbored anti-fat bias. Sabrina Strings further asserts that "in a *Time Magazine* cover story from 1961 . . . he claimed that obesity did not necessarily cause coronary heart disease. It was nevertheless, in his view, 'ugly.'" Obesity became an arbitrary measure of fatness designed to vilify Black and poor people, strategically dispossessing certain groups to elevate thin bodies—in short, to further exalt white, cisgender, able-bodied people as the norm.

Even today, people have experienced a great deal of misdiagnosis and maltreatment, some even losing their lives fighting for basic care in a system that places more value on thin white bodies. The histories of fatphobia, anti-Blackness, and ableism are intrinsically linked.

My students carefully selected photos of people they were attracted to, only to realize that the selection had already been made for them by fatphobic and ableist algorithms and media. People living with chronic illness and disabilities are worthy of love and desire, worthy of being someone's type, of being fucked (if they want and however they want). I had grown used to people not seeing my body as worthy of love or pleasure, but post-mastectomy, I had entered new territory—now I was the world's inspiration porn.

Although I was in round two out of six rounds of chemotherapy, I was determined to attend the Afropunk Festival. Despite the humid, sticky Northeast August heat, I wore a dress and a blanket around my shoulders—partly to look cool, but mostly because I was freezing, one of chemotherapy's diverse side effects being chills. I stood in line, shifting between hot flashes and chills, hoping my water bottle wouldn't be confiscated despite the larger-than-life signs reading NO OUTSIDE FOOD OR DRINKS. My friends likely thought I should have been home in bed, but since I had attended this music festival—which feels like a Black weird-kid punk mecca—for the past two years, they supported me not missing it. I leaned my body against theirs as we waited in the long line to get in; chemotherapy exhaustion happens on both a spiritual and cellular level. I had my water with me, tucked slightly under my blanket. When I got to the gate, the security guard stopped me.

"No water bottles allowed," the guard said.

I thought it would be simple to explain. "I'm on chemo," I said. "I need to drink a lot of water. I can show you my catheter if that helps prove what I'm saying." The port was right below my collarbone and stuck out two to three inches from my chest.

"No exceptions."

"It's just water in this bottle. You can smell it. I can't be for too long without water." I knew the lines for water at the festival would be a lot, so I wanted to have some emergency reserves for when I would inevitably have to wait in line. The security guard would not budge, foreshadowing how they would treat us when they started to invite white-owned companies to sponsor. He was concerned the water might actually be tequila even though, demonstrably, it wasn't. Was that the first sign I noticed that Afropunk didn't care about the whole community, that it wasn't all that alternative in the end? Maybe. Because, really, how punk is it to be ableist? It's ironic, to say the least, that Afropunk's brand is "no racism, no homophobia, no transphobia, no fatphobia, no xenophobia, and no ableism." My desire to have a moment of normalcy overrode logic, so I gave in and gave up my water. I convinced myself that I'd find a water vendor right away, maybe some shade. Outdoor music festivals often don't make the list of spaces that are accessible. Joyous and carefree Black people were all around me, but even the balm of their company could not mute the side effects of chemo. I lasted just thirty minutes at Afropunk in 2014, wilting under the sway of the chemical cocktail in my veins.

By the summer of 2016, I had been finished with chemo for six months and had completely healed from my double mastectomy and reconstructive surgeries. But my soul was tired. I was tired of being treated like inspiration porn, tired of not seeing Black people in breast cancer advocacy campaigns, and tired of the medical institution's complete disregard for my pain. Doctors would say to me, at twenty-eight, "Oh my God, you're so young."

To this day, at thirty-nine, they still say that. But other people my age, and much younger, live with cancer. We are not anomalies, and it is infuriating to be treated like one. When I asked the plastic surgeon to show me pictures of what scarring might look like on Black skin like mine after breast reconstruction, it took her two weeks to find the one image she thought she might have. Had I been white, my plastic surgeon would have had a *range* of images available at the ready. As she flipped through the plastic-covered photos in what looked like a family album, I kept patiently waiting for an image of a Black person. She seemed to be looking for one, too, turning the pages so quickly as if surprised everyone was white. It seems to me that white people tend to think of their whiteness only in the presence of someone who is not white.

I didn't feel anything while this was happening—it just felt familiar, yet another time where I was not anywhere. I have mastered masking any emotion other than a smile around white people, fearing I will be directly targeted if I express how I actually feel. This leaves me often disconnected from my true emotions. The lack of representation of queer, trans, and nonbinary Black people in all aspects of the breast cancer experience was stunning. Black people, as a whole, were mostly left out of any sort of breast cancer awareness or advocacy campaigns.

By the summer of 2016, I had had enough.

"I'm going topless at Afropunk this year," I told my friends. "I want people to be educated about breast cancer. I want them to know what a Black person with breast cancer looks like. I want them to check their own breasts. Afropunk is a space for Black queer and nonbinary young folks, for trans young folks. And I know they aren't seeing this. Because I didn't see it." My "get ready, I'm gonna be naked in public" announcement didn't surprise my friends. As much as I love clothes (and I *love* clothes), I feel happiest and most at ease without them. I'd just met East Oakland native award-winning writer and poet Ebony on a Tinder date three weeks prior and like many queer relationships, we were falling fast. I shared with him that I wanted to go topless at Afropunk and he became an instant hype man. He loved the idea and wanted to go to Afropunk with me, but he couldn't afford to be away from his life and work in Oakland any longer, and I couldn't afford to help him stay. 2016 was the first year Afropunk cost money to get in. But 2015 was a year of change for the festival too. It had started to lose its very grunge, very Black, and very punk identity. *Vogue* had sent a reporter to cover it that year and ran a Best Dressed at Afropunk 2015 listicle. More kinds of people began anticipating going to Afropunk. When you add a cost to anything, you are inevitably sending the message that certain people can and should not access said space/item. The bands started to get a bit bigger, the names, the stars—all bigger. And press. Afropunk was becoming less Afro and more commodified by whiteness.

In 2016, I was frustrated about the changes and I was also excited to feel safeness in my Black girl quirkyness, not on cancer meds or healing from surgeries; I was happy to be alive. That first day at Afropunk in 2016, I wore lacy sunshine-yellow short shorts edged in tiny pom fringe from Target. My braids were piled in a bun atop my head and dotted with bright yellow gerbera daisies. A red silky scarf tied around my breasts served as a top. To accessorize, I added a beaded, bib-style necklace in shades of blue, white, green, yellow, red, and orange. I felt beautiful and nervous. But why should I be nervous? This was a festival! People go topless at festivals all the time, I reminded myself. My good friend Zuri, also a sex educator, walked in with me to Afropunk that summer day. "Are you going to do it?" she asked as soon as we were through the gate.

Suddenly, it just didn't feel right. I changed my mind. "You know what? I think I can't do it. I'm just too shy. I'm scared."

Zuri gave me a look. "You're naked all the time. What the hell?"

"I can't." And then a presumably cisgender man walked by us, shirtless. Zuri and I glanced at each other. That was my cue. My nerves were still wild, but I took my top off anyway. And I just stood there, shoulders back, feeling instantly free and fine. All anxiety fell away. My breasts were a natural part of my outfit. As I settled into myself, I saw someone taking a photo. Since I felt so utterly at ease at that moment, it didn't occur to me that this person might be taking a photo of me. But that image was one that would go viral and never stop.

That image was the one that would mean that no doctor would ever have an excuse not to show a Black person what their breast reconstruction surgery scars might look like. Zuri and I began to walk through the festival. I tried to catch everyone's eye almost as a way to brace myself for their shock that I was topless, but they would eventually break eye contact and stare at my chest. People looked at me strangely, but that was familiar. Being topless at Afropunk after a double mastectomy and reconstruction was a perfect microcosm of all my life experiences as a Black queer nonbinary person. I felt wonderfully at home.

People stopped me constantly, many of them telling me how brave I was. But what I heard the most that day was this question: What happened to you? And that was heart-wrenching to hear. It told me that people didn't know what breast cancer looked like. Now, everybody's scars look different, and every body is different, but for the most part, I thought people would recognize the catheter scar. They did not. I thought they would read my body as familiar in terms of what happens after a double mastectomy as opposed to how breasts look after just getting breast implants. But no. My post-mastectomy reconstructed Black body was a revelation to the people around me. They cried and thanked me for being visible. I decided when I returned to Afropunk the next day, although the outfit I'd planned months before wasn't intended to be topless, I would bare my chest again.

Breast cancer survivors are too-often painted as selfless, inspirational beings, thus erasing any room for being sexy. I rejected the notion that just because my nipples were now long, stunning scars, I was no longer a sexual being. Walking Afropunk topless was about *that*. The lack of Black visibility in the breast cancer world, the ways in which we are left out of the conversation and, therefore, the treatment. The continued subtle slights and blatant medical apartheid that result from that erasure. Walking Afropunk topless was about all of that. The mortality rate for Black cisgender women diagnosed with breast cancer is 42 percent higher than that of white women. My mother, a Black woman who died of breast cancer when I was thirteen, is one of those numbers. And a universe more. Walking Afropunk topless was about her.

Punk cannot be bought. (Though Afropunk got lost on that point, a topic for another essay.) Punk is a feeling, a sound, an expression of self. You know it when you see it or hear it. To the non-punk on the outside looking in, it might seem like a performance. Like something someone does solely to get attention and make other folks nervous. That's okay, even if it's not the truth. I want people to look. I want people to see my scars, my skin, and my power. I want them to see a Black femme standing in truth and resisting white supremacist patriarchal notions of existence.

That's punk. Going topless at Afropunk changed my life. I was featured in countless magazines and publications, but when I noticed that I was being pushed into the role of Ms. Pink October, I had to strategically pivot, forcing people to see me as a sexual being. Just like the bouncer who was unwilling to bend and allow me to bring water into the music festival, people can be unmovable in their perception of those living with chronic illnesses as inspiration and nothing more. Living in a society steeped in capitalism has taught me which bodies the state will discard—those that exist outside the parameters it deems worthy.

After going topless at Afropunk, I felt as though I had healed from breast cancer. The first time I stepped into a kink space, I had no idea that healing in a whole new way was on the horizon. This particular play party, a space where people engage in kink, was in an old church building, so it was really tapping into my church traumas. I had gone with a few friends from my master's program; some had lots of experience in kink, and some were new to the scene. I didn't always identify as kinky, but I enjoyed certain sexual activities—like spanking—which is impact play, though they've become normalized in vanilla sex spaces. I always had an affinity for spanking, but I never knew there were spaces where people could just bend over and be consensually spanked, among other things. All play parties are not the same, but this one was laid out perfectly, with various areas with ample space to play and areas for voyeurs to watch without interrupting. I wrestled with a friend and watched someone get flogged and punched, mostly observing to determine what I would want to experience next time. I left that party wanting to experiment more intentionally with impact play. I started dating someone who had an extensive background in kink.

Eventually, we entered into a 24/7 D/s (Dominant and submissive) dynamic. We had entirely too many rules for everyone to remember. I'd get a text in the middle of the day while working at my nonprofit job, "Send me a nude now." I felt immediately aroused by the inconvenience of having to figure out how to do this at work, without getting caught or losing my job. When we were together, we'd role-play different scenes, and all scenarios led to me being spanked one way or another. After being poked and prodded by doctors and nurses, being bent over and spanked until her palm print was an accessory to my ass was healing. I'd go home and sit on the hard train seats and wince in pain if I sat down too fast, but this time the pain felt good, a reminder of the time we had, rather than an oncology office or a hospital. With every hit, I was reclaiming a moment where I had to work through the pain to get to the other side; by contrast, I was experiencing pain in my body on my own terms.

The very first time I underwent chemotherapy, I was in a private room, a "luxury" that this breast cancer clinic gives to all first timers. The nurse walked me through all the potential side effects, let me know how long the session would take, and then presented me with the largest needle I had ever seen. She had a squeaky but sweet voice; she moved slowly, which annoyed me as someone who had lived in New York City too long and who also just wanted to get it over with. She told me to take a deep breath, and on the count of three, she would insert the needle into my catheter; when she inserted the needle, it felt like she had punched me in the chest; the wind was completely knocked out of me.

When I immediately hunched over, gasped for air, and began to cry, she asked, "Wait, did you numb your port site two hours before coming?" No one had told me to numb my port before receiving chemotherapy. This was one of the most painful experiences of my entire cancer journey; yes, more painful than my double mastectomy. Kink offered me solace, a soft place to land, the ability to submit to someone I trusted with my body, rather than doctors and nurses who could so easily neglect to tell me about a numbing cream. Before cancer, my body was being used for someone else's pleasure, but kink offered an opportunity to be worshiped—and not just a part of me, but *all* of me.

Stepping outside of my comfort zone by sending a nude or attending a play party forced me to challenge the ableist assumptions I had about my own body. I do not think a play party needs to be or even is everyone's ministry, but finding ways to move beyond what we have inherited from the world is essential. I am constantly trying to lift my inherited views. Looking into feminist, queer-led-and-run porn sites has been so helpful in how I view bodies. Seeing a fat Black femme masturbate or even be bent over and fucked by her leather Domme not only brings me pleasure but also affirms my own body.

Finally, understanding how white supremacy has long determined who is deemed attractive—marked by disability or fatness—can help anyone begin to decolonize their ideas of desirability. Learning that who I find attractive or what I hate about my body isn't unique or original allows me to interrupt these harmful thoughts (present tense, as I haven't arrived anywhere, and this work is ongoing). Furthermore, desirability is a tool to keep us all on a spiral about how something looks.

I speak about pleasure expansively. I hope you understand by now that pleasure amid oppressive systems must begin with examining why some people are intentionally kept from having their material needs met and thus unable to access any level of pleasure, including but not limited to sexual pleasure. A truly inclusive world of pleasure is not complicit in white supremacist systems and doesn't create conditions that actively push disabled and fat folks out of society. It goes beyond hanging a nondescript sign about honoring all bodies—it interrogates and radically reorganizes itself around the bodies it has worked so hard to discard. A sexually free world is actively decolonizing and anti-racist. It means the end of wealth disparity, safe and affordable housing for all, disruption of cisgender heterosexual identity as THE standard, restorative justice, and the end of STI stigma. It means fat bodies exist without contest, and accessibility for all bodies, abilities, and ages. It is very Black, queer, Indigenous, pro-slut, and supportive of sex work. It celebrates asexuality and trans femmes thriving. It demands reparations from the state for Black people.

Standing in the mirror trying to avoid looking at my double mastectomy scars, as I got dressed to do labor for a job that did not care about me, has now morphed into me using those same scars to resist the notion that we are only valuable for what we produce. Even when I went topless, people still tried to confine me to their narrow imagination of chronically ill people—our bodies serving as constant reminders to able-bodied people that they are "better off." Sitting alone at chemotherapy appointments made me realize how much my body had been used by the very people who claimed to desire me. It wasn't until I was tasked with honoring my body holistically that I felt liberated as a sexual being.

I had to sit with the fatphobia I had internalized along the way to really unearth the harmful thoughts I had about my body and, thus, any other fat body. What if all of us were forced to sit with all the biases we have about our own bodies and those around us? How might the world look different if we took the time to interrogate those beliefs rather than just accepting them as unique? At every moment, the institutions that comprise society are flooding us with messages that say we need to be thin and able-bodied in order to have our material needs met, let alone receive pleasure. Believing that everybody deserves clean water, air, quality hospitals, food, and free health care should not be a radical thought. All of us collectively dismantling the systems that teach us to hate ourselves is how we triumph and live freely, content in our bodies, knowing no one body is better than another, ensuring everyone has what they need not only to survive but thrive on this floating rock.

- Who benefits from you hating your body? Consider how the beauty, diet, and medical industries profit from your self-doubt.
- Trace the lineage of your body. What ancestral stories are written in your curves, your features, your movements? Which parts of you carry the resilience of those who came before?
- How have you been conditioned to view your body as something that needs fixing rather than something to be celebrated?
- What would it mean to see your body as more than its productivity or appearance—as a site of joy, pleasure, and radical self-determination?

# 4

# That's So Gay!

> "'Queer' not as being about who you're having sex with (that can be a dimension of it); but 'queer' as being about the self that is at odds with everything around it and has to invent and create and find a place to speak and to thrive and to live."
>
> —bell hooks

CONTENT WARNING:
*sexual assault, homophobia, transphobia*

What do Beetlejuice, Oprah Winfrey, and Jerry Springer have in common? Honestly, not much, but they were my babysitters. At seven years old, I was a latchkey kid. I'd come home, throw my backpack on the table, boil water, act as if I were a gourmet chef sprinkling the seasoning packet over the Oodles of Noodles before I plopped them in a bowl, and turn on the TV. Jerry Springer came on first, and I knew I had made it just in time if I turned on the TV and heard that familiar chant: "Jerry! Jerry! Jerry!" The premise of *The Jerry Springer Show* was to bring on regular people who were doing something that would be considered shocking to the masses; queerness and transness fit that criteria of '90s sensational televesion, with episode titles like "I'm gay and I'm leaving you," "Straight boyfriend sleeps with men," and "Dude, try a transexual." The episode "Straight to gay in a week" was about a man who was cheating on his fiancée and subsequently wanted to end the engagement after a week to be with the person with whom he had been having an affair. When Jerry said, "Let's meet the person you have been cheating with," the crowd erupted with laughter, pointing and cheering when a man turned the corner and appeared on stage. The crowd screamed even louder, in a mix of disgust and surprise, when the two men kissed. The messaging was clear: Queerness was a joke, its only utility to provide shock value on a show where the presumption was that everyone in the audience and watching at home was straight and cisgender. My seven-year-old baby queer self took this as further evidence that the thoughts I was having about girls were wrong. In 2022, after being on television for three decades, Jerry Springer would give a lackluster apology for the impact his show had on culture but the damage had been done.

I did my homework with *Beetlejuice* in the background, as it didn't hold my attention quite like the shows I had no business watching. *Oprah* had similarly controversial episodes that did the same thing to queerness and transness as the *Jerry Springer Show*, just with a more even keel. Her audience was never as rowdy as Jerry's, and Winfrey is a skilled journalist, so she was able to be objective, but the use of queer and trans people as content for cis-hetero people's entertainment was still prevalent.

In an *Oprah* episode that I don't think I ever saw but which aired October 11, 1988, on the first official National Coming Out Day, guests came to the mic and shared that they were gay, with no further distinction as to where they saw themselves within what we now recognize as the LGBTQIA+ community; almost as if their coming out had been tailored to fit the audience's understanding. Oprah asked follow-up questions like "Do you feel better now?" or "Is it easier to share here than to confront people in your life in person?" There was no speculation as to why coming out is hard nor the potential repercussions of doing so on national television. Having a segment on National Coming Out Day may have seemed like a progressive thing to do, but without acknowledging the impacts of homophobia, it landed inauspiciously as the ratings grab it was intended to be. These episodes of *Jerry Springer* and *Oprah* unintentionally fit right into the popular debate of the '90s: Are you born gay or is it a choice? This half-hearted, nonsensical chicken-before-the-egg debate positioned queerness as an unfortunate consequence of childhood harm rather than just a completely normal way to love.

Precisely how old I was when I was sexually assaulted by a family friend is blurry. I was no older than ten. I still had a great deal of innocence and trust in the people around me. Trauma has a way of erasing the memories that your brain doesn't want to face. Although I was always told that no one should touch my genitals, what do you do when it feels good? My mom's Lifetime movies taught me that a big scary man would try to assault me, and it would be painful; not a twenty-year-old woman who I idolized. I wanted to be just like her; she wore lace bras with underwire and knew all the lyrics to Salt-N-Pepa's "Shoop." I'd practice "Shoop" so that I could impress her the next time we saw each other. She was the granddaughter of my dad's best friend's parents. She happened to live with her grandparents, and whenever they watched us, she acted more like a babysitter than they did due to their age. I wish they had actually watched us; maybe then the assault would never have happened.

They lived in a row home in Baltimore City; maybe it was Maryland weather patterns or just a gloomy foreboding, but there seemed to be a perpetual cloud that sat over their house. I don't ever remember the sun peeking out. Walking up their entrance stairs seemed like they would never end. I'd count the steps and avoid the cracks, hoping to slow time. Mr. Wilson walked with a cane in his right hand and a tobacco pipe in the other. Ms. Gene was always quiet; you wouldn't know she was coming if the floorboards didn't creak beneath her. She embraced my dad like he was her own child. Their granddaughter wouldn't come to the door to say hello or goodbye to my parents; she would appear after they left and disappear right before they arrived. Like clockwork, my parents would drop my brother and I off, the grandparents would disappear, and she would appear in the living room with her boom box and Salt-N-Pepa CD. We'd listen to music, and then I would end up in her room. She'd invite me to play upstairs, and every time I would oblige without hesitation even though I knew what she meant. My brother stayed downstairs. I was being assaulted every time we went to their house, for a little over a year. It may have been longer, but my brain only held on to snippets of memories:

> Um, you're packed, and you're stacked 'specially in the back
>
> Brother, wanna thank your mother for a butt like that
> (thanks, Mom)
>
> Can I get some fries with that shake-shake boobie?
>
> If looks could kill you would be an Uzi
>
> Or a shotgun, bang! What's up with that thang?

I still get jolted back to that time when I hear that song. For seventeen years, I would guard the secret that I was sexually assaulted. I didn't think anyone would believe me, I wasn't sure whether it had been assault, and I was connecting my newfound interest in women to that early experience. I felt like a question mark. If I told people I was bisexual, would I also have to reveal that I was assaulted? Would they link the assault to me being queer as a way to delegitimize who I am? What is wrong with me? Why did this happen to me?

I would eventually stop watching *Jerry Springer* and *Oprah*, but their impact endured. Showcasing transness and queerness as a mockery or a spectacle is homophobic even when done with the best of intentions. There is no way to measure the impact that these popular shows had on queer people today, but I grew up believing that I must keep my bisexuality a secret. Bisexuality and assault existed on the same plane for me: I was ashamed of feeling a certain way and ashamed that a certain thing had happened, so I kept them both a secret. When I eventually came out, that did not magically erase all the ways I had been indoctrinated by the straight agenda—nor my internalized homophobia. It would take me years to uncouple my assault from my queerness, and in some ways, I am still unearthing internalized queerphobia and transphobia.

My mother's favorite movie when I was growing up was *Waiting to Exhale*. She saw it in theaters on opening day with her friends, and she listened to the soundtrack nonstop. When she eventually rented the film on VHS, she would hurry to fast-forward the sex scenes so that I wouldn't see. Because I knew I wasn't supposed to see, I would sneak back into the living room later at night to watch those parts. As a kid, I could not relate to Savannah, Bernadine, Robyn, and Gloria, but I learned that men are sneaky; that they lie, cheat, and will leave you for a white woman. I couldn't articulate why at the time, but I thought it was incredibly hot to stand watching all your ex's belongings burn to ash while smoking a cigarette. Bernadine was probably my first crush, though I didn't realize it. I found pixie cuts, being pissed at men, and having a ball with your friends everything I wanted to be when I grew up.

I begged to have a TV in my room, so that I could play Super Nintendo late into the night. Until I discovered porn. I'd wait until my parents were asleep before flipping to the channel with the pixelated screen. I could see shapes and hear moaning and knew that something salacious was occurring. When I was tired of pixels, I'd switch to HBO's *Real Sex*. But it wasn't just sex, it was a deep dive into people's sex lives, their fantasies, and their fetishes. I preferred the porn because it didn't require me to learn about people's most intimate proclivities. As a thirteen-year-old, I had already formed beliefs around what was "normal." *Real Sex* felt too niche for me, likely because it focused on real people as opposed to pandering to white cisgender male fantasies. Anytime I stumbled upon a porn scene with two women (though it was never Black women) I fine-tuned my attention, wanting to see more. Around this time, I began admitting to my journal that I could imagine being intimate or sexual with a woman, but that that was all I wanted—no romantic connection.

The first time I saw a Black lesbian dynamic was while watching the movie *The Color Purple*. Shug dresses Celie up, guiding her to the mirror and encouraging her to smile. The way Shug gazes at Celie is filled with such deep admiration; I never interpreted her expression as sexual. They then sit together on the bed, where Celie confides in Shug about her lack of experience with real love and consensual intimacy, sharing, "He just gets on top of me and does his business," as she laments the coldness of her abusive husband. Shug responds with a gentle laugh and then leans in to kiss Celie. Steven Spielberg received pushback for including a kiss in the movie. My porn and *Waiting to Exhale* conditioning had taught me that two characters kissing would quickly escalate into something more. But Celie and Shug's kiss felt friendly to me, not sexual, and maybe that was the point of Spielberg's direction. I had to read the book to learn that Celie and Shug were lovers; the movie completely obfuscated this narrative. It's deeply telling that we live in a society where vivid depictions of sexual assault are more acceptable than a queer romance.

The only other dose of queer visibility I got was in the movie *Set It Off*, and the scene in question lasted no more than thirty seconds—but felt like hours considering how many times I rewound and replayed the VHS with delicate precision. Played by Queen Latifah, Cleo, a masculine-presenting lesbian, languishes in her garage on top of a vintage Cadillac in a sports bra and baggy unzipped work pants while her girlfriend Ursula, a deaf femme-presenting light-skinned Black woman with a blond buzz cut (played by a hearing actress, Samantha MacLachlan), gyrates seductively above her, clad only in fishnet stockings and a thong bodysuit. The other three characters—Stony (Jada Pinkett Smith), Frankie (Vivica A. Fox), and T.T. (Kimberly Elise)—enter the garage and interrupt the scene, confronting Cleo about her changed behavior since their first bank robbery. Unfazed, Cleo kisses Ursula's leg and quips that she's been acting differently because "look what I have in front of me." Then the scene ends. There is no narrative development of their relationship. We don't see Cleo using ASL with Ursula, going on dates, holding hands; and when Cleo is murdered, there are no extended visuals of Ursula's grief. Jada Pinkett Smith's character was the only developed love story; she went on elaborate dates with Keith, the character played by Blair Underwood; they had a sex scene; and their romance would extend until the end of the movie. The hypersexualization of a queer relationship that takes on a binary appearance, given that Cleo was a stud and Ursula was more feminine presenting, occurred to my twelve-year-old, developing, prepubescent brain as a more typical (read: *legitimate*) queer relationship than Celie and Shug's friendly dalliances, because it mirrored my only other visual representation of queer relationships: porn. The tension herein is that it was important to see, but it was no different than how *Oprah*, *Jerry Springer*, and other shows would exploit and denigrate queerness and transness.

These TV shows and movies continued to make queerness taboo and shield everyone from seeing the richness of a queer relationship or a trans person in love. They played it safe, in a way that wasn't intentional. Of course, Takashi Bufford and Kate Lanier, the Black cis man and white cis woman who wrote *Set It Off*, could not imagine Cleo in a loving relationship as a Black, fat, dark-skinned masculine person. Their limiting beliefs were no different than my own: Black lesbians were only valuable in their expression of hypersexuality. Before I had my first lesbian relationship, I wanted to be with someone who was masculine, and all I could imagine for our relationship was us having sex. I have wrestled with my fascination with the scenes in *Set It Off* and *The Color Purple*, how what was hidden and subverted and sanitized by the Hollywood machine actually resonated with me. While it felt significant to see Black, fat, or disabled queer people in a sexual context, it also did not feel good. There was something else under the surface; the depiction was limiting and lacked the richness of actual Black queer experience. As my good friend and sexologist Cindy Lee Alves reminds us, we have to make space for "both and," leaving room for nuance. The tension of the unexplored in these scenes made me feel claustrophobic. No making space here.

I came out to my boyfriend when I was fifteen. He was the person that I spoke to the most, who made me feel safe enough to reveal even my deepest secrets. My relationships with my close girlfriends were centered around boy talk, so coming out to them didn't occur to me as an option. My dad and brother already had a lot to say about my boyfriend (read: *they didn't like him*), so I knew I couldn't tell them that I was interested in girls too. My other family members were life-on-earth-is-Sodom-and-Gomorrah-get-prepared-for-the-rapture-coming-in-the-new-year religious. And, if I came out to my boyfriend, who also liked girls, maybe he would understand? (Wishful thinking.) My interest in girls at the time was strictly sexual, and I assured him of that. Coming out as bi-curious seemed like the safest way to identify and still maintain what most high schoolers want: a romantic relationship.

"I have something to tell you, and I don't want you to judge me," I told him. "I think I am bisexual." I held my breath and bit my lip, hoping that he'd break the silence before I had to speak again.

He was still quiet. "Did you hear me?" I whispered.

"Yes, I heard you, but what does this mean?" I went on to reassure him that I still liked him and asked if maybe at some point down the line, I could experiment with girls, as if he had the power to grant me permission. We stayed together through high school and the first year of college; I even moved to be closer to him in hopes that we would stay together forever in a very toxic, Disney kind of way. Spoiler alert: We didn't stay together forever. By the time I transferred to a new college at nineteen, I had grown more confident than the nervous fifteen-year-old who had stumbled over their words when coming out. Moving away from him seemed like the perfect opportunity to have my first bisexual experience. We had fought like cats and dogs, as he felt threatened by my desire to explore, and I grew tired of assuring him that I still liked him. I didn't have the language to articulate that I felt stifled by his insecurity over not being enough. The relationship would eventually fizzle after a long game of friends with benefits, when I solidified for myself that I deserved more than catering to the sexual needs of a man.

The term "gay agenda" has been bandied about—when children watch television shows with visible gay characters, if the word *gay* is even mentioned in a school (Florida is a mess!), when drag queens read at the library, or when I made a video singing "gay baby" while my child wore a rainbow onesie. People's fear of being overtaken by gayness is rooted in the fallacy that everyone is inherently heterosexual.

Clearly the only agenda that exists is heterosexuality. TV and film depictions of queerness are generally hidden behind R ratings or late-night spots, suggesting they are a disruption to the media's regimen of heteronormativity. Before a child has language, adults will make comments about who they will attract, or comment that a little girl has a boyfriend because she meets a boy at the playground. Contrary to popular essentialist and ahistorical analysis, heterosexuality is not inherently pure or any more natural than queerness. Yet this has dictated a prevailing belief system for thousands of years, due in no small part to the colonial impacts of Christianity. And no, Christianity is not the only homophobic organized religion, and there are atheists who are homophobic, and its impacts have been vast, leading most of us growing to believe the lie that heterosexuality is the way, the truth, and the light. In *Queering the Color Line: Race and the Invention of Homosexuality in American Culture*, Siobhan B. Somerville writes, "'homosexual' or 'heterosexual' emerged at the same time that the United States was aggressively constructing and policing the boundary between 'black' and 'white.'" Historically, there has been a concerted effort to make queerness a "savage" identity, much in the same way that Blackness was created to be by the early white European imperial power structure, which, during its conquests of land and human beings, endorsed a dominant narrative that queerness was perverse, backward, and a sin and therefore linked to the Black and the Indigenous, the base and hypersexual peoples. As time went on, and social mores changed, the permeability and malleability of whiteness would erase Black and Indigenous histories of queerness, portraying it as an evolved sexual identity that only white people have access to.

Popular sayings like "girl crush" or "bromance" are rooted in homophobia; instead of just stating that you have a crush on someone that is a girl while you are also a girl, there is this need to cover it up by not just saying it's a crush but also embedding your sexual identity for fear of being questioned. Heterosexual women will lament that they feel so much safer at gay bars, simply due to the fact that they are not being hit on. Without the gaze of heterosexual men, heterosexual women feel free. So why minimize queerness by claiming a "girl crush"? A sexual identity where people feel unsafe is spoken about in more valid terms than the one in which people find a haven.

Many cisgender heterosexual women will share with me their fantasies of being with other women like they're dirty little secrets. They express concern for what a departure from heterosexuality would entail, but the assumption that queer or lesbian women will fulfill your sexual needs is an assumption rooted in the heteronormative agenda. It diminishes queerness to treat it as a tool that can be manipulated for heterosexual exploration. Discovering that you are queer through unsatisfactory sexual experiences is valid, and queerness is so much more than sex. Sexuality is fluid, even when you identify as heterosexual. You are not confined to one type of sex—explore! But know that queerness does not exist simply to satisfy your curiosities. Same message for queer folks: Sex does not have to look one way based on harmful gender tropes and heteronormativity. Queer people have to divorce ourselves from heteronormativity just as heterosexual folks do, as we have all been trained inside of the same messed-up circus tent.

I once thought my queerness existed only as a distant sexual fantasy. Queerness was something I witnessed when I was sneaking around to find it. I thought it should not be seen in the light of day and should remain a dark-shrouded fantasy, only sexual, not a deep knowing of who I was as a human being.

We attended the University of Miami, a campus in Coral Gables, Florida, that resembled a resort designed for the predominantly wealthy, predominantly white student body from the East Coast and Midwest. Every patch of grass that caught the sun became their personal tanning bed. Coral Gables isn't the Miami most people picture, endless rows of hotels, beaches, and expensive cars. Coral Gables is a suburb of Miami and while the wealth is palatable, the racial lines of gentrification dividing the Haitian community from the Cubans is stark. The first time I saw my first girlfriend, Brandy, I nearly walked into a bush. High cheekbones, dark skin, lip piercing, shaved head, and carrying a skateboard. She looked like Grace Jones and Pharrell Williams had a baby. I didn't know how to approach someone I liked. My *Waiting to Exhale* upbringing taught me that men are supposed to make the first move, so I was left wondering—how does this work when it's two women?

I resorted to Facebook. It was new at the time and fulfilled on allowing people to express themselves behind a keyboard than in person. I already had a profile set up, but it listed me as "interested in men." I hovered over the "interested in men and women" option in the drop-down menu, sweating with nervousness. I called my roommate for advice, and without hesitation, she encouraged me to share my truth with the whole school (this was back when Facebook was just for college students, before every auntie and cousin joined). It felt like a coming-out experience in itself. After making the change, I walked around campus, half expecting someone to come up and ask me about it. I would have even appreciated the congratulations, but I got nothing. It took me a week to request my new crush as a friend. I squealed and ran away from the computer. The friend request went unheeded.

My next plan was to get a job in campus security, where she also worked. I asked for the same shift as her. It was the graveyard shift, and I fantasized about us talking all night, her walking me back to my dorm room and sealing the evening with a kiss under the Miami night sky. But on the night in question, somebody else was filling in for her. I was deflated.

I begged a mutual friend to introduce us, and I kept making my intentions known until, finally, having a girlfriend was checked off of my "bisexual to-do list." I was so smitten to have a girlfriend that I could barely contain myself, skipping class just to make out or have sex. She was sort of like a stemme, a few lineups short of what the early 2000s deemed a stud, and I presented as femme. I was finally living an extended version of the Cleo and Ursula scene. I fell into a dynamic where sex happened on her terms, whenever she wanted to initiate. Our relationship mirrored how I viewed lesbian relationships—purely sexual, transactional, you do for me and I will please you, mostly through sexual means, and use sex as a way to dominate you, keep you near, give you what you think you want or what you deserve, as I am incapable of giving you love, care, and affection.

Queer people are not exempt from being homophobic. Internalized homophobia shows up in how we try to be with each other in an amorous way, with little to no examples of how that should look. For me, it became about provision: Here's what I can give to you or get from you in exchange for companionship so I don't have to be lonely. Said another way, my first serious queer relationship had a heteronormative dynamic—one of utility, convenience, duty, and exchange, rooted in capitalist institutions. There is nothing queer about using people, and if we consider queerness as deviant from what bell hooks calls the "dominator culture" or mainstream society, there is nothing queer about capitalism. We were both lonely, and a lot of people are lonely, but there is a particular loneliness that comes with marginalization. Neither of us could articulate this. Nor did a predominantly white institution (PWI) offer us the time, safety, or space to untangle it all. We had to play roles that were already at our fingertips.

Our conversations were surface level, and Brandy spent most of our time together obsessing over clothes. If we weren't in her dorm room, or in class, we were shopping. She was born and raised in Miami by her grandmother. After her grandmother passed away, her mother became more involved in her life. Brandy never knew her father, and her mother had always been openly lesbian. She was attending our school on a full scholarship, and she would wait for her refund checks to buy books or new clothes from Urban Outfitters. When Brandy couldn't afford to shop, I eagerly helped out, even though it meant racking up credit card debt. My desire to stay in the relationship was stronger than my concern about the growing financial burden. This was a barely concealed analog for the transactional nature of our relationship.

I always prided myself on being good with parents, so I wasn't scared to meet her mom for the first time, I was excited. The three of us were in Brandy's tiny dorm room when Brandy started dancing behind me, pulling me to grind on her to "You" by Lloyd and Lil Wayne, as if her mother wasn't sitting three feet away from us. Brandy wasn't usually into PDA. "We shouldn't be acting like this in front of your mom," I whispered. She ignored me, like she was trying to prove a point. She danced around me, aware of the awkwardness, but rather than stopping, she smiled, leaned in, and kissed me before I could even process that her mother was watching us like she was one of our peers. To Brandy, I think she was. But it was my internalized homophobia that left me feeling as though dancing and sharing a kiss in front of a parent was somehow risqué.

We didn't talk much about her relationship with her mom, but we didn't need to say much: Her mental health revealed what words couldn't. She often had crying spells, spending entire days in bed, overwhelmed by everything, by life. On good days, we'd go out and enjoy each other's company. On bad days, I'd tiptoe around her mood, afraid that I might trigger another crying spell. I didn't know how to ask what she needed or how to support her; I just stayed quiet until it passed, which sometimes took days. At the time, there were very few resources on how to support a partner with depression. Sex became a catchall solution for everything—arguments, tough mental health days, her mother's reappearance in her life, and any other unresolved pain.

A Black queer person is not just navigating life being queer but sitting at multiple intersections of oppression. So many queer and trans people are navigating mental health struggles, and it is no different for Black queer people, if not even more heightened and compounded by perpetual racial and systemic violence. As queer visibility increased in the media, this did not result in the material conditions shifting or much visibility for Black queer people. There is often the belief that visibility equals safety, acceptance, and a post-homophobic world, but often what visibility really looks like is the media's attempt to capitalize off the most marketable (read: conventionally attractive cis-hetero-adjacent queer representation). For example, in the late 1990s and early 2000s, media began elevating an image of queerness that was white, wealthy, and, if viewed after 9 p.m., included pelvic bones peeking out of ultra-low-rise jeans, turkey basters, and erect nipples in white tank tops sitting poolside at the Dinah Shore Weekend. Not to mention the rapid ascension of the crystalline-blue-eyed second coming of late-stage-capitalist-lesbianism herself, Ellen DeGeneres, and the crossover popularity of shows like *Queer as Folk*, *The L Word* (which only had one Black character), and *Will and Grace*.

My life was dramatically different from the narratives perpetuated by the mainstream media although I had worked so hard to have it match up. I was constantly worried about my severely depressed partner, opening credit cards to have consumption express my love, hiding who I was to my family, and constantly searching for Black queer community. My experience was similar to those of so many other Black queer people, but how could we know? Not seeing ourselves represented anywhere made so many of us feel invisible, and vulnerable to the lie that Black people are inherently homophobic. This fallacy was created to place blame on Black people for homophobia, using our forced ties to Christianity. Once it was no longer mainstream to be homophobic, white people began to place that responsibility on the Black community's shoulders and conveniently hid their hands behind their backs.

If Black people are inherently homophobic, then once again white people get to be seen as civilized. This was best exemplified in California during the 2008 elections, which heralded the emergence of the widely controversial ballot Proposition 8, seeking to ban same-sex marriages, an initiative that passed in the third largest state in the country. White cisgender gay men placed the blame of Prop 8's success on Black communities, and as the young people say, that "math is not mathing." In 2008, sex and relationship advice columnist and journalist Dan Savage said, "I'm thrilled that we've just elected our first African American president . . . But I can't help but feeling hurt that the love and support aren't mutual. I do know this, though: I'm done pretending that the handful of racist gay white men out there—and they're out there, and I think they're scum—are a bigger problem for African Americans, gay and straight, than the huge numbers of homophobic African Americans are for gay Americans, whatever their color." While Barack Obama was against gay marriage at the beginning of his presidency, so were all forty-three white presidents before him. Black people do not have the institutional power nor the population numbers to single-handedly overturn any ballot. The reason why gay marriage passed was largely due to white cis men wanting marriage to legitimize their queerness, to better assimilate into mainstream cishet society. The deliberate erasure of the long history of queerness among Black and Indigenous people serves as a tactic to position white queer identities as the default. I think this is an important place for white people to toggle with, since whiteness is pedestalized and queerness is inherently the opposite of that position, what is queerness truly to a white person? This gentrification of queerness has led to the false notion that queerness can be reduced to a single narrative, appearance, and expression. Yet another example that white cisgender men are still white, even if they are gay.

I see my students struggling with a desire to "look the part," questioning whether they should mimic the common expressions of queerness seen among white queer people: shaving the sides of their heads or hanging keychain links from their jeans. Because whiteness is so powerful, white queer people have more freedom to alter their physical appearance to express their identity without fear of scrutiny. Their whiteness shields them from the level of judgment others might face. Understanding that Black people are not inherently homophobic and that whiteness does not need to be at the center of our expression of queerness is crucial for us to unlearn and undo the indoctrination that we are agents of our own subjugation. Buying into the fact that Black queer people are inherently wrong results in us relating to each other as if we are disposable in our platonic and romantic relationships—holding ourselves, and therefore each other, in low regard.

"I really like what I used to do with my ex," Brandy told me. My heart sank, and my mind started to race. Why was she thinking about other girls? Was I not enough? "We used to go to sex shops and pick out dildos and vibrators together." My brain raced to a solution, not wanting to deal with the humiliation that I could potentially be doing bisexuality wrong.

"We can do that! Let's go to a sex shop!" There was nothing her ex could do that I could not also do, and my ego was in a secret competition with her. While deliberating which sex shop to go to, we landed on one in South Beach, away from campus so nobody would see us.

We went to a sex shop in the middle of the workday. We walked around the store, mostly silent, occasionally pointing and giggling at lingerie or whips. When we got to the dildo section, I put my head close to Brandy's and whispered, "Which one do you like?" She smirked like she was a pro at shopping at sex-toy stores, lifted her finger, and pointed to a conservatively sized baby blue dildo. I thought it was cute and didn't want to dally too long, so I whispered back, "Let's get it."

"Did you two want to get anything else, maybe a strap on for the dildo?" the sales associate asked, as if she knew we didn't really know what we were doing. Brandy said yes louder than she had spoken all day.

We walked out of the store in silence. "Do you want to go to the beach?" I asked, unable to bear the awkward quiet any longer. We didn't have swimsuits or towels, but for college kids with a beach practically in our backyard, showing up unprepared wasn't unusual. We lay back on the shore, cupping our heads in our hands to keep the sand out of our hair, listening to seagulls squabbling over scraps from an overflowing trash can, small jet planes buzzing overhead with ads for upcoming parties and car dealerships, and the ocean waves crashing. "That was fun," I said, my voice betraying uncertainty.

"Yeah," she replied flatly.

"Are you okay?" I asked, breaking the silence for the second time, now wondering if going to the sex-toy shop had been a mistake.

"I'm okay, I just kinda miss my ex, we used to come to this beach when she visited." *This beach* being the main destination for all spring breakers in Miami. There was nothing special or secret about this beach. I couldn't hide my frustration, and we began to argue. I don't remember exactly what I said, but our argument continued ineffectively, two people who had not learned how to be in conflict or express emotions. Two people who, it turns out, barely knew each other at all.

We were interrupted when a group of teenagers approached us and asked, "Are you two dykes? Who is the man and who is the woman?" As they ran off, their laughter roared above the ocean waves, but their question illuminated my own internalized homophobia.

There's a persistent assumption that being queer means you're automatically free of homophobia, but as mentioned, in a homophobic world, it's impossible not to absorb heteronormative expectations. Brandy wanted to be penetrated, something she missed about her ex, and I felt like I couldn't provide that because I was a femme. She was masculine; wasn't she supposed to be the one doing the penetrating? Heteronormativity is a powerful force. I was so focused on replicating heterosexual roles in our queer relationship that I couldn't really hear what my partner was articulating about her sexual desires. I wanted to be in a relationship with a girl, but I hadn't fully questioned or challenged my own ingrained preconceptions.

We eventually ended our emotionally unstable relationship but would remain friends like good anxiously attached queers do. I would go on to have other partners, who I also subconsciously expected to play heterocentric house disguised as queerness. When Prop 8 was overturned, I celebrated with my white partner, taking to social media to share how important the ability to marry was for us.

The first time I actually considered who I was as a queer person was when I was twenty-eight and I was forced to sit still, under fluorescent lighting, in a La-Z-Boy chair, hooked up to a chemotherapy IV. I was married to a white person who I had fought to be with. She'd told me I wasn't "her type," and I told her, "I will change that." She was everything I was fed about whiteness and queerness, all wrapped up in one; she even looked like Ellen and, just like the world I tried to fit into but which never accepted me, she wasn't interested in me. I'd eventually convince her to date me, and she obliged either out of pity or her selfish desires to be seen as the white lesbian liberal with a Black girlfriend. I'd believed we fell in love, but sudden chronic illness/disability has a way of unearthing that which is hidden below the surface. She never truly wanted to be with me, she just wanted to be with the idea of me. We had an apartment in gentrified Brooklyn that we only secured because of her whiteness, full of IKEA furniture and trinkets from our time in the Peace Corps. On the surface, we looked like a lesbian dream, but our relationship had no politic. I wanted to be with her to be seen as beautiful in the eyes of whiteness and valid as a queer person. It took a year of chemotherapy and a double mastectomy for me to realize that my queerness certainly was not going to be found in whiteness, or my marriage. After eight years together and one and a half years married, we divorced.

My queerness was here all along, but I needed to define it for myself and honor all of who I was, especially my Blackness. Okay, I also slept with a Black queer person who woke up in the morning and asked, "Where is your bonnet at?", found it, and secured it on my head, which was the intimacy I had been craving but couldn't articulate. I had been searching for my queerness, and it was there all along in my Blackness. The honor of existing as a Black queer person is that our existence is a radical act. Holding a queer identity requires us not just to love but to invent.

Queerness demanded imagination and creativity, I was looking for myself in media representations that wanted to fit queerness into a cis-heterocentric palatable box. As bell hooks said, "'queer' [is] about the self that is at odds with everything around it and that has to invent and create and find a place to speak and to thrive and to live." I had always been me, but I was hiding from myself in hopes that I could be or be with Ellen. And—this is likely a chapter for another book—but can whiteness be queered? I stepped into my queerness powerfully the moment I began to question everything around me. As Cathy Cohen writes in *Punks, Bulldaggers, and Welfare Queens*, "at the intersection of oppression and resistance lies the radical potential of queerness to challenge and bring together all those deemed marginal and all those committed to liberatory politics." I identified as bisexual, which then evolved to lesbian, then to queer as I became less and less fixated on what was going to make me appear LGBTQIA+ versus how I could upend the systems that directly attack anyone who does not conform. It wasn't until I saw that I was queered in every way, not just the way I love, that I began to shift into myself.

Are you gay, yet? Just kidding. This chapter was not intended for people to take on an identity that does not honor who they believe themselves to be. More queer people does not inherently end cis-hetero supremacy, but destroying the idea that all of us should be and are straight or that any of us have fixed ways of being is an effective place to start. A few questions to ruminate on:

- How does cis-heteropatriarchy show up in your relationships?
- Are there certain roles in relationships that you apply to masculinity and femininity?

- Are you assuming young people in your life are straight?
- In what ways could you be harboring homophobic bias? Yes, even in your queer relationship.
- Do your relationships feel more like a business deal than a reciprocal exchange of communication and intimacy?

Our relationships are political too.

# 5

# A Read: White Womanhood and the Maintenance of Power

> "I will cut off this right arm of mine before I will ever work or demand the ballot for the Negro and not the woman."
>
> —Susan B. Anthony

I will be honest with you: I did not know that the Peace Corps was a magnet for liberal newly college-graduated white women who did not want to jump straight into corporate America like their white cis men counterparts and were determined to spend two years being saviors of people they ultimately saw as beneath them. I also did not know that it was a lesbian hotspot. I can admit that I joined the Peace Corps after college with similar savior aspirations. I grew up watching infomercials depicting famished Black children in unnamed countries, giving viewers a myopic depiction of an entire continent and a xenophobic view of the United States. It worked on me; I watched those commercials and thought that because I lived in the US, I was somehow better off. They didn't, however, completely brainwash me, because as a Black American going into "civil" service, I hated the United States, a sharp distinction between myself and the other, white, volunteers. I wanted to use the Peace Corps to get away from a country in which I was born but never felt welcome.

At the time, I did not have the language to articulate that the forces causing starvation in African countries were the same ones relegating Black people to food apartheid in the United States. I believed that our US government–sanctioned program was created to do good around the world. Beyoncé may work hard, but cognitive dissonance works harder. It wasn't long before my xenophobic altruistic fantasy came to a screeching halt.

I was one of two Black people in my Peace Corps cohort. There was one Asian person, and the rest of the forty volunteers were white, mostly women. I dreaded service training. The forced togetherness felt like neoliberal bratty whine-offs mixed with poop stories and assessing whose access to water was the worst. For the first time in my life, I was living in a place that was predominantly Black, and it was a balm, but our service training disrupted that reprieve. Being white in Ethiopia is like being Black in a predominantly white space anywhere in the world: Someone is always trying to talk to you, staring at you, objectifying your body, hair, looks, and speech. There is a popular saying on social media, "When you are Black you are never really alone," but the reverse is true in a predominantly Black country or space. No one ever bothered me.

We opened training sessions by sharing how we were feeling being alone on our respective sites all over the country. A white woman would share her frustrations about the food, street harassment, latrines, or lack of running water. She missed the comforts of US life, and she felt like she wasn't helping Ethiopians because she had decided that she knew more than an Indigenous population that fought back against being colonized by the Italians and survived famine by using their natural resource of tef to make injera, a nutritionally dense spongelike bread. The other white volunteers would nod in arrogant agreement.

In contrast, I shared that for the first time in my life, I did not feel like a conspicuous outsider; people often assumed I was Ethiopian. Sacrificing running water, pooping in a latrine, and eating injera on a regular basis seemed like a small price to pay for this level of comfort. The same white woman, who had just been on the verge of tears sharing her struggles in this open forum, suddenly lashed out at me. "You do not look Ethiopian! Your life is totally different." Before I could respond, she continued, "You are American, just like me." I was so accustomed to white women and their fragility that her response did not surprise me. What stayed with me, though, was that in a room full of white women who signed up to "help" in another country, not one of them spoke up for me—not even the volunteer that I was dating. She spoke with so much convinction, as if our ancestors arrived to the shores of the United States in the same way.

I want to say that American white women experienced a sudden shift to the right as part of an unexplainable conservative rebrand when national exit polls for the 2024 presidential election showed 53 percent of them voted to re-elect Donald Trump for his second presidency. But that would deny the long-standing legacy of white cisgender women, across the spectrum of political and cultural identities, colluding with white cisgender men in their bid toward world domination in exchange for a little power of their own. This collusion represents not an end to patriarchy, but a new beginning for it—one that makes space for all white women. From Ariana Grande speaking AAVE to the point where she is nicknamed "Blackiana," to the Kardashian-Jenner family dynasty of culture vultures profiting billions from appropriating Black aesthetics, to the white lesbian who identifies as a "stud," to the well-meaning Zionist self-help guru with millions of followers, to the budding content creator marketing Christian ethnonationalism under the guise of the "tradwife" social media trend—the provenance of which is a nostalgic longing for 1950s post–nuclear war white upper-middle-class prosperity and chlorpromazine-induced oblivion.

After all, the building blocks of a nebulous white "womanhood" were built on the backs of others. The manufacturing of an innocent, sexually submissive, quiet, and demure white woman functions as a differentiation from, response to, and othering directed only and intentionally in comparison to Black women. As a trade-off for their complicity in white supremacist violence in all its forms, white women seem to await the promise of a cultivated position as the ultimate "real" woman—contingent upon their adherence and allegiance to the state's cis-heterocentric agenda tailor-made specifically with white people in mind. A Donald Trump reelection increased anti-trans legislation; the overturning of *Roe v. Wade* and affirmative action were all overt, demonstrative acts of the continued policing of bodies that the state deems as threats to not only whiteness as the standard-bearer for humanity but also as the economic, political, social, and cultural superior.

While there seems to be more evidence to support white men's propensities toward violence (perhaps driven by a self-fulfilling, though false, gendered presumption that men are inherently more dangerous), white women—whether they identify as conservative, liberal, anarchist, trans, queer, disabled, or abolitionist—benefit from a perceived innocence by virtue of their whiteness. J.K. Rowling's public, near-constant transphobic screeds in opinion pieces and across the internet are seen as innocuous at best—she has received little to no material consequence and, in fact, has likely made more money since coming out as an avowed TERF (trans-exclusionary "radical" feminist).

Meanwhile, Elon Musk's transphobia aligns with the "evil genius" persona that most liberals and progressives despise. Both of their banal perspectives on "real women" essentially follow the same pattern, and neither has faced accountability. However, there is a growing concern that Musk's harmful words could quickly translate into actions, a risk that the still-loved British fantasy author could never anticipate.

It often comes as a shock when white women who are liberal, queer, or trans are caught, accused of, or implicated in racist, violent behaviors—juxtaposed sharply with the assumption that their whiteness is merely an impediment to their political, gender, or sexual identities, that they are a safer option in the "who's an ally and who is not" paradigm. Historically and contemporarily, Black people, particularly Black women, intimately understand that a liberal white woman is not significantly different from a conservative white woman; they are essentially two sides of the same spectrum. As you've learned, my ex-wife was a self-proclaimed liberal; she'd canvassed for Obama, served in the Peace Corps, and could recite the definition of "racism," but when it came to attending chemotherapy sessions with her Black fiancé, being seen as anti-racist was more important than actually showing up. "I don't think I will be able to take much time off," she said in response to hearing my chemotherapy schedule. She worked for a real estate agent who would have offered her as much time off as she needed. Three months after I finished chemotherapy, attending many sessions alone, she told me that I was "mean" while I had cancer. When I asked her to explain further, she told me that she couldn't put her finger on precisely how, but that she just felt that I was mean. While I did push back on the things she was saying and about her not coming to chemotherapy treatments, I related to her as I've been taught to relate to all white women, especially liberal-leaning queer ones: that they are mostly well-meaning and their intentions are good, so it took me many years to process her marked absence during that difficult period in my life.

Countless studies have shown that when one person in a romantic relationship is diagnosed with a disability or chronic illness, relationships tend to end due to our society's ableist indoctrination that people living with disabilities and chronic illnesses are a nuisance and challenging. What's missing from these studies are insights into how this shows up even more so in interracial relationships. If white people feel they are making a sacrifice by dating a person outside of their race, then that Black or non-Black person of color needs to be perfect in their eyes, and any element of struggle has them leave likely even faster than if they were with another white person. When I told other white women in our lives that I believed that my ex-wife was racist and that was why we were divorcing, most of them defended her and ended their friendships with me.

White women can easily move between a Daughters of the Confederacy–level of conservatism and bra-burning radical feminism without losing opportunities or facing the same backlash and scrutiny that their non-white counterparts experience. Well-known twentieth-century suffragist Susan B. Anthony famously said, "I will cut off this right arm of mine before I will ever work to demand the ballot for the Negro and not the woman." She said this while also claiming to be "besties" with Sojourner Truth, a Black woman suffragist, civil rights activist, and formerly enslaved person. Her comments did nothing to deter people from lauding her as an icon in the movement for women's suffrage nonetheless one hundred years later.

Planned Parenthood founder Margaret Sanger worked with

W. E. B. Du Bois, renowned Black scholar and sociologist of the nineteenth and twentieth centuries, to develop talking points justifying the sterilization of Black women to affirm the necessity of birth control. Only in the last decade has there been growing criticism of her eugenicist past, and to this day she remains widely regarded in many circles, unironically, as a "pioneer" in sex education and women's reproductive rights. This continues to exist without an actual reckoning with the fact that her plan to popularize and advocate for birth control's use and availability to white women was to scapegoat Black women as unfit to bear children.

The myth of hypersexuality has been attached to all Black people but manifests in especially harmful ways for Black women. While Black cis men benefit from patriarchal protection and have gained power by exploiting Black women, their privilege hasn't protected the community as a whole. This is evident in how W. E. B. Du Bois, NAACP founder, supported Margaret Sanger's eugenics agenda to create birth control by claiming "the mass of ignorant Negroes still breed carelessly and disastrously, so that the increase among Negroes, even more than the increase among whites, is from that portion of the population least intelligent and fit, and least able to rear their children properly." Though Du Bois addressed all Black people, his rhetoric particularly targeted Black mothers, as Sanger used these arguments to promote birth control for white women. Before her campaign ended, thousands of Black people and Puerto Ricans with uteruses were forcibly sterilized.

From 2014 to 2021ish, white women crowned their heads with pink pussy hats, put Black Lives Matter signs on their lawns, put pronouns in their email signatures, followed Black organizers on social media platforms, and attended racial and social workshops—all while the material conditions of Black people remained virtually unchanged as white-owned businesses and corporations amassed wealth and capital gains not seen in decades in the midst of a global pandemic that claimed the lives of mostly marginalized peoples. Many people vocalized how shocked they were that white women would vote for Trump again in 2024, that they were essentially voting against themselves. Or were they? It is certainly worth positing: Why might white women side with white men seemingly against their own interests? And what interests do white men have that white women also share? The answer might not be so surprising when taking even a cursory glance at chattel slavery in the United States.

Contrary to the strategic, ahistorical rendering of them as innocent, white women owned slaves, attended lynchings, and were regular members of the Ku Klux Klan—not just as a casual expression of their anti-Blackness, but because their livelihoods and financial solvency depended on the exploitation of Black people's unfree labor. Are there outliers, white women who have resisted white supremacy? White people are often able to deal with systems in ideological, intellectual terms, not at the level of impact, so even the most well-meaning white women—outliers to this system who appear to outwardly resist white supremacy, repudiate it in their classroom land acknowledgments, decry it in their nonprofit board meetings and social media posts—still benefit from the unfree labor of Black and non-Black people of color.

The wealth gap between white and Latinx women is stark, with Latinx women making the least out of all groups, earning 26 percent less than white women. White women make up high numbers of tenured professors at universities where mostly Black and non-Black people of color comprise the landscaping and janitorial/custodial staff. Despite benefiting from and relying on Black nannies, domestic workers, and housecleaners, these same white women remain oblivious to the paradox of their political leanings and the disparity between themselves and other women. Rather than giving up power or advocating for Black people to receive reparations, they'd rather volunteer at the soup kitchen. Is it feasible then to say that even the most left-leaning white women fear what a total systemic shift in the balance of power might mean for them? How can white people fancy themselves as radical when the system is designed with them in mind?

Robin DiAngelo, author of the book *White Fragility*, has profited handsomely from scholarship built by Black thinkers. It remains unknown how much she gives to Black communities, and even if we had the number, a white woman is still being used as a source and profiting from racial and social justice. When given the opportunity to uproot racial violence, white people are still looking to do so in a way that centers them and generates profit. Glennon Doyle has built an entire platform around "having hard conversations" where Black scholars and educators are invited as guests to teach Doyle, her wife, Abby Wambach, and listeners to lift up marginalized voices. The irony is not lost that these calls to action are coming from guests while Doyle and her wife remain at the center of who we are tasked to listen to.

A podcast mic or a book deal is just another way that white people have leaned into the belief that they should always have access to Black people. Being able to make money off of Black pain seems to be the only vehicle for white people to care about Black existence. The lines of racial capitalism must be maintained by the appearance of neoliberal gestures, niceties and "civility" that appear to signal some "post-racial" optimism and unity but actually reveal a deeper discomfiture with the kind of shared spaces that an actual "post-racial" society might require. I notice this in everyday interactions with white people, especially white women, that I call "white people compliments." When I am boarding a plane, lugging bags and my body through narrow aisles, there is always a white woman saying how much they love my hair. When I am in the grocery store in sweatpants and a T-shirt, my clogs are the coolest thing they have seen all day. Although these compliments typically come from white women, white men are not exempt, as they will do a "love the hair" drive-by compliment as well. I find that this typically happens when I am in a space white people have deemed as "white only."

Segregation signs may have gone away, but due to the continued organizing structure of racial capitalism, the lines of segregation did not. Some white people are discomfited by Black people's presence, so instead of dealing with their discomfort, they make a compliment to appear safe, as "one of the good ones," and to demonstrate their entitlement to a Black person's space. When I talk about white people giving compliments, there is frustration on the other side: "What's wrong with a compliment?" "Should I just not be saying anything?" "I love complimenting people." Growing up around white people and being in predominantly white spaces has shown me that white people rarely talk to white people they don't know, let alone compliment them. Instead of sitting with the discomfort that their compliments are likely coming from a place of wanting to look good rather than authentic interaction, some may get defensive, which in many ways proves my point. Is complimenting someone for you or that person? Can a Black person respond to a compliment from a white person in any other way besides being thankful? The short answer is no. White women are using Black people in public space as some sort of anti-racism sporting match where they attempt to prove to themselves that they can talk to Black people.

A Black person's presence being able to dysregulate a white person's whole nervous system shows the extent to which the latter desires to keep white spaces white, thus maintaining racial capitalistic class structures. The displacement myth—the belief that white people will become the minority—benefits, encapsulates, protects, and safeguards all white people, even those who do not agree with it. This myth propelled neo-Nazi white supremacist Dylan Roof to murder nine Black people and severely injure six at a Charleston, South Carolina, Bible study, stating before he fired his gun that "we are becoming second-class citizens, and that is why you have to go." It would also propel Kyle Rittenhouse to travel across state lines, with his mother escorting him, and ultimately kill two people at a Black Lives Matter protest in Kenosha, Wisconsin. Whether they take the lead, remain silent to challenge the beliefs of their neo-Nazi children, or directly influence them, white women are not innocent in these violent acts. White women need not separate themselves from these injustices but locate themselves as benefactors of such violence.

Christian nationalism has enjoyed a rebirth in the cultural zeitgeist, providing the foundation for why we have a gender binary. In the Bible, God says that Eve is made from Adam's rib. So, who are white women going to be other than a creation made from a man? Oyèrónkẹ́ Oyěwùmí, author of *The Invention of Women*, posits that Western society relates to gender as a biological function; its function is a predisposition rather than an individual choice to define for yourself—a woman is supposed to breastfeed because that is her biological function. As long as identity is connected to biology vis-à-vis the church, one is more "real," but this is a fallacy made up to further control bodies. Not every woman will bear children, and females are not the only gender that can have children. The subjugation lies in not being able to subvert this institutionalized program.

White supremacy gives white women power but fewer options as to their identity formation of who they can be. Given the context of how this country was created, are you GI Jane, Judy Garland, Audrey Hepburn, or are you a descendant of unskilled settlers? Of colonialists who were unable to define who they were and had to do so in relation to the others who were here before them? If I am taught this for hundreds of years, it will begin to stick and spread through colonization across the world, forcing non-white societies and groups of people to endorse this illegitimate singular worldview to legitimize it.

White women became the missionaries and nuns who caused immense physical and sexual violence toward Indigenous children forced into colonial gender programming at Indian boarding schools from the eighteenth century through the twentieth century. It is University of Pennsylvania's Amy Wax asserting that "embracing . . . cultural distance nationalism means in effect positing that our country will be better off with more whites and fewer non-whites," and the *New York Times* publishing an article about it with the headline: "UPenn Accuses Professor of Being Racist; Should She Be Fired?" Wax claimed that "everyone wants to go to countries ruled by white Europeans" because of their "superior" mores. Despite making these comments and being subject to a mountain of documented exchanges and reports of other racist, xenophobic, homophobic, and bigoted statements since her tenure at UPenn began in 2001, she did not face disciplinary action until 2018. Even then, she has neither lost her job nor her prized tenure status at the Ivy League university, with some suggesting that relieving her of her duties would impinge upon "academic freedoms."

It is Governor Kathy Hochul saying in 2024 that "there are Black kids growing up in the Bronx that do not know what the word computer is. They do not know these things." Although she faced backlash, she still holds her gubernatorial seat. It is Carolyn Bryant Donham admitting to lying about Emmett Till, which resulted in his murder and public funeral, yet receiving no consequences for lying, and dying peacefully at the age of eighty-eight. Much of the focus on the salaciousness of her claims centers around her belated admission to fabricating the entire story. But it wasn't just that she, as a twenty-one-year-old adult, lied about a fourteen-year-old child, accusing him of whistling at her. She was a willing participant in not challenging the sheer existence of a vigilante system of laws created to protect white women at the expense of sexualizing and vilifying Black men and youngsters.

These laws predated that fateful day, and, completely aware of them, what more could Donham have done in her sweet, innocent, matronly nature to have advocated for the end of Jim Crow segregation? What actions did she take to disrupt the status quo at the time? Why was radicalism a historical expectation of Black people but not white people? How have white women weaponized being held and seen as harmless in the Western public imagination, contrasted very sharply with the well-documented realities of their violences or their role as bystanders in the face of it?

Donham and her husband, Roy Bryant, who killed Emmett Till, rose to fame in their hometown, earning her the titles "Roy Bryant's Most Attractive Wife" and "Crossroads Marilyn Monroe." Consider Amber Guyger entering Botham Jean's apartment in 2018, allegedly mistaking it for her own, murdering Jean while he was eating a bowl of ice cream and watching television. Guyger was sentenced to ten years in prison beginning immediately after sentencing—a much lower sentence than what the jury was expecting—but not before Jean's brother and Judge Tammy Kemp, the Black woman judge, hugged her, gave her a Bible, and wished her well. Botham Jean was the only person who needed protection as he was ambushed in his own home eating a bowl of ice cream. If we continue to rush to protect white women, who is seen as suspicious and less worthy of protection? If white women are automatically assumed to be innocent, we will continue to meet each other with suspicion.

The resistance that white women likely have toward challenging notions around their gender and race is similar to uncovering a family secret—once it is revealed, things can never be the same. There is no pussy hat parade thrown for white women who actually want to end the weaponization of the gender binary instead of wielding it to be seen as innocent perpetual victims who get away with literal crimes, sometimes murder or otherwise harmful complicities.

Elizabeth Holmes scammed investors out of hundreds of millions of dollars, selling them on a machine that would detect diseases with just one drop of blood—without actually having created it. To make herself appear more credible, she perfected a deep, monotone voice and wore a black turtleneck to emulate Apple founder Steve Jobs. While this may appear to many as a harmless attempt by a woman to anticipate and overcome misogynistic doubts about her expertise and worthiness in a predominantly white male–dominated tech industry, it could also represent Holmes's aspiration to one day emulate the power-hoarding condescension and authoritarian persona necessary to amass billions of dollars in personal wealth, as Jobs did. Powerful and iconoclastic for his trailblazing inventions, Steve Jobs did nothing to challenge the exploitative and exclusionary white male boys' club that would come to define Silicon Valley for decades to this day.

Often, white women leverage the gender binary to conceal crimes and misdeeds (such as Ms. Holmes) in a manner that other racial groups cannot, thanks to the advantage of being perceived as innocent—a phenomenon that historians have dubbed "the cult of true womanhood." But instead of "piety, purity, domesticity, and submissiveness" being hallmark features of this myth, what was once relegated to private home life now extends even to white, educated, working women in the public sphere, given their kowtowing to white cis men for the approval to rival their success.

Where white supremacist notions of being seen as "pure" and "true" racially have been created and preserved by white people, so, too, has the historical figure of the "pure" and "true" woman, the ideal—delicate, soft, maybe even weak—and in present times, these tropes seem to be deployed conveniently and strategically when they can garner white women praise or protection. To embody the ideal of a "perfect" woman, a "bad" woman was necessary. Where Black women specifically were the proverbial "bad" women, untrue, barely woman enough, Black trans women have reemerged in the white cishet imagination as the ultimate threat/scapegoat to their scheme: not women at all. White women relish their dominance in the cult of womanhood, ensuring no one else can reap the same benefits.

Increased transphobia in the media and legislatively is a central piece to maintaining white women as the blueprint. In a capitalist world, trans people getting more attention threatens white women's importance culturally, socially, and financially. J.K. Rowling's whole transphobic take is that men are biologically stronger than women. If there are more than two genders, then how will she, as a white woman, maintain her desire to be seen as inherently innocent and thus weak? J.K. Rowling uses "J.K." as her pen name because she wanted to see how far her books would sell if the name appeared to be associated with a man. She even authored crime books under the pen name Robert Galbraith for the same purpose.

Rowling creates fantasy worlds in her books with people flying on brooms, wizards, and magic, but contesting the limitations of white supremacy was something she was unwilling to do. Instead, she resisted defining herself to profit from the very system that kept her from writing her full name on her books. It should come as no surprise that most of the people J.K. Rowling targets are racially Black women, many of whom are athletes. Black women and those gendered as such fail gender by virtue of their Blackness—Rowling makes this plain with incessant tweets saying the quiet part out loud. If Black women are seen as the outlier to gender, then white women once again get to maintain their position of privilege. This highlights the reason why Black trans women are a threat to white supremacy: By just existing, they subvert the white gaze and reveal a long-standing fallacy about gender—it is not biologically based.

Removing biology from gender does benefit white women, although they won't see it that way as long as the gender binary remains their foundation for identity—their innocence is no longer innate, their access to power revoked by having to be who you say you are rather than how people assume you to be. White women could not even handle being nicknamed for their violence.

"Karen" became the nickname for white women following the 2020 election, created by Black people who were constantly interfacing with white women who jumped at the opportunity to call the police on Black people, asking for the manager to complain when they did not get their way, or even using their Black partner as a cover for their racism. "Karen" served as a means to challenge the perception that white women, unlike their cis male counterparts, should not be associated with white supremacy. From 2020 to 2024, "Karen" slowly morphed into a term that white women fought to separate themselves from, going as far as calling out other white women for being Karens.

White women honing in on being called a "Karen," rather than uprooting what would necessitate the need to characterize white women as Karens, was yet another indication that white women will do anything to hold on to their power. Being identified by a marginalized group and linked to the harm they inflicted was not consistent with their brand image. The goal is to be powerful like white men, seen as victims to patriarchy but never associated with being aggressive or violent—after all, that would be a departure from how they are perceived to be naturally as white women. Aggression and violence are reserved for Blackness.

White women will do anything to distinguish themselves, which is why they make very little effort to uproot transphobia. Sarah McBride was the first trans woman elected to Congress, but before she could be sworn into office, Congress created a ban to stop trans people from using bathrooms that corresponded with their gender, forcing them into bathrooms that corresponded to their sex assigned at birth. Instead of McBride, a known Zionist, standing up against this bill, she stated, "I'm not here to fight about bathrooms; I'm here to fight for Delawareans and to bring down costs facing families. Like all members, I will follow the rules as outlined by Speaker Johnson, even if I disagree with them. This effort to distract from the real issues facing this country hasn't distracted me over the last several days."

While I do not disagree that transphobia is used as a distraction, transphobia is in fact a real issue that directly impacts people's everyday lives. Was holding a seat in Congress more important than fighting against a blatantly transphobic bathroom ban? It surely does not rest on McBride's shoulders to uproot transphobia, but her willingness to fall in line with federally mandated transphobia in an effort to secure her hard-won spot in the war machine effectively set the stage for second-class citizenship for any other trans would-be civic leaders who might succeed her. Despite her best intentions, her complicity in this matter endorses white cis-heterosexist values, which will undoubtedly harm trans and gender-expansive Delawareans and people across the nation.

In an effort to improve declining literacy rates and encourage children to play with gender, Drag Queen Story Hour was created in 2015 by white, queer author and poet Michelle Tea. Although children enjoyed these events and they were well attended, effectively providing a safer space for children to read and explore gender and sexuality, there was pushback. Alt-right, neo-Nazi, conservative, and white supremacist groups protested outside libraries and event spaces where Drag Queen Story Hour was occurring, their central complaint being that drag queens were causing gender confusion and were too sexual for children.

A small sect of white second-wave feminists lodged their criticisms of drag queens as a whole, seeing drag "as the reproduction of a specifically sexualized rendering of feminine identity," states E. K. Smith referenced in "Gender on Stage: Drag Queens and Performative Femininity" by Galyna Kotliuk. These criticisms of an initiative whose main purpose was to make learning and reading fun for children were roped into the transphobic quest to define who is a man and who is a woman, largely in response to increased trans visibility and tropes of gays/trans people being hypersexual and therefore not safe to be around children lest they also "turn" them gay. A drag queen is not someone who is necessarily trans (although they can be), but their expression of femininity was in direct contradiction to the exalted way white womanhood has been pigeonholed: tame, demure, and preserved for a man's sexual interest.

In *Ain't I a Woman*, bell hooks writes, "modesty, sexual purity, innocence, and a submissive manner were the qualities associated with womanhood and femininity." These qualities were also intrinsically linked when defining race. Black women were not seen as sexually pure or modest; their Blackness erased that possibility. Instead, they were the antithesis to whiteness: wild, hypersexual, uncouth sites of labor. One could argue that drag queens express a type of femininity that is reserved for Blackness.

There is an element of drag queen performance—intricate makeup, formfitting clothes, high heels, and big hair—that is all to highlight gender fluidity. I worry that by associating gender fluidity only with the stage, people might think expressions of gender fluidity are only reserved for drag queen brunch. It seems as long as drag queens stay on stages where adults can opt in or out, avoid being around children or existing in public space, then the fragility of the gender binary can remain intact. Similar to media reports on increased viewership for online trans pornography alongside heightened anti-trans legislation, as long as trans people and drag queens stay tucked away like a dirty little secret, distant from white cishet existence, then they can be (marginally) accepted.

Only in the eyes of white supremacy would the presence of a drag queen be threatening to children, since children are to be seen-not-heard, controlled, and much less able to explore and name their gender on their own terms. Control is the main objective in an oppressive structure; freedom is a threat against the prospect of more chains. An increase in trans visibility was severely hampering the ability to maintain the false but nonetheless prevailing sentiment that there are only two genders.

The first recognized drag queen in the United States was a formerly enslaved Black man, William Dorsey Swann, who led Black queer resistance spaces called House of the Swann in the 1880s–1890s for other enslaved peoples to dress in clothes they felt affirmed in, all while directly resisting arrest and police raids. Drag is a salute to the folks who, by virtue of being Black, fail gender. Black femininity is othered regardless of whether it is performed by someone who is cisgender or trans. In *Black on Both Sides*, prolific gender scholar C. Riley Snorton writes, "Captive flesh figures a critical genealogy for modern transness, as chattel persons gave rise to an understanding of gender as mutable and as an amendable form of being."

Drag queens being seen as inherently sexual is no different than how Black women are perceived. Like Snorton posits, the treatment of Black people laid the groundwork for how anyone who subverted gender would be treated. The parallels between how drag queens, trans people, and Black women (cis and/or trans) are regarded are not lost in this moment of heightened visibility and resistance, but also the lengths that white people will go to in order to distance themselves from gender-expansive identities. With every shift toward freedom, there are many more steps back toward rigidity.

As of December 2024, there are 669 anti-trans bills across the country designed to stop trans people from having access to medical care, housing, legal support, and existence in public space. The presence of trans people, in particular Black trans women, serves as a threat to white womanhood, which, when threatened, uses the police state to minimize that threat. That state is defining over and over again who is a man and a woman—a definition that is not void of race. Anti-trans legislation attempts to stop Drag Queen Story Hour, and overturning *Roe v. Wade* and DEI were all overt measures taken to solidify that there are only two genders and one superior race that must be maintained.

The covert quest to maintain this reality is embedded in popular fashion trends like the "clean girl aesthetic," which rose in popularity in 2022, currently with 700 million likes and reposts on TikTok. To be seen as a clean girl, one had to wear one's hair slicked back, gold hoop earrings as the main accessory, minimal makeup, and simple clothes—oversize slacks, a white T-shirt, and a jacket. The emphasis on dressing this way was attributed to being seen as classy, chic, off-duty model outfits, like you had old money.

Most of the articles and tags for the style focus on white, thin, cisgender women, like Hailey Bieber, who came under fire when she claimed that lining her lips and adding gloss was her unique style—a trend that Black and non-Black people of color have been doing to accentuate their lips for decades. The clean girl aesthetic was criticized by fashion critics for being fatphobic, classist, and anti-Black. Most of the "off-duty model" outfits were tailored oversize slacks or jeans, which are rarely made for fat bodies, and the idea of "looking clean" all day where hair or makeup is never out of place shows the privilege in being able to focus on how you look all day.

One aspect that I felt was missing from the critique was the transphobic presence this trend also carried out. The clean girl aesthetic is an active distancing from hyperfemininity, which is associated with hypersexuality and thus marks anyone expressing their gender in this way as othered. The message that less makeup and oversize clothes that don't show cleavage or thighs signify cleanliness is loaded—if someone is clean by following this trend, then those who don't are dirty? Putting emphasis on how much makeup someone is wearing intentionally pushes out trans people, especially trans women who utilize cosmetics to hide facial hair and increase facial feminization.

The gender binary is further enshrined by this trend, situating who is a "real" woman versus who is trans by simply distancing oneself from hyperfemininity and locating power in dressing masculine. There is privilege in wearing less makeup, oversize clothing, not showing cleavage and still being seen as a woman. There is no shred of coincidence that this trend is happening on the heels of increased anti-trans legislation and critiques of drag queens reading to children.

Transphobia does not always look like an inherent hatred of trans people, but a desire to elevate oneself to a level of whiteness by showing that you can operate as an apparatus of the state. Drag queens and trans people are a much easier target for cisgender people to scapegoat for gender confusion and sexualizing children; the latter requires introspection and accountability to name the gender binary, patriarchy, and white supremacy as the culprits. White people would have to be honest that the gender binary is completely made up, risking the realization that everything they know about themselves is a lie—an admission that requires a disavowal of privilege and power.

When *Roe v. Wade* was overturned in 2022, white women seemed to band together in their frustrations with white men prohibiting bodily autonomy. Although Black and non-Black people of color of all genders are controlled by the state via their reproductive capabilities or lack thereof, white women organized only when abortion access would directly impact them. If you only care about justice when it impacts you, do you really care about justice, or is it just another opportunity to signal virtue?

The idea that cisgender men alone dictated the overturning of *Roe v. Wade* would deny the presence of Trump-appointed Supreme Court Justice Amy Coney Barrett, a long-time fangirl of late Supreme Court Justice Antonin Scalia, known for his hatred of everything that is not white, cisgender, and heterosexual as well as for his love for the Constitution's ability to legally enshrine that hatred. It comes as no coincidence that Barrett is blond-haired, blue-eyed, married, and has seven children (two of whom are adopted Black children from Haiti).

In remarks about *Dobbs v. Jackson*, Barrett stated, "If you can give up your baby when it's born, why does forcing a woman to go through pregnancy affect her life at all?"—a damning but unfortunately unsurprising statement from a white woman who has two adopted Black children, showing clear disregard for the Black carrying parent who likely had a great deal to sort through when it came to putting their children up for adoption. This rhetoric also ignores the fact that people have a whole host of life-threatening complications while pregnant, in addition to fatigue, vomiting, changes in memory and cognition, and discomfort from an expanding uterus.

Barrett's intentional ditziness around pregnancy, even though she has been pregnant several times, is why she was the perfect Supreme Court justice pick for a white supremacist patriarchal country. Although she navigates the world as a woman, she has disavowed her gender for her race. In an article titled "Amy Coney Barrett's Gentle Deceptions," Melissa Gira Grant makes the case for how Barrett's performance of femininity serves/d as a political tool before Barrett was confirmed as a Supreme Court justice: "It may not matter how successful Barrett's performance of nonthreatening, perfected femininity is, given how much precedent Republicans are willing to blow past to confirm her nomination. And even if this was a fair fight, convincing anyone that Barrett is who she presents herself to be isn't the intention. It's meant to lend others around her plausible deniability, to claim she doesn't have an agenda and, by extension, neither do they."

Between 2021 and 2024, there was a heightened focus on Mormons and "trad" (traditional white families and housewives) content. Mormon moms dancing off-beat to rap songs on TikTok were so popular that they garnered a primetime spot on Hulu. Their show followed them around while they created content, planned baby showers, and had surprise pregnancies, all under the age of twenty-five.

Nara Smith, a mixed-race, light-skinned Black woman, is one of the most popular people on TikTok, famed for cooking intricate meals while wearing couture for her white husband, Lucky Smith, a suspected Trump supporter, with whom she has three children. Her comments are filled with people remarking on how astute she is that she is able to cook and care for three children—the ultimate accomplishment in a post-*Dobbs* world. Tradwives have one of the most popular tags on social media, full of mostly white women standing in a kitchen wearing an apron professing how much feminism is ruining the traditional (read: *white*) family.

Hannah Neelman, another extremely popular Mormon/tradwife content creator, has amassed a cult following of ten million followers on TikTok. A former professional ballet dancer and Mrs. America in 2023, she had dreams of being an actress. But she traded those dreams in for a farm; "homesteading," they claim. When the federal government created the Homestead Act of 1962 to forcibly remove Indigenous communities from their land, they'd probably be pleased to know it was all so their descendants, like Hannah Neelman, no longer actually had to "live off the land" but instead could live in a 1950s Americana wet dream replete with a ring light, eight children, and an egg apron gifted by her uber-rich husband for her birthday (assuaging her desires to go to Greece would have likely been easily achievable—his father is the founder of JetBlue, after all).

The support for this type of content is neither niche nor happening in a vacuum; it's inside of white conservative hysteria around procreation to address declining birth rates and increasing divorce rates among white people. The institution of heterosexuality was created as the bedrock for the white nuclear family, contributing to white purity and thus presenting a narrow image of the American dream.

White people, especially white women, are in a crisis of consciousness around who they are as white people. The task here is not to end the chapter with some readers feeling guilty that it is in fact more of the same rigmarole that changes nothing. If you happen to be a white woman reader, consider asking yourself: Who are you without the exploitation and subjugation of Black people? Who are you without the presence of a white man to emulate, to be in a relationship with, or to be in competition with? Who is the white woman without whiteness?

When we look at white women as inherently good, who gets left behind? Who goes unprotected? No one was there to protect Botham Jean when he was murdered in his own home eating ice cream. The state's machinery of protection activates swiftly and decisively for white women—from law enforcement to media narratives to institutional policies—while systematically leaving Black, brown, and trans bodies vulnerable. The state has neatly divided the world into good and bad along racial lines, creating a system where white womanhood is synonymous with virtue, safety, and protection.

The examples I've shared here barely scratch the surface of how white womanhood, also known as the cult of domesticity, has shaped our society, reinforcing the idea that "woman" by default means "white woman." From owning slaves to packing lunches for lynchings (and the dance parties that would follow in the evening), white women have a long history of willing and unwitting complicity in a white supremacist patriarchal police state. This system was, in part, sustained by their own loss of autonomy, forcing adherence to absurdly restrictive gender norms that many of them would be driven to great lengths to uphold (my fingers ache just thinking of all that embroidering and white sheet sewing the Daughters of the Confederacy had to do to just to be seen as "women"). Given this violent history, it is no surprise that the present moment finds many white cisgender women playing ignorant to white cis men's machinations for control, trading autonomy for the impunity that whiteness affords them.

But at what cost? Not just to them personally on moral grounds, but to those othered in the name of their Madonna status since, as Hitler reasoned, a white woman's reproductive labors to the white supremacist cause make them the center of a fictional universe of racial purity. Though a total fabrication, its material and real-world impacts particularly on Black people of marginalized genders cannot be denied, as famed philosopher Charles W. Mills writes in his essay "The Racial Contract": "White supremacy is the basic unnamed political system that has shaped and made the modern world what it is today . . . [and] covers more than two thousand years of Western political thought." Central to that thought is the public excoriation of Black people, specifically Black women, trans, and cis as part of the state mapping its sociopolitical nationalist agenda onto our bodies in order to hide, scapegoat, distract, and deflect from its atrocities domestically and abroad.

From the US touting itself as a great liberator of the free world during WWII—rescuing Europe from the scourge of Nazism only to be practicing a form of apartheid against Black people at home—to the present day, the incessant pitting of the Black woman against a moral compass for what is deviant sexually and intellectually, as a symbol of progressive orthodoxy masked as mere "identity politics," an imposition upon sensibility, respectability, and common decency positing that the barbarians are too sensitized by their subhuman status, too politically correct, and too stupid to appreciate the great smart white man's admonishment of anyone and everyone (except himself and other white men). Cementing this point, white billionaire Harvard alumnus Bill Ackman stated, with dramatic flair, that the first Black woman president of the prestigious predominantly white university "has done more damage to the reputation of Harvard University than any individual in our nearly 500-year history," which would naturally include several of its slave-owning presidents.

It didn't take much for Republican state representative of New York Elise Stefanik, a self-proclaimed MAGA warrior, to happily spark the witch hunt to discredit and oust Claudine Gay, former president of Harvard University. These actions are a part of a cultural war to further entrench white male superiority via specious and banal claims that the woke left are "weaponizing" historical narratives for political gain. But the right are angelic, righteous sportsmen whose racially motivated identity politics are somehow more justified. It can be said with certainty that many white cisgender women work in cahoots with white men, the goal being to uphold oppressive power structures even at the expense of contributing to a wave of anti-intellectualism and attacks on critical thought. They do this just to be seen as likable to white men, who have historically punished white women for any semblance of intelligence that could challenge theirs.

Even the most progressive white women are not immune from this predation by white men. I recall once prolific YouTuber and sex educator for Planned Parenthood, Laci Green, defending her desire to have open dialogue with white supremacists online and reportedly being in an intimate relationship with a content creator who attracted a large alt-right audience while still calling herself a feminist inside of the neutral "all sides, all opinions matter" rhetoric. An argument can be made that she, too, was used as a vehicle for the same white racist and sexist cis audience who previously subjected her to a barrage of threats and harassment for being what they called a "social justice warrior." Many of her fans have argued she was being manipulated, but detractors posit that she played along because it served her interests—more views from the screen-addicted incel crowd held the promise of boosted ad revenue on her then-widely popular platform. Perhaps she was simply learning to lean into her perceived online persona: that of a smart, pliant, blond-haired, blue-eyed feminist, with a newly minted willingness to "hear both sides." Opinionated just enough not to alienate her new audience—the cult of domesticity meets Betty Friedan's *The Feminine Mystique* meets racist women's suffrage movement organizer all wrapped up in a girlboss bow.

White women's complicities have been written about extensively by many Black radical feminist scholars throughout time. We can only reaffirm what has already been said about the sort of dichotomous space that white women across the ideological, class, and political spectrum tend to occupy either as incredibly bigoted and antagonistic or as liberal, progressive, well-meaning beneficiaries of incredible antagonism toward marginalized groups. I think that white women will have to decide: Who are you going to be? Are you going to be yourself, what a white cis man wants you to be or a caricature of the thing you revile the most?

At the core of the widespread parroting, mimicking, and lampooning of Black girlhood, and Black working-class aesthetic popularized on social media, is a hatred of Black women, undergirded by a thinly veiled thought: "I can do it better because I am better." The assumption that solidarity can be hedged on gendered lines never really existed, because white women have been too interested in consuming and profiting from Black women and femmes, unsure of how to view or engage us other than as saviors and/or laborers from whom they can derive their identity—whether directly or in sharp juxtaposition to. Whether it's Alex Consani, a white model and the first trans woman to win the prestigious Model of the Year Award, accepting the honor thanking Black trans women, notably absent from the space, for having "fought for the space," in a bizarre, butchered blaccent, or Drew Barrymore donning the then second in command of the world's top imperial power the country's "momala" to a reticent former Vice President Kamala Harris. Or famed white gay cis fashion designer Marc Jacobs's Blackfishing to the umpth degree, replete with long nail extensions, pursed lips, and head cocked, just like the white models he had walk the runway in faux "dreadlocks" for his Spring/Summer 2017 show. Or the white women who date and produce children with Black cis men for sport in some imaginary pick-me competition with Black women. Blackness is an object to possess, and the caricaturing of Black people has nearly the same deleterious impact as the actual historical possession of Black people. Do not easily dismiss the outrageousness and cringe of the small sample of aforementioned examples as innocent or superfluous; white women will need to give up power much in the same way that white cis men will need to, despite their simultaneously protected and privileged status as white—cis, trans, or otherwise.

Many have already made their choice: Marjorie Taylor Greene has made her choice. But what about those deemed less extreme (read: *overt*) in their loyalty to the cult of whiteness and white womanhood, those who (ostensibly) despise the Marjorie Taylor Greenes, who seek to be a departure from Marjorie, if not completely, at least marginally?

The path forward isn't through performative allyship or guilt but through dismantling allegiances to anti-Blackness, colonialism, and the gender binary—the very systems that created the false belief that white women are more beautiful, more worthy, more deserving of protection, and inherently virtuous. This myth was built at the grave psychic, physical, and emotional expense of Black people, and its consequences persist to this day. The question isn't whether we measure up to them, but why we ever accepted their definition of "good" in the first place.

Here are some questions for us all to consider moving forward:

- In what ways do you see white women maintaining power through performances of innocence and victimhood?
- How do you benefit from others being forced into rigid gender roles? What privileges would you have to give up for true liberation from oppressive racialized socioeconomic institutions and structures?
- When have you gained social or material benefits by enforcing gender norms on others? What would it cost to stop?

# 6

# Realness: You Are Because Black Femmes Is

"I'm poor, black, I may even be ugly, but dear God, I'm here!"

—Celie, *The Color Purple*

"I always dressed like this around my people."

—Mary Jones

"The slave system defined Black people as chattel since women, no less than men, were (re)produced as socially dead, such that they might as well have been genderless."

—Patrice D. Douglass's interpretation of Angela Davis's quote, from *Women, Race and Class*

I realized that I am a nonbinary femme because of Black (cis and trans) women, as Black womanhood (cis and trans) is an inherently queer(ed) existence. Identifying as a Black nonbinary femme exists for me as a love letter to the people who molded me as a human—Black women. There was nothing about whiteness that offered me the freedom to be my full self. If anything, I felt more constrained in my attempt to fit into mainstream, white-washed expressions of queered gender and sexual identity. There were spaces wherein my Blackness was ignored and treated like a contradiction to being a nonbinary, queer femme. It seemed the aesthetic was always more important than substance and meaning; devoid of a sociocultural and political history I could relate to. As a nonbinary child without the language to name it back then, Black cisgender women taught me—through their flourishing, fantastic failing, their destruction of and ascent above binary notions of gender—that I get to name myself for myself, and that Blackness is instrumental to that process. But it took years to experience such in its fullness.

Black women and femmes, and those perceived to be, have sublimated our bondage and all that the gender binary created us to be: a receptacle that people can see themselves through but also be above, our freedom of artistic, cultural, sexual, and/or bodily expression disparaged and also imitated, meme-ified by a world hellbent on leaving us for dead literally and figuratively while getting their whole life from it (literally and figuratively). Despite unimaginable odds, Black women created themselves out of the nothingness they were imagined to be. "Black" and "woman" are juxtaposed to each other much in the same way that "Black" and "white" are, and the earliest adherents of the latter would first begin to fashion themselves into a mythic dominance, civility, normality, and benevolence that gave way to another emergent binary even more salient than "man" and "woman"—that of race. This construct proxied Black people as the penultimate other whose evil deviance made these new philosophical, theological (albeit fictional) differences so stark that they simply had to be natural, if not sufficient enough to justify their seizure and conquest. Just as those who would come to designate themselves as white created race for their sole benefit, "woman" and "man" are similarly created designations, or different means to the same end; thus the gender binary is no more than a made-up trap squarely rooted in anti-Black racism and used as a way to not only reify difference between white and Black people but also to naturalize the subjugation of women, specifically Black transgender and cisgender women alike. Black femmes negate the gender binary entirely, especially in coveted expressions of "femininity" like sensuality, innocence, fragility, sentience, etc., which under this structure are falsely associated with—reserved and gatekept for—white women. Without any scientific or scholarly agreement on it, "femininity" is an arbitrary marker of supposedly orthodox, biological-essentialist "female" behaviors, though the Eurocentric manner of labeling certain practices or characteristics as "feminine" did not emerge in the English language until the fourteenth century.

This social construct was another fabrication to relegate those who could now easily be gendered as women (per these newfound attributes of the so-called "fairer sex") to the lower rungs of society, rendered incapable of self- or political governance, property ownership, bodily autonomy, and all the other attributes conveniently better suited to "masculine" "males." Without the gender binary as a developing colonial process to enshrine imperialistic notions of a nation-state, which is only made real by those who enforce it, there would be no white men and women at all; so, what is most glaring about colonization in Europe and spread across the Atlantic is that whiteness and womanness and manliness, the very personhood of those privileged by these newly minted social constructs of gender and race, are hinged on the denigration of those who are not and can never be either white or man, much less "feminine" or "masculine." While white women are rewarded with humanity under the white male gaze for successful performances of femininity, they are harshly punished if/when they fail to do so precisely because it leaves room for Black women to be seen as feminine according to white supremacist, Eurocentric standard—which would disrupt the whole social order of the nation-state built on anti-Blackness: the false but highly effective premise that Black people are nonhuman. As scholar and author Frank B. Wilderson III posits, "anti-Blackness is not merely a form of racism, but a fundamental structural and ontological antagonism that positions Black people as perpetually outside of humanity and civil society."

Our Black women, femmes, and those gendered as such lay the ruse bare; their very existence exposes the contradictions and hypocrisies the gender binary is utterly reliant on for its survival: A woman is only a woman if she has a uterus or vulva, takes care of and nurtures children, submits to men, cooks, cleans, is emotionally aware but never to the extent that it embarrasses a man, is feminine, and is sexually available to men. A man is only a man by having a penis, being dominating to women, aggressive, a financial provider, emotionally unavailable beyond anger, and is sexually promiscuous with women. Any deviation beyond these flimsy constructions created by old white cisgender men results in forced assimilation, or else physical violence. On the basis of their Blackness, Black women (cis and trans) and those perceived to be, especially those who express themselves in feminine ways, are punished, policed, and excluded from expressions of femininity to maintain the anti-Black imposition that femininity is not attainable for Black people.

Many of our families have inherited beliefs about how women should be seen, heard, and experienced, which was transferred from their own learned misogynoir from dominant culture. I can remember the first time my uterine lining shed (also known as a period); it marked a pivotal moment. Now, how I performed gender needed to be more closely surveyed and policed. The

Black women in my life were constantly making corrections to what I wore, how I walked, sat, ate, slept, played, doted on crushes, and danced. I mimicked them: swaying my hips and butt when I danced, standing with my hand on my hip, speaking my mind boisterously, being a listening board to other people's problems, sleeping with my hair in a headscarf, bonnet, or even underwear, and then my head on my arm to never mess up a new 'do. But nearly every facet of my being was still nitpicked. It was as if they didn't want me to become like them but to become some version of womanhood that they did not live up to.

Although they were commanding that I shift my behavior, it felt contradictory, since the women around me did not abide by the rules they were expecting me to follow. Even more confusing in the eyes of seven-year-old Ericka was that my uncles, their husbands, their boyfriends, and other Black cisgender men in my life were not held to the same standard of "excellence." They watched trash cans overflow and did not take them out, saw dishes in the sink and did not offer to wash them. They treated their homes like restaurants where their wives were servers, they slept all day but still woke up to a meal and cleaned laundry. I did not have the language at the time to explain that "womanhood" never felt like something that I could live up to. It honestly felt at odds with my Blackness. Instead of trying to fit myself into an impossible box, I got to know myself beyond what I was being told I should be.

I started to identify as a Black nonbinary femme when I could give language to the fact that Black women were not being hypocrites in their criticism of my own unwitting or natural subversion of the binary. Instead, they were victims of a violent world that made them its footstool at any given moment regardless of how fast they chased the ever-shifting goalposts of or abided by the restrictions of confined womanhood.

Therefore, the control, at once protective and corrective, that I experienced from the Black women around me, no doubt influenced by the cis-heteropatriarchy sold to us as the organizing (civilizing, normalizing) principle of the world and humanity itself, was simply a forced, prescribed way of being that was passed down to them like a family heirloom. Although countless Black feminists have created expansive frameworks on gender theory and the unique experiences of Black womanhood, this work has been largely inaccessible, rarely discussed beyond the classrooms of an ivory tower. I wasn't introduced to Audre Lorde, bell hooks, June Jordan, Saidiya Hartman, Angela Davis, or Dr. Joy James until I was well into my bachelor's program. But you do not have to be a Black feminist to understand that the de jure abolition of slavery all across the Americas, but especially in the United States, did not end the subjugation of Black women.

Blackness, especially Black womanhood, is often seen as an oxymoron to queerness, as if an inherent distance exists. But the people who have had to carve a name for themselves out of nothing and against all odds while also navigating the constraints of the world—for me, that is the experience of being queer. In the same way that Black womanhood is a creation, queerness is a creation of itself.

Before it became a limitless expression, the word "queer" was used to describe Black people, regardless of gender or sexuality. In *No Mercy Here: Gender, Punishment, and the Making of Jim Crow Modernity*, Sarah Haley writes, "Imprisoned Black cisgender women were labeled queer in the years immediately preceding the word being used to describe homosexual desire and homosexuals. The imprisoned Black female subject was in some ways, one vestibule to queerness; she was 'the principal point of passage between the human and the non-human world' or the route by which the dominant modes decided the distinction between humanity and 'other.'" Black women, and those perceived to be inherently queer, exist on the margins, perpetually failing the contract of the gender binary. There are consequences to being perceived as queer: being subject to increased surveillance, other identities attempting to pilfer Black women's expression for their enjoyment, and being susceptible to violence from both individuals and the state.

Black women are the blueprint for so many people's identities, explorations of style, language, music, and culture and rarely do they receive the credit; treated as if they are only to be taken from but not acknowledged. When people steal from Black women, they act as if it had no source; they are rendered invisible. All that is pedestalized about femininity on a white woman is demonized when attributed to Black women and those perceived to be.

When I teach all across the country, I often ask my students to describe how a girl or woman is supposed to act. What are the behaviors that are traditionally reserved for and assigned to girls, women, and those gendered as women? You would think I was teaching the same class over and over in a time loop because the responses are always the same: be proper, speak when spoken to, sit with your legs closed, be submissive to men; be agreeable, pure, innocent, and sensitive. When I ask if these descriptions apply to Black women and girls, there is always a resounding no. Witnessing the dynamics and learning the histories of my mother, grandmother, and great-grandmother (Gran Gran) opened my eyes to the unique place that Black women hold in the world.

• • •

My mother spent most of her life on a narrow street in East Baltimore, lined with row homes inhabited by Black families. My grandparents had bought a two-bedroom, one-bathroom home for themselves, my two uncles, and my mom. After giving their youngest son a bedroom and their other son the basement, they then told my mom there was no room for her in that house and asked her to live with her grandmother, five houses away on the same street. How does a family choose a home and not imagine their entire family living there? How does it come to pass that the only daughter of a family is told to live elsewhere? I only learned of this story when I started noticing that my grandmother treated me much differently than my cisgender boy cousins and my brother. I wanted to understand why it felt like I was singled out. Perhaps it was too painful a recollection for my mom; my dad offered up this history. I was told that my uncles were my grandmother's pride and joy. My mom's older brother was a soft-spoken, cake-baking karaoke-singing enthusiast who never had children and whose marriage ended due to his drug addiction most tried to hide, and my mom's younger brother was doted on the most. He was light-skinned, loud, arrogant, tall, and married multiple times—a guaranteed way to curry favor with my grandmother. My mother eventually grew up, married, had two kids, went to church, sang in the choir, left Baltimore, and begrudgingly moved to the suburbs—a class-status change that is typically celebrated. But my grandmother still found things about her to judge and critique.

I grew up hearing stories about my mother and grandmother not getting along, but my mom was very connected to my great-grandma, Gran Gran. Gran Gran acted as a mother to my mom, although she didn't have a good relationship with her own daughter. My grandmother may have been repeating unhealed wounds, and my great-grandmother was doing the same: trying to make up for how she failed her own daughter by bonding with my mom. I will never know the full story, but what I do know is that my mom fought for her mother's love even though she likely understood that you shouldn't have to fight for anyone, much less your parents, to love you.

My grandmother used to say that a man can sleep in the gutter and wake up the next morning and still be a man, but if a woman sleeps in the gutter, she is less of a woman. I was very young when she first said this to me, so I didn't entirely comprehend its meaning, but the sentiment was clear. I wonder if she realized she applied that same double standard with her own daughter and granddaughter. Perfectionism was a big tenet for my grandmother: Her house was always clean, her church clothes pristine, even her jeans had iron creases! She drove a burgundy early '90s model Mitsubishi Eclipse, always blasting country music, singing off-key (her voice raspy from her daily short box of Newport menthols), and waving to the people she liked, though she mostly kept to herself. Her perfectionism seemed to be a shield for what she intended to hide: All of her children had different fathers.

By contrast, Gran Gran was a fat, tobacco-chewing, vegetable-gardening, avid believer in Christ, and a fishing country girl—night and day from the child she raised. Gran Gran shuffled when she walked around in her customary housedress and curlers, chewing snuff, always tending to her rose and vegetable gardens. Gran Gran shares the last name of a major tobacco plantation owner in Sumter, South Carolina, where she is from, and chewing tobacco was likely her reprieve from the deep pain she held, or a habit adopted as a result. Being raised to be a Black girl by my mother, grandmother, and Gran Gran, who were also groomed to be Black women, I experienced firsthand how my Blackness seemed to cancel out expressions of girl/womanhood. I felt lost trying to live up to its constraints, and so did they. Yet they struggled and strived their entire lives at home with their children, their partners, in the workforce, at the grocery store, everywhere they went, to be afforded the humanity that femininity or womanhood grants women, including challenging and policing one another. Black women by virtue of being Black transcend gender, oftentimes without even realizing it.

Although they lived on the same block, just five homes apart, Gran Gran and Grandma might as well have been in separate countries. Their mutual dislike of each other wedged a terribly strong divide that even their own shared misogyny failed to close, and in what was an intentional departure from her forebears, eschewing the cycle of misogynoir under which she was reared, my mother was elated to be having a daughter and, according to my Dad, told him that she was going to treat me better than she ever was. Even when my brother Austin was born, we were never treated differently, an indication of my mother's steadfast commitment to healing a generational wound before pop psychology made it popular to do so—and maybe before she healed her own.

During my mother's funeral, my grandmother turned to me and said, "I know you are hurting, but you will never know what it is like to lose a child." I found this to be a completely bizarre sentiment to share with your granddaughter who will now grow up without her mom. My grandmother's guilt was evident. She tried to be more of a mother to her daughter in death than when she was alive, gloating about how close they were and how much she missed her, never acknowledging the pain she caused.

Black people upholding a system doesn't validate the system or let its white creators off the hook. The upholding is a survival tactic, striving for acceptance by mimicking a world that is constantly rejecting you. My grandmother and great-grandmother were led to believe that upholding misogynistic beliefs would elevate them or mitigate their own feelings of powerlessness. My mother, Grandma, and Gran Gran were all focused on how things looked. I think they hoped that in doing so they could preempt any misogynistic critiques of their identities, related to hypersexuality and poverty, that they were accustomed to experiencing.

How do you treat Black women when you don't value your own humanity as a Black woman? I think it's vital to note that this is really hard for me to write. I don't want you, the reader, to walk away feeling that my grandmother and Gran Gran were exclusively horrible to each other (and my grandmother to my mother). Instead, I want you to read between the lines and consider why my grandmother and Gran Gran chose misogynoir as their weapon. What life experiences and conditioning must have convinced them that misogynoir was a valid tool?

In a patriarchal society, misogynoir is used as social currency: People gain power and even respect from certain circles by suppressing and subjugating Black women. Even if you identify as a Black woman, you are not exempt from being misogynistic toward that end. Patriarchy is the structure which grants men and masculinity power, and there are women who would rather be like men than dismantle patriarchy and misogyny. History has shown us how Black women are used to propel others to positions of power and become collateral to the desire for power of white women, Black men, and white men, the latter of whom may be the most demonstrative of this fact: the most privileged by direct contrast to and through the marginalization of the least privileged under global white supremacist notions of gender and race.

. . .

In 1965, Daniel Patrick Moynihan, a white Democratic senator from New York, posited in his infamous, poorly researched racist screed "The Negro Family: The Case for National Action," commonly called the Moynihan Report, that Black people suffer from "matriarchal societies" which create single-parent households and thus cause Black people to depend on the state, rather than progress like white people whose socioeconomic success he attributes to a nuclear, heterosexist familial structure with the "man" at the helm. Filled mostly with salacious conjecture and racialized psychobabble, Moynihan's screed claims that Black families had a destructive impact on the white race, specifically dogpiling on Black women. Not coincidentally—and during the zenith of the Civil Rights and Black Power movements the same year his report was published—the former statesman was catapulted by what the late historian and professor Dr. Cedric J. Robinson calls the "particularistic forces of racism and nationalism" (that depend upon and commercialize the othering of Black women as a sort of forced industrial labor itself, in this instance under the guise of public policy) to a professorship at Harvard University, one of the world's most prestigious collegiate institutions (and also built and buttressed by the forced and unfree labor of Black people).

The Moynihan Report, like many other examples of white-authored propaganda in historical archives, had far-reaching, devastating impacts on the Black community. Its politically motivated use of social science as an authenticator of racist beliefs that undergird a global history of patriarchy, anti-Blackness, transphobia/misogynoir, fatphobia, classism, and ableism wielded especially against women and children was an attempt to circumvent much-needed civil rights legislation and quell dissent by shifting the blame for racial tensions away from an objectively racist system and onto a demonized Black subject. This legacy of negative perceptions deeply affected my family across generations. My grandmother internalized these pressures, carefully crafting an image that pushed against these stereotypes—driving a sports car and maintaining a meticulous appearance while attempting to take to her grave that her children had different fathers. The weight of these social prejudices was so powerful that my great-grandmother internalized sex-negative, anti-Black myths of Black women's perceived hypersexuality, severely criticizing my grandmother for having children with multiple men. This conflict completely destroyed their relationship and led my grandmother to reject Black women as a whole—including her own daughter, my mother.

I wonder who my mother would have been if she felt loved by her mother. How do you relate to your gender as a Black woman if you are a reflection of what your mother hates? There was a valid reason for the pain that my grandmother carried; the world kept showing her that a Black woman was an experiment, a means to an end. She happened to use capitalism and the binary to enshrine her pain, which inevitably caused more harm. The long history of removing bodily autonomy from Black women was directly reflected in how the Black women in my family treated each other and themselves. Their actions were harmful but nowhere near as violent as the histories held in their bodies, and that has only continued by way of structures including but not limited to invisibilized police brutality, intimate partner violence, and the abuses of the medical industrial complex by which Black women are exceptionally and excessively targeted.

. . .

In the 1930s, Margaret Sanger created birth control after nonconsensually sterilizing thousands of Black American and Puerto Rican women. She justified doing this with insight from the misogynoiristic information she received from W. E. B. Du Bois that Black women were unfit parents. This unfounded belief conveniently came into common parlance post-slavery when Black women could no longer be forced to mother white children. To make it appear that white women were the blueprint for motherhood or that they had any skill in doing so, negative narratives of Black women were made. In the 1960s, sterilization was such a common practice in Mississippi that it was nicknamed the "Mississippi appendectomy," which also victimized civil rights activist, breast cancer survivor, and disability justice organizer Fannie Lou Hamer. She had her uterus removed without consent during what was supposed to be tumor removal surgery.

Removing Black people's reproductive capacity was done in response to the white replacement myth, the belief that white people would be outnumbered. Black people had been forced to birth children during slavery, which increased the population; in order to quell this, they were subjected to forced sterilization. As Dorothy Roberts documents in *Killing the Black Body*, "During the 1970s sterilization became the most rapidly growing form of birth control in the United States, rising from 200,000 cases in 1970 to over 700,000 in 1980 . . . Teaching hospitals performed unnecessary hysterectomies on poor Black women as practice for their medical residents." Although Black people had been used as chattel to nonconsensually build an entire nation for two hundred and fifty years, white people began to see that they were being outnumbered and thus took more harmful measures to halt Black people from having children on their own terms. Black reproductive capacity was judged a threat to the state in order to pedestalize white cisgender reproductive capacity. Ironically, and unlike for their white cis counterparts, biological essentialism did not insulate Black people gendered as women from medical apartheid but actually had the opposite effect, in that it made them the target/subject of experimentation using genitalia, reproductive capacity, the uterus, etc. to cement the border between Black and white women, much in the same way this pseudoscientific focus on "biology" has been weaponized against Black transgender people then and now. Similarly, the state has been on a campaign to convince people with uteruses that their main objective in life is to have children, so stripping Black people with uteruses of the choice to do so is institutionalizing this rhetoric. White women are only actors in fictional television shows like *The Handmaid's Tale* that mimic the horrors of reproductive injustice that Black women, and those perceived to be, have actually experienced. The crux of the harm that has been caused by reproductive injustice has all been on the same theme of "you are not a real woman."

This history has not ended; it continues in the prison and bail system by sterilizing incarcerated Black people, who comprise some of the highest numbers of those detained, and through medical institutions that are killing Black birthing and chronically ill people. In December 2020, Dr. Susan Moore, herself a physician, documented her mistreatment at an Indianapolis hospital, stating, "I put forth and maintain that if I were white, I wouldn't have to go through that." Despite her medical knowledge, doctors refused to treat her pain, suggesting she would abuse narcotics. She died of COVID-19 two weeks later. These violent acts are tactics to cement the idea that Black women are biologically distinct from white women, less than and subhuman.

How Black women exist in the white imagination has been nothing short of deadly, serving as a way to position white women as "real" women. As bell hooks further notes, "Most people tend to see the devaluation of Black womanhood as occurring only in the context of slavery. In actuality, sexual exploitation of Black women continued long after slavery ended and was institutionalized by other oppressive practices." This idea that someone's genitalia determine how they are going to be is the continuation of oppressive practices. The gender binary subsists off of racism, it is in fact the culprit for the violence Black women have endured.

Linking genitalia with gender identity has been used as a way to make someone real, strategically linking man-made assumptions about nature to explain nurture. Furthermore, Black trans women are often denied their womanhood, not only because of their Blackness but falsehoods that link gender to genitalia. In 1995, Tyra Hunter, a Black trans woman, died after a car accident because firefighters, upon discovering her genitalia, made derogatory statements instead of providing immediate care. The ways that Black cis women or those with uteruses have been and are treated is not a departure from how Black trans women experience violence. In every example, one's genitalia are either failing to prove womanhood, or "womanhood" is intentionally being removed as a way to assert that Black (cis and trans) women are not real women.

Cisgender people have been led to believe that they are nothing without this flimsy, made-up structure, so they fight tooth and nail to keep it in place, because otherwise, they'd have to ask the question: Who am I without the gender binary? What would I be if colonialism did not exist? Does being cisgender only exist in opposition to being trans? Trans people exist beyond the bounds of cisness. Being cis is formed in opposition to being trans, so who are you without constantly asserting your fabricated normality vis-à-vis having a clitoris or penis?

Chimamanda Ngozi Adichie, author and speaker, became world renowned after her viral TED talk "We Should All Be Feminists." In it, she spoke explicitly about the contradictions and gendered expectations placed specifically on girls. She would later be featured on Beyoncé's 2013 self-titled album; an excerpt from "We Should All Be Feminists" was used as the intro to Beyoncé's song "Flawless." In a 2017 interview, when Adichie was asked how feminism applies to trans women, she argued, "I think the whole problem of gender in the world is about our experiences. It's not about how we wear our hair or whether we have a vagina or a penis. It's about the way the world treats us, and I think if you've lived in the world as a man with the privileges that the world accords to men and then sort of change gender, it's difficult for me to accept that then we can equate your experience with the experience of a woman who has lived from the beginning as a woman and who has not been accorded those privileges that men are."

When she was called out for being transphobic, she took to Facebook to write a post to clear up any confusion; unfortunately, she only added insult to injury. She wrote that she supported trans people's existence, that they should be "allowed to be," but continued, "I don't think it's a good thing to talk about women's issues being the same as the issues of trans women because I don't think that's true." What Adichie failed to reckon with is the idea that there is not one universal truth about what makes a woman. She claims that "trans women are trans women," asserting that they are not women but something else entirely.

Although she claimed that she was referring to the differences in the early socialization and treatment of different women, Adichie fell into using an age-old colonial tactic called biological essentialism, in which biology is used as a tool to assert who or what is real and who is not.

As Oyèrónkẹ́ Oyěwùmí notes in *The Invention of Women*, "The idea that biology is destiny—or, better still, destiny is biology—has been a staple of Western thought for centuries . . . In the West, biological explanations appear to be especially privileged over other ways of explaining differences of gender, race, or class. Difference is expressed as degeneration." Adichie's feminism rests on the hope that women will someday wield the same power as men, a common ambition among white feminism, not an eradication of the structures that position one gender over another. As Oyěwùmí says, "from a cross-cultural perspective, the more interesting point is the degree to which feminism, despite its radical local stance, exhibits the same ethnocentric and imperialistic characteristics of the Western discourses it sought to subvert." Gender is neither stagnant nor fixed, it is everchanging and experienced differently for each and every person; what we all have in common is our socialization and trauma from misogyny, transphobia, and sexism.

Trans people, especially Black trans women, have endured extreme violence due to a widespread subscription to Adichie's worldview throughout the United States and the Western world. In 2023, Nigeria passed one of the harshest LGBTQIA+ laws, essentially surveilling and jailing anyone who wore clothes that did not correspond to their assumed gender, in addition to laws that stopped gay, lesbian, and queer people from being affectionate with a partner in public. There were mass arrests in October 2023 following the law's implementation. One of Adichie's former students and colleagues, esteemed author and speaker Akwaeke Emezi, spoke against Adichie's transphobic rhetoric, saying, "In the context of widespread anti-LGBTQ sentiment in Nigeria, this situation has provided anti-trans and anti-queer forces another opportunity to attack those communities." These colonial understandings of gender don't just harm theoretical discourse—they create deadly conditions for the most marginalized.

Countless Black trans women have lost their lives at the hands of people who are so deeply insecure about their own gender that they are compelled to take the life of someone who appears to cast light on their own discomfort. Trans people have been kept from jobs and housing. Trans people have been left to die in hospitals after medical staff discovered that they were trans. The only reason people are mostly silent about the blatant genocide against Black trans women is that they use the erasure of Black trans women to make themselves whole.

As Jules Gill-Peterson writes in *A Short History of Trans Misogyny*, "the more viciously or evangelically any trans misognynist delivers invectives against the immoral, impolitic, or dangerous trans women in the world, the more they admit that their gender and sexual identities depend on trans femininity in a crucial way for existence."

The extreme vulnerability of Black trans women in our society stems from a long history of hatred toward Black women. I am deeply concerned about how transmisogynoir has erased society's consciousness regarding the protection of Black trans women. The public response to violence against Black trans women is markedly different from reactions to harm against white women, whether cis or trans. When a white woman is kidnapped or a white trans person is harmed, there is significantly more public outcry, highlighting how society discards

Black trans women. The truth remains: If Black trans women are not free, none of us are free—yet too few people grasp this connection.

• • •

In my teaching, I center Black trans women—not to place them on a pedestal, but to challenge the idea of being cisgender as the standard. This approach enables everyone to see themselves while highlighting those who are intentionally excluded from most institutions, only to have their culture and experiences appropriated by the white and cisgender gaze. This also interrupts the desire to "study" trans people—as if there is one central way to be trans—and instead focuses on the system that singles out trans people and impacts everyone regardless of their gender identity—*cis-heteropatriarchy*. Cis-heteropatriarchy is the systemic assumption that women exist solely for the purpose of attracting or being in relationship with a man, which demands that men subjugate women in order to affirm their masculinity in order to be seen as men.

Black trans women challenge the gender binary by demonstrating that Black people are autonomous beings that get to say who they will be in the face of constant violence. They embody resistance against state control, proving that choice and discovery of who you are is a right, not an invitation for speculation, debate, or harm. Yet the violent pushback against this self-determination has intensified, reinforcing harmful biological essentialist views that deny Black women and girls their right to softness, love, respect, and bodily autonomy.

Throughout history, white supremacist capitalist patriarchy has viewed Black women and girls as threats to social order, subjecting their bodies to relentless scrutiny, criticism, and violence. Mary Jones was a Black trans woman in the late 1800s, living in New York's free society and working as a sex worker. Jones passed as a Black cisgender woman to the world around her, and sex work further solidified her gender. One night in 1836, one of her clients noticed that his wallet was missing, but that he had the wallet of someone else. He was able to track down the person who owned the wallet, and they teamed up to have Jones arrested. The police officer met with Mary Jones but pretended to be a client, he then restrained her and searched her home and body. When he searched her body, he discovered Jones's genitalia. Mary Jones was put on trial shortly thereafter for theft. She appeared in court dressed as she normally would have. When she was questioned in the courthouse, she was told to share her "right name," to which she responded, "Peter Sewally, I am a man." She was then asked: "What induced you to wearing women's clothing?" In Jules Gill-Peterson's book *Transmisogyny*, she details Jones's response: "I have been in the practice of waiting upon girls of ill fame and made the Beds and received the Company at the door and received the money for the Rooms etc. And they induced me to dress in women's clothes, saying I looked so much better in them, and I have always attended parties among the people of my own Colour dressed in that way—and in New Orleans I always dressed in this way." Jones was sentenced to five years in prison for grand larceny; they used her deadname, Peter Sewally, claiming that Mary Jones was an alias. She was not on trial for being trans or cross-dressing, but that did not stop the press from being transphobic. Posters of Jones dressed in a beautiful dress, wig, and headdress were plastered on businesses with the caption "The Man-Monster." As Gill-Peterson asserts, Jones was humiliated in the courtroom and in the press, not simply because she was dressed in women's clothing, but for something even more threatening to the white imagination: "She was Black and free."

To keep structures of oppression in place, there must be agreement for the structure in the first place. Jones shared that she was free with other Black people, threatening white people's belief that although New York had abolished slavery, Black people were still to exist as second-class citizens. As a sex worker, Mary Jones threatened whiteness by passing as a woman and working with white male clients. She subverted the notion that Black women were only to be relegated to hypersexualization and demonization. As previously discussed, the increase of anti-trans legislation from 2020 to 2024 is in direct connection to the racial "reckoning" (I put that in quotes because can we really call it that?). The trend we can trace from Jones's story almost two hundred years later is that Black womanhood, especially in boldfaced expressions of femininity, is still a threat to the state, exposing white people's attachment to manufactured differences used to elevate themselves. We have to consider why so many of us have likely never heard of Mary Jones but are deeply familiar with transphobia and misogynoir. The erasure throughout history of Black women's resistance is an intentional tool of subjugation.

Black cisgender women fail the constraints of cishood as much as Black trans women do. Being Black transmutes cishood, as Black women were never meant to be seen as human—an experience that is most demonstrable of Black trans women's societal treatment and survival.

In Nikki Giovanni's documentary *Going to Mars: The Nikki Giovanni Project*, she declares, "I'm a big fan of Black women. 'Cause in our blood is space travel. Because we've come from an unknown, to an unknown. And that's all that space travel is. If anybody can find what there is in this darkness, it's Black women." This metaphor of space travel resonates deeply with the historical experience of Black women in America, as articulated in Hortense Spillers's pivotal work, *Mama's Maybe, Papa's Baby*. Spillers observes that "those African persons in the 'Middle Passage' were literally suspended in the 'oceanic' . . . removed from the indigenous land and culture, and not yet 'American' either, these captive persons, without names that their captors would recognize, were in movement across the Atlantic, but they were also nowhere at all."

• • •

Black women's (cis and trans) very existence exposes the contradictions and hypocrisies the gender binary is utterly reliant on for its survival. Throughout history, Black women have done what have been deemed male activities (strenuous manual labor in cotton, sugarcane, and rice fields) and what have been deemed woman activities (breastfeeding, caretaking for white children, domestic work, skilled labor like dressmaking and textile work, etc.). Therefore, Black women have worked to subvert those colonial scripts of gender and instead have improvised and self-invented gender for ourselves. Our inherent failing of something so stupid and violent as the gender binary makes us the most exemplary. We stand as a constant reminder of what it means to be human, as being human is a queered existence, not a rigid, confined expression.

Being a Black woman is its own insurgent gender that, paired with a performance of femininity, is dangerous to the state. Femininity is seen as weak in a patriarchal transmisogynistic capitalist society, so that these omnipotent, godlike figures calling themselves men can be seen as powerful. Without people who are feminine seeing themselves as less than masculine folks, masculinity loses its power. Black femme folks have flipped this on its head and have carved out femininity for themselves, not necessarily exclusively free of the male gaze but certainly not centering it.

When that person is Black and identifies as a woman, that flamboyant, free exercise of self-possession, a body used for its own benefit, whether it is soft, nurturing, maternal or not, done on its own terms and not necessarily for a man, white man, or any partner at all, this Black femininity is villainized for its unassailability in spite of the grave risks associated with living outside of the heavily state-mechanized notions of binary gender that mandate how we are ultimately supposed to be or if we are even human beings. Said another way, Black femmes are badass.

So much so that the African American linguistic and cultural advent of studs, AGs (aggressives), and bulldaggers has always been a space within and beyond white heteronormative masculinity for Black lesbians and queer women. Even though masculinity under patriarchy is celebrated and protected, the presence of these outliers challenges commonly accepted but fictive gender modes and norms all throughout American history. They have become their own new and creative identity marker, a significant presence in the Black community then and now.

Black women transcend colonial binary gender and are a living reminder that no amount of antiquated (yet effective) Eurocentric, imperialist conditioning over thousands of years can change the fact that gender is fluid. As Black trans rights pioneer, performer, and organizer Marsha P. Johnson famously said in response to questions about her gender identity, "Pay it no mind." It was as an act of defiance; Johnson was not willing to be pigeonholed into rigid forms of gender. She wanted people to see her for her humanity; no one needed to know the ins and outs of her identity to honor who she was, especially an identity that was constantly in flux, not just for trans people. Black womanhood is a creation, and it needs to remain that way. It is continuously evolving and stands as an opening to explore beyond coloniality.

. . .

Understanding that Black women were never thought of in the limited scope of womanhood, I began to explore who I was instead of trying to fit into a concept that never included me in the first place.

I don't know the exact moment I started saying out loud that I am a nonbinary femme. The thought was clear in my head before I had the language to articulate it. I get asked all the time why I identify this way, as if it was a choice and not a conscious grueling effort to name myself rather than just agree and fall in line with the label the world has placed on me. Not having the language to explain my gender can feel daunting at times. I try to appease everyone (a function of being gendered and raised as a Black cisgender girl) and explain anyway. "But doesn't the word 'femme' mean 'woman' in French?" People proffer these pointedly insulting statements as questions and still expect me to answer. I do anyway. Although I speak English and *femme* meaning "woman" in French has no bearing on my identity, I still have to make my gender "make sense" in every language. Trans, nonbinary, and gender-variant folks are led to believe that we belong to the world, not to ourselves. Even cisgender people are performing their gender for each other despite their identities being perceived as unquestionably normative. Is cisgender identity authentic or just a performance of obedience? Learning the stories of Mary Jones and Marsha P. Johnson, attending KiKi balls and witnessing the Black women in my life, gave me the spaciousness to understand my gender as nonbinary. Being nonbinary is an opportunity to reclaim what was removed from my ancestors, releasing the binaristic, white cis man-made conception of womanhood that was offered as the only avenue for me to be seen as human, as worthy of life, and that ultimately did not fit how I saw myself.

Being nonbinary is a reminder that I belong to myself and that I get to say how I exist in this temporary body. I get to buy an overpriced matte-red lipstick from the makeup aisle just because it accentuates my full lips that I spent most of my life trying to hide. Being a nonbinary femme has me consciously interrogating how I have been taught to perform gender. It's a reminder that despite what the world says, I get to be soft and held.

Desirability is not the main focus of being nonbinary, and I'd argue it is not a focus at all. In Monique Witting's piece "The Straight Mind," she posits that "to reject the obligation of coitus and the institutions that this obligation has produced" defies cis-heteronormative design. I am affirmed by the fact that being nonbinary is an act of resistance and refusal to center my existence around the idea that I am less than because I am not desirable or consumptive.

It's reclamation work. I get to take back all the "musts" and the outright policing of who I am perceived to be; how I dress; how I speak—too loud/too angry; how I fuck—too little/too much and too fat. It's a reminder that I deserve to be loved in all the ways Stevie Wonder describes in his song "As." It's the fullness you feel after hugging someone you have been yearning to see. There are times when I resonate with being perceived as a Black woman. When that bassline for D'Angelo's "Lady" drops, I am completely okay with misgendering myself for D'Angelo. And I am clear that the world sees me as a Black woman; that is how I will be gendered as long as gender is a function that people think that they can see. There is a level of privilege that I am afforded from being able to pass as cisgender that has to be acknowledged and that my Blackness will inevitably subvert.

The way that Black women have been able to carve out their identities beyond constant dehumanization has always been queer to me. When I say my mom's existence informed my non-binary identity, her identity transitioned beyond the expectations placed on her; she was soft and sharp, and she could read the girls who danced with liquor-filled cups making the dance floor slippery without skipping a beat. Her presence brought a hush over a room before she even opened her mouth. The way she played with fashion and wasn't held down by perceptions of masculine or feminine—if it looked good it looked good, her Black womanhood was nonbinary to me. My mother is my queer and gender-expansive icon, and it's okay if that only makes sense to me.

- How have you internalized anti-Black notions of gender? What would it mean to fully reject those standards?

- When do you find yourself policing Black gender expression, even subtly? What fears or assumptions drive that behavior?

- How do you participate in systems that deny Black people freedom of gender expression? What would real solidarity require?
- For cis people, how can you begin or continue to interrogate how you came to know your gender and how your gender identity and expression are contingent upon someone else's being suppressed?

# 7

# A Country Not Founded on Consent

> "Decolonization, which sets out to change the world's order, is, obviously, a program of complete disorder. But it cannot come as a result of magical practices, of a natural shock, or of a friendly understanding. Decolonization, as we know, is a historical process: that is to say, it cannot be understood, it cannot be intelligible nor clear to itself except in the exact measure that we can discern the movements which give it historical form and context."
>
> —Franz Fanon, *The Wretched of the Earth*

> "I am sick and tired of being sick and tired."
>
> —Fannie Lou Hamer

CONTENT WARNING:
*Sexual violence, r*pe, lynching, xenophobia, racism*

When I lecture on consent, I use an exercise to engage students and demonstrate how consent conversations are endemic to everything, not just sex. Students are asked to stand and shake each other's hands if they can. They will usually begin to do so without uttering any words, and some will turn it into a competition, rushing to shake as many hands as possible, including mine. After everyone has shaken at least one other person's hand, I will pause and ask if their handshakes had consent. Most shrug their shoulders, never having considered that sticking out your hand and assuming it will be received with a shake is not entirely consensual. Then I asked if they had ever shaken someone's hand and it was super sweaty, held for too long, or squeezed too tight? Was there perhaps ever a time that you would have preferred to do a fist bump, side kiss on the cheek, or a hug? They will usually begin telling stories about times when they wanted to pull away but worried it would be rude if they did.

Next, I instruct them to ask if they can shake their classmate's hand and instruct the other person to say no. We then process how it felt to hear no. Some students share that, although this is just an exercise, they felt rejected. I then asked them to go around the room again, shaking each other's hands with consent this time, which would include a negotiation. The second time around takes longer, and students have to high-five or hug after talking through what is best for them or feeling empowered to just say no. The nervous laughter that was present the first time around transforms into conversations about what works best for their bodies.

When I ask students to share about the difference between the two experiences, they reflect that if asking for a handshake was commonplace, perhaps they would have been able to avoid so many awkward situations; how hearing no or negotiating could build the muscle for other interactions. This consent activity lasts roughly twenty minutes, but in that short amount of time, it becomes evident that we live in a society that lacks consent. The assumption is that you put your hand out and that should signal to receive a handshake; but what about extending your hand to allow for someone to opt in or opt out?

Oftentimes, handshakes occur in professional settings, where one person may have more institutional power than the other: Is consenting to the handshake your only option, or would it cost you your job if you said no or even attempted to negotiate? In a sexual setting, you are naked in bed with someone. The assumption is that sex will eventually happen, but there exists the possibility that that's not what you want at all. Our assumptions about how to engage with other people's bodies are largely funneled through how certain bodies are perceived. Our anti-Black-capitalistic-transphobic-ableist society determines whose bodies are worthy of consent. Consent is often removed before any words have been spoken, the assumption being that bodies, especially marginalized bodies, are to be controlled by those in power.

Not existing in a marginalized group does not leave you exempt from experiencing the ways in which we have all been socialized to think our bodies exist under the permission of someone else, not our own. Consent must begin with an acknowledgment of all the ways the state has actively removed bodily autonomy to create and maintain a dominant group. In order for there to be a dominant group, marginalized people have been forced under a constant state of duress, our narratives, bodies, and culture vulnerable to being manipulated at any moment. When a Black person walks down the street, what are the perceptions people have of them? What preconceived narratives are attached to them?

Ours is a society built on the transatlantic slave trade, genocide, and dispossession of Indigenous Americans, medical apartheid, prisons, and the continued removal of Indigenous people from their land across the globe—most notably Palestine. Our understanding of consent is shaped by historical contexts and present social dynamics, which often lead to problematic assumptions where the mere perception of agreement is treated as sufficient justification for the action. While this chapter will address practicing consent conversations in intimate settings, we must first examine the profound historical and contemporary contexts of sex education and consent—a narrative that is deeply challenging and often troubling. It is paramount that we engage in conversations about consent, lifting it toward the light without turning our eyes away from the truth and without compromising rigor or historicity.

Sex ed conversations cannot be all about blow jobs, spankings, flavored lube, and shit (no, literally, scat play is a fetish). Consent conversations have been rebranded as fun and sexy to convince the masses that they are necessary, but that's like slapping icing on a mud pie and calling it cake; it does not address the root issue of why people do not value consent conversations in the first place. Consent is, in fact, fun and sexy, but not everybody is granted the same access to that reality. If you exist in a marginalized body, consent is often removed the moment you step outside of your home. The origins of finding clever ways to talk about sex likely can be traced back to sex ed, but what is often missing are the experiences of marginalized voices as they relate to consent. How we view bodies and, thus, how we have been socialized to treat them greatly informs our relationship to consent.

The sex ed field is overwhelmingly white; from academia to sex tech, sex ed is used as a tool for a predominantly white industry to hide behind its own racist proclivities. Talking about sex becomes the new anti-racist checkmark, lowering the litmus test threshold for radicalism—all it takes to be radical in a white-dominated sex ed field is yelling "penis" in a room full of people. Engaging in a conversation around consent/bodily autonomy must include the racial implications, as it is not just a simple yes or no in a world where people feel entitled to other people's bodies. It is no coincidence that Black, Latinx, and Indigenous people experience higher rates of sexual violence; this does not happen simply due to a lack of consent conversations.

The United States and many other Western countries have created conditions under which only certain bodies matter, which has had a detrimental impact on how we all view our own and others' bodies. This wound does not go away when we engage in romantic or sexual intimacy; if anything, this is when our inherited thoughts about other people's bodies and our own are even more heightened. Consent cannot be separated from the racist notions that fuel how people relate to other people's bodies. Bodily autonomy is a concept typically introduced to students in their teens, but these conversations must begin as soon as people acquire language. A handshake may seem innocuous, but it reveals so much about our culture of consent (or lack thereof). As a society, we must acknowledge what has informed our relationship to bodily autonomy and engage in consent in every interaction.

As of 2024, white people own 98 percent of private agricultural land in the United States. Although the word "treaty" is derived from the Anglo-French word *treté*, meaning negotiated, bargained, or discussed, that is not a truly accurate rhetorical description of how white people came to own most of the land in the US. As early as kindergarten, most of us are sold a neatly packaged lie that when white people colonized Pawtuxet Village, renaming it Plymouth Colony, they had a cordial conversation with the Wampanoag people; and though they were unable to grow their own food and were completely reliant on the Wampanoag for survival, the Pilgrims magically learned to speak Wôpanâak overnight in order to negotiate a plan to live in harmony. When this negotiation ended, they celebrated over a feast of unseasoned food.

My one-year-old child came home from daycare with a laminated sheet that had stenciled drawings of people with braids and feathered headdresses and others wearing captain hats; between them sat a giant smiling turkey and a table full of vegetables. Every year, on the last Thursday in November, millions of Americans celebrate Thanksgiving—a holiday created by white settlers to perpetuate their sanitized version of history. This narrative portrays peaceful treaty signings through which Indigenous peoples supposedly willingly surrendered their lands to white settlers. Thanksgiving's status as a national holiday demonstrates how controlling the narrative can reshape the perception of lands taken by force. Unfortunately, Thanksgiving is not unique in being a holiday designed to control historical narratives. It was only in 2021 that the White House first recognized Indigenous Peoples' Day, only slightly shifting away from the false notion that Christopher Columbus discovered the Americas. As of 2025, Indigenous Peoples' Day has not yet achieved status as a nationally recognized federal holiday. These small governmental acknowledgments stem from Indigenous peoples' persistent advocacy for historical truth: Colonization involved the violent suppression of language, religion, and culture; theft of land; devastating spread of unfamiliar diseases that decimated Indigenous populations; sexual violence; and warfare—all in pursuit of territorial conquest and power.

The practice of closing schools and businesses to commemorate a sanitized version of history compounds this historical injury. However, holidays represent just one of many ways the state has worked to maintain its preferred historical narrative. *Pocahontas* was the first Disney film "inspired" by a true story, but even Disney would have to admit the only true parts are in these lyrics from the theme song: "You think you own whatever land you land on" and "You think the only people who are people are the people who look and think like you." In the movie, Pocahontas, an Indigenous woman, is depicted as putting her life on the line for John Smith, a white settler, which then results in them falling in love. This story is based on the real-life white settler John Smith, who wrote a recounting of his time in the Americas after returning to England.

The "true story" of Pocahontas, like the telling of her life through a white settler's lens, completely removed her agency. The *real* true story of Pocahontas, whose real name was Amonute and also Matoaka, is tragic and short. Amonute was kidnapped by John Smith and his group of white settlers who sought to displace the Powhatan from their homeland in present-day Virginia. She would have been ten years old when she was kidnapped, raped, and married off to another John, a twenty-six-year-old John Rolfe. In the movie, John Smith and Pocahontas are depicted in the final scene riding off into the sunset. In real life, she was brought to England, where she was poisoned and died at twenty; her remains are still in England, while her descendants still live in Virginia. Disney conveniently distorted the story of an Indigenous woman to make a profit while also feeding the propaganda machine that white settlers had compassion and that Indigenous women were benevolently resilient. Disney, a multibillion-dollar company, has indoctrinated an untold number of children, including the author and possibly the reader. Disney is often dismissed as children's entertainment, but the role that it plays in propagating how we view people's bodies is insurmountable, lasting for decades.

The story of Pocahontas was not an isolated tragedy or merely a relic of the past—this violent history continues today, with murder being the third leading cause of death for Indigenous women, who also face increased rates of kidnapping and are 2.5 times more likely to experience sexual assault than any other group. In 1978, the Supreme Court ruled that no non-Indian committing violence on Indigenous reservations could be tried in courts there; this legislation singlehandedly has left Indigenous people subject to much harm, in particular sexual violence, of which white cisgender men are the primary perpetrators. The fallacies that we are fed via Disney, our educational system, and other media outlets are designed to absolve white people of their atrocious past (and present) by perpetuating racist notions of Indigenous people, maintaining the narrative that their bodies are not worthy of agency, respect, dignity, or consent.

While Thanksgiving might be easily dismissed as just another federally recognized holiday centered on consumerism and sweet potato pie, the story of how it became nationally recognized reveals key ingredients of our country's legacy of disregarding bodily autonomy, particularly in relation to gender. Abraham Lincoln established this national holiday—ostensibly meant to reflect and express gratitude for the dispossession of Indigenous peoples from their land—after thirty-six years of persistent pressure on a succession of presidents from Sarah Josepha Hale, a widowed white woman who campaigned tirelessly for its recognition. When Hale's husband died, she was left with five kids to care for, and she used the money left to publish two very popular poetry books, including the well-known nursery rhyme "Mary Had a Little Lamb." Hale's advocacy for the Thanksgiving holiday was rooted in her work to teach upper-class affluent white women how to comport themselves as ideals of the perfected "Anglo-Saxon" Protestant women. She became the editor for *Godey's Lady's Book*, one of the first magazines geared toward wealthy Protestant white women to convince them that believing in God, being fashionable, being submissive to men, and maintaining a thin physique by not eating too much would cement "racial superiority."

Gender plays a significant role in determining whose bodies are more vulnerable to having their agency removed, and the intersection of race cannot be excluded. As we've covered, white women have not only benefitted from the gender binary, but they are also progenitors of its presence, advancing the notion that they are the blueprint for "a woman." The idea that women are inherently submissive to men and also must cater to their needs at the expense of their own has only made white women more susceptible to violence. The irony is not lost on me that Thanksgiving became a holiday during a time when enslaved Black people, especially women (and those perceived to be), were the primary source of domestic labor; their bodies were used nonconsensually for everything from planting the foods that would eventually end up on dinner tables, to then serving said food, to their bodies being sexually assaulted to build an entire nation.

In the mid-1830s, when the Thanksgiving holiday was established, white people in the North were debating the morality of slavery, garnering them the title of abolitionist, although many of these Northerners would have still benefited directly or indirectly from the economic exploits of slavery. Even if an abolitionist believed in the abolition of slavery on economic, political, or logistical grounds, that did not mean they felt that all races were equal and morally deserving of life. As an abolitionist, Hale felt that the institution of slavery was not allowing the country to progress and that enslaved Black people should be sent to Liberia so as to eliminate the possibility of miscegenation and to complete the project of ethnonationalism that undergirded the idea of white purity, an ideal she worked so hard to protect.

The institution of slavery stripped agency from Indigenous Africans, forcibly displacing them from their lands, cultures, and languages. While enslaved Black people were compelled to cultivate the land, white people created new social markers to distance themselves from Black people, establishing a hierarchy of inferiority. They constructed gender identity roles deeply informed by anti-Blackness and, by extension, fatphobia, to set themselves apart. Hale served as a foot soldier for white supremacy—her pursuit of white superiority earned her a false sense of protection from having her own agency removed, unlike the Black people she sought to distance herself from. Though Hale intended Thanksgiving to be a holiday promoting racial superiority, many enslaved Indigenous Africans were able to escape captivity on this day while their captors and abusers were distracted by overeating and drinking alcohol, inadvertently undermining their own efforts to maintain control of the plantations.

In a speech at the University of California, Santa Barbara, in 2008, Black scholar and educator Cedric Robinson mentions, from his seminal work, *Black Marxism: The Making of the Black Radical Tradition*, that in tracing a lineage of African diasporic resistance against capitalism and other forms of systemic oppression, it was critical to debunk ". . . the notion that freedom is the reserve of the privileged classes . . . the sensitivity to, the urges, the impulse, the necessity to [freedom] is unusual or unique [to them]." The concept of freedom is paradoxical in a country founded on the mass genocide and enslavement of Indigenous Americans and Indigenous Africans, land theft brokered via abrogated, illegitimate land treaties and all manner of continued disenfranchisement. This paradox would naturally need to be shrewdly and steadily reinforced via a barrage of targeted, highly racialized, and gendered propaganda canonized throughout American history.

The lengths enslaved Indigenous Africans took to be free to regain their bodily autonomy exemplify the human desire for agency and are also terribly obscured in the historical record. The immense amount of flesh being dumped into the Atlantic Ocean during the transatlantic slave trade completely altered the hunting paths of its sharks. Enslaved Indigenous Africans were thrown overboard, but they also jumped, an option that may seem a macabre option to some, but may have felt like freedom to those who had had all decision-making power abruptly stripped away through the very nature of their bondage; not to mention the deplorable conditions on the long journey from the west coasts of Africa to the Americas and Caribbean. Once on land, the conditions of chattel slavery were not any better than those at sea. Henry Box Brown was an enslaved man who had been separated from his wife and children due to them being sold, so he shipped himself from North Carolina to Philadelphia in a three-by-two-foot box, unable to tolerate the inconceivable conditions of slavery any further. Harriet Jacobs was also enslaved in North Carolina; when her kidnapper threatened to harm her children if she did not submit to his sexually violent advances, she hid in the crawl space of her grandmother's attic for seven years, unable to stand and only being able to see her children through the cracks in the wood. Harriet Jacobs writes about her experiences being enslaved in what is considered a seminal American text: *Incidents of a Slave Girl, Written by Herself*, under the pseudonym Linda Brent; her book provides a firsthand account of the atrocities of chattel slavery:

"Women are considered of no value unless they continually increase their owner's stock. They are put on a par with animals. This same master shot a woman through the head, who had run away and been brought back to him. No one called him to account for it. If a slave resisted being whipped, the bloodhounds were unpacked and set upon him to tear his flesh from his bones. The master who did these things was highly educated and styled a perfect gentleman. He also boasted the name and standing of a Christian, though Satan never had a truer follower."

In the 1840s in Alabama, three enslaved people—Lucy, Anarcha, and Betsey—were nonconsensually experimented on by James Marion Sims. After his reputation faltered in South Carolina due to patient deaths, Sims, like many white physicians, used Black bodies to improve his social position. In Montgomery, he leased enslaved people to experiment on, seeking a cure for vesicovaginal fistulae, a bladder condition typically occurring from labor. Lucy, Anarcha, and Betsey had allegedly been exiled from their plantations due to an inability to control their bowels after childbirth. Sims conducted these experiments without anesthesia, believing Black people didn't feel pain like white people did. As Harriet A. Washington writes in *Medical Apartheid*:

"Betsey's voice has been silenced by history, but as one reads Sims's biographers and his own memoirs, a haughty, self-absorbed researcher emerges, a man who bought black women slaves and addicted them to morphine in order to perform dozens of exquisitely painful, distressingly intimate vaginal surgeries. Not until he had experimented with his surgeries on Betsey and her fellow slaves for years did Sims write an essay to cure white women."

Sims would invite other aspiring white doctors to watch Lucy, Anarcha, and Betsey restrained naked to medical tables, unable to move although they were kept awake during these extensive procedures. Lucy, Anarcha, and Betsey did not consent to being used like lab rats, and Sims did not care. When he later operated on white women, he used anesthesia. Sims would eventually move to New York, but not before performing medical experiments on enslaved Black children, prying open their skulls from their brains to prove that the size made them intellectually inferior. And yet he still went on to be named the "Father of Modern Gynecology," with statues erected in his honor, most notably in Harlem. As C. Riley Snorton writes in *Black on Both Sides*, "Anarcha, Betsey and Lucy, and the unnamed other captives were rendered as raw materials for making the field of 'women's medicine,' from which they were excluded as women according to the attenuating frame of plantation medicine's sexual economies." Though their bodies were used to advance "women's medicine," they were not considered women, nor worthy of the relief these medical advances were purported to provide.

As their legacy, we have illustrations of their genitals in precarious positions during these gruesome experiments, but we don't know their last names or gender identities or have their own account of what happened to them. The lengths that Sims went to remove bodily autonomy from Lucy, Anarcha, Betsey, and so many other unnamed people can only be described as pure evil. That he still received accolades for his medical "advances" shows how forcibly controlling a Black person's body was rewarded.

On November 6, 2024, Donald Trump was elected president by a landslide of voters committed to getting him back in office, conveniently overlooking accusations of rape that led to a conviction of sexual abuse in civil court just a year prior. Many people expressed upset at Trump winning, arguing that an accused rapist and convicted felon should not be able to run for the nation's highest public office, but this country routinely rewards white cisgender men for their uncanny and largely unchecked ability to usurp the bodily autonomy of others. It should come as no surprise that Trump is also a white supremacist. In a white supremacist police state, one only needs to demonstrate support for the state's authority to remove bodily autonomy to be granted power over others' bodies.

Roughly thirty years ago, Anita Hill, a lawyer, who worked as a legal adviser for Clarence Thomas in the US Department of Education's Office for Civil Rights and later at the Equal Employment Opportunity Commission (EEOC), was grilled in a Senate hearing by all-white cisgender men for her leaked accusations of sexual harassment against conservative Judge Clarence Thomas. In the process of Thomas being confirmed as a Supreme Court Justice, a live TV hearing showed white senators, including former president Joe Biden, treating Hill as if she were on trial, questioning her motives for coming forward. Anita Hill shared that Thomas asked her to go out with him on multiple occasions, described his sexual experiences as well as the porn that he watched. The senators questioned why Hill did not stop working for Thomas, and she had to reiterate multiple times that she feared retaliation. Even Thomas's former special assistant, Jane Campa "JC" Alvarez, a Mexican American who spent most of her career working on behalf of Latinx communities, testified on behalf of Thomas, stating, "Women who have really been harassed would agree, if the allegations were true, you put as much distance as you can between yourself and that other person. What's more, you don't follow them to the next job—especially if you are a black female, Yale Law School graduate. Let's face it, out in the corporate sector, companies are fighting for women with those kinds of credentials."

In a country founded on sexual violence, coming forward often makes survivors susceptible to more harm and re-traumatization. In the end, Thomas would be confirmed as a Supreme Court justice; within his first year, he would vote to overturn *Roe v. Wade*, and he would succeed in doing so in 2022. Hill had to endure scrutiny from members of the US government, her former colleagues, and also the court of public opinion—she received countless death threats. Although Clarence Thomas is a Black man, his conservative views align neatly with white supremacy. Anita Hill did what so many survivors of abuse are terrified to do: She spoke out against the harassment she experienced, creating an opening for countless survivors to come forward with their experiences. Anita Hill speaking her truth to an all-white Senate hearing was revolutionary, a kick in the teeth to the ways that Black women have been silenced, forced to hold and reckon with their pain alone.

The horrors that Lucy, Anarcha, and Betsy experienced did not disappear with the abolition of slavery; they instead had a ripple effect that extended through time. Hill's was a high-profile case in which her body was blamed for causing the sexual harassment that she experienced. The impacts of a country founded on a lack of consent echo in the screams from survivors of sexual assault demanding to be believed, some of whom are Trump's and Thomas's survivors. Jacobs adding "Written by Herself" to the title of her book speaks to the level of erasure and complete removal of agency, even in the retelling of experiences of harm. White people stole Indigenous Africans from their land, with the clear intention of controlling their bodies for profit in every way, the brain and tongue often the first to be shackled. Although Jacobs was able to publish her book, there are so many accounts of the enslaved that we will never hear, especially in mainstream discourse, and those that we do know of have been watered down to make white people more comfortable. Even in the retelling of a deplorable institution, white people's agency is centered over the people who poisoned their kidnappers, chose to kill their own children to keep them safe, camouflaged themselves in swamps, ran from dogs, folded their bodies into boxes and attics—all to reclaim what had been taken from them: their agency.

The narrative that white supremacy still holds on chattel slavery places slavery as a two-hundred-fifty-year moment, frozen in time, abolished due to the heroism of a white President. In reality, slavery has only changed shape: Prisons became the replacement, removing agency from those who were criminalized by the state—a history steeped in racism. This country has built more prisons—torture shrines to hoard wealth and resources—than any other country in the world, controlling the bodies of the most marginalized with law and order, medical and environmental racism; and discarding those who cannot use their bodies to produce labor for the capitalistic machine. The treatment of Indigenous Americans and Africans is not simply wrapped up in the hatred of these groups. Rather, it has always been informed by how white people could make a profit, capitalism laying the groundwork for nullifying bodily autonomy.

Racial capitalism is defined by Cedric Robinson as "capitalism that develops and operates within a racist system and regime. Fundamental for the reproduction of violence to thus create capital." During slavery, Black people were the capital for white people to amass wealth and continue the colonial quest; this structure has continued to the present day through the subjugation of Black life, most notably the prison system. Although Black people make up 12 percent of the US population, they are disproportionately represented in the prison system at 38 percent. The fact that the state has the power and the privilege to remove a person's agency for an arbitrary length of time based on a vast array of circumstances creates the conditions for a society that does not value consent. Believing that prisons should exist is antithetical to bodily autonomy; prisons are not only sites of bondage but also immense sexual violence, criminalize mental illness, and death. They deepen the pockets of those who own and invest in them, furthering the social inequities that lead people to prison in the first place.

I, too, struggle with the notion of abolition; I consider myself a student of abolition, actively working through my own contradictions. When it comes to people who harm children, commit wage theft, doctors who intentionally harm patients, and those who commit sexual violence—these are instances where I have a hard time not believing some people belong underneath the jail. However, a country founded on sexual violence, bondage, control, and forced assimilation of Black and Indigenous peoples does not hold the moral compass to determine who should be removed from society. There are far too many people who have committed countless crimes who walk free, and many people who did nothing wrong but are punished for being born Black, trans, poor, or neurodivergent, proving prisons to be ineffective and reserved for a particular person, not a certain crime. My evolution around consent has expanded to include systems of oppression subsisting on the removal of bodily autonomy. I didn't always see it this way, I thought oppressive structures like anti-Black racism were distinct from bodily autonomy, simply because they are never talked about as connected. I remember debating classmates in high school about rape that happens in marriages, they did not believe this was possible; I was clear that it did but did not have the language to further explain. I wish I could go back and have the conversation with them so they can see that they didn't believe marital rape is possible due to the patriarchal belief that a woman belongs to a man in marriage, that her autonomy is revoked in many instances that are seen as traditional (name changes, expected housework, and sex).

As Angela Davis writes in *Are Prisons Obsolete?*: "We must think about imprisonment as a fate reserved for others, a fate reserved for the 'evildoers,' to use a term recently popularized by George W. Bush. Because of the persistent power of racism, 'criminals' and 'evildoers' are, in the collective imagination, fantasized as people of color. The prison, therefore, functions ideologically as an abstract site into which undesirables are deposited, relieving us of the responsibility of thinking about the real issues afflicting those communities from which prisoners are drawn in such disproportionate numbers."

The origins of the police are directly linked to chattel slavery. White people took it upon themselves to form vigilante groups to chase enslaved Black people, training mastiffs and bloodhounds to hunt Black people to recover what they viewed only as property. Lynchings, the original corporal punishment, are the removal of bodily autonomy in its final form. Attended by white men, women, and children, the spectacle of lynching was to act as a warning to other enslaved Black people to stay in line. Today, Black people experience police brutality in high numbers and, as mentioned above, make up a large percentage of prison populations, speaking to the ways that white America is committed to still having lynchings under the guise of law and order. The term "criminal" was defined before the word "crime," so what or whom is being punished?

Black people's agency and bodily autonomy became even more threatening to white people after slavery was abolished. White people transformed Black people's freedom into an imagined threat to their quest for racial purity, claiming that Black people's desire for freedom was actually a desire for romantic and sexual relationships with white people. This particular accusation was directed at Black men. While sexual violence had long been a tool of control and dominance that white people used during chattel slavery, they were now asserting that it was Black people who had a proclivity toward sexual violence. When slavery was abolished, lynchings increased, as though Black men were viewed as a sexual threat to white masculinity and heterosexuality that needed to be eradicated. The bloodstains still remain, etched into the soil of cities across the US, Black people removed from the earth due to false accusations of sexual violence or sometimes even an innocuous glance at a white person.

Casting Black men as sexual maniacs who needed to be controlled and kept away from white women has endured: Stereotypes about Black men having large penises and being inherently hypersexual are propaganda that can be found in pornography today. Porn is a multibillion-dollar industry across which racist sexual fantasies are displayed freely under the guise of sex positivity, revealing the porn industry's willingness to exploit anti-Blackness as a lucrative form of desire. "Ebony" and "interracial" categories have garnered increased interest in recent years, including a spike in 2017 that was concurrent with a rise in white supremacist groups and Donald Trump's first presidential election.

The porn industry also saw a rise in the popularity of "cuckold" porn in 2017, when alt-right groups resurfaced the thirteenth-century term "cuck." "Cuckold" describes a man who is emasculated and humiliated by not being able to sexually please his wife or partner but derives pleasure from the experience of watching someone else do so; "cuckservative" was used in alt-right circles as an insult toward white men who had "betrayed" their whiteness/white supremacy. The prevalence of interracial and cuckold pornography featuring Black men with white women perhaps reveals that fears about racial purity mask underlying sexual fantasies. Cuckold pornography specifically employs racist stereotypes to depict white men being "emasculated" by Black men with large penises having sex with white women and, in some scenes, penetrating the white male actors as well. These scenes represent the ultimate performance of Black body fetishism—the white man's humiliation simultaneously produces arousal. The white men's displays of humiliation position them as innocent bystanders incapable of using their bodies to provide pleasure, paralleling their claimed "inability" to use their bodies to build an entire nation.

These scenes beg the question: What is whiteness without the subjugation of Blackness? Cuckold pornography typically depicts white women as victims of the Black man's advances or as willing participants in racist imagery, highlighting the sexually perverse ways that Black men have always been portrayed. White women will often be the only voices that are heard in a cuckold scene, vocally egging on their white scene partner's feelings of humiliation or using racism to taunt the Black actor. In 2017, Black porn star Moe the Monster sued the porn company Dogfart.com, which specializes in interracial porn, when they inserted a soundbite of him being called the n-slur by a white woman actress, although he had blatantly refused to be called that on several occasions. The production company noted that viewers like hearing the n-slur used in their porn videos. The porn industry often uses Black bodies to satisfy racist proclivities. Performer Ana Foxxx told *Cosmopolitan* she was cast in a scene that was later titled "black booty points toward the Union," in which she knelt on concrete and performed multiple blow jobs on white men wearing Confederate flags. Black women are portrayed as ghetto, angry, and solely as accessories in scenes with white people. According to an article by *Vice* magazine, "What 'Interracial' Cuckold Porn Reveals About White Male Insecurity," white women porn actresses are paid more to be in scenes with Black men, citing the belief that they have larger penises that therefore require more work. Black women, on the other hand, receive no such increased pay rate.

Porn is a white-dominated industry; its categories are not created by the viewers but through the imaginations of mostly white cisgender men. A white man being "emasculated" or threatened by a Black man is greatly informed by white cisgender men building their entire identities off of the subjugation of the Black body. The porn industry exemplifies the ways that Black men have been made to be the wet nurses to white people's sexual perversions and overall obsession with Black bodies. The cuckold fantasy illuminates the insecurities and fears that fueled lynchings, police brutality, and prisons in hopes for racial purity but also so that Black men would not be seen as more desirable and thus more powerful than white men. In September 2024, Andrew Shulz, white supremacist comedian and podcaster, appeared on the show *ShxtsNGigs* with James Duncan and Fuhad Dawodu, two award-winning Black podcasters, where they discussed the "Black girlfriend effect." The concept, which trended on TikTok, suggests that a white man dating a Black woman will have a "glow up" by growing his beard and getting a fade; in simpler terms, grooming like a Black man. As Duncan and Dawodu explained the trend to Shulz, he responded, "They shave their hair because they start losing it, because he's so stressed to be around this Black girl complaining all the time."

James and Fuhad laugh along as Schulz continues: "They grow their beard because they need a cushion when they get slapped. I think the black girlfriend effect might be a protective instinct."

While I have critiques of the "Black girlfriend effect," this idea that white men are again unable to groom themselves without being in a sexual relationship with a Black woman, this feels a bit too on the nose for me. But the focus here is two Black men laughing at a white man making disparaging remarks about Black women. Again, cuckolding is happening beyond the porn category; Black men are seemingly willing to be used for the pleasure of white men. Black men think they will have access to the same level of power as white men if they degrade Black women. Later that year, rapper Kendrick Lamar called out Shulz on his album, rapping in the song "wacced out murals," "Don't let no white comedian talk about no Black woman, that's law." Schulz responded by questioning whether rappers really care about Black women and insisted that his comments were just a joke. He then made sexually violent comments about Lamar:

"But, just Kendrick? I would make love to him, and there's nothing he could do about it," he said. "I would make love to him. And the only thing that he could do is decide if it's consensual or not . . . I would go so far as to say he couldn't stop most people on the planet from having sex with him . . . He's talking a lot of shit, but if it came down to it, I could put him on my lap, I could feed him a bottle."

Schulz's comments reflect a common pattern in a country that has sexualized Blackness as a form of power and control. Although Pornhub's analytics showed that "Ebony" was the most searched category in the US, one has to consider the thin line between fantasy/desire and fetishism/violence. Porn trends reveal an indelible impulse to separate Black people from their agency. The lacy veil of sexual fantasy may be shrouding ugly and deep-rooted prejudices that lead to further violence against Black people. As Sherronda J. Brown writes in *Refusing Compulsory Sexuality*, "Blackness negates the need for consent in the social imagination since we are constructed as always consenting—either passively or enthusiastically—to the sexualization imposed on us."

Recy Taylor, a Black twenty-four-year-old sharecropper from Alabama, was kidnapped and raped by six white men as she walked home from church in 1944. In an act of great bravery, Recy Taylor came forward and named her rapists. But even with eyewitnesses, national advocacy, and plenty of media coverage (thanks in part to Rosa Parks mobilizing her resources to ensure the story was known), all six men were acquitted and suffered no consequences for their actions. Taylor would go on to outlive most of her assailants, and she never stopped telling her story. Taylor's story illuminates how the Black body is a site of perpetual disregard, laying the groundwork to continue to institutionalize the removal of consent from Black people.

In 2011, NYPD reported 700,000 stops under Stop and Frisk, a law that permitted police to approach and pat down anyone who they felt was suspicious. NYPD would rarely, if ever, stop and frisk a white person. Due to our racialized conceptions of criminality and the continued effects of redlining, police presence is always in high numbers in Black communities (although the social inequities that create the conditions for a Black neighborhood are what cause crime, not being Black itself). Black trans and gender-nonconforming individuals are disproportionately affected by Stop-and-Frisk legislation. Police and prisons have their origins in correcting and reinforcing gender standards: profiling trans people, especially in predominantly Black neighborhoods, was just an extension of their main objective, reminiscent of cross-dressing laws from the 1830s to 1940s, which were designed to enforce normalcy. If a trans or gender-nonconforming person was profiled and their identification didn't match the officer's perception of their gender, this would lead to sexual violence in the form of groping to confirm genitalia. If trans people, especially women, carried condoms, they would be accused of participating in sex work. Feeling entitled to knowledge of or control over someone else's body because they are different only serves to justify more harm toward that group.

If the image of a seventeen-year-old white girl being stopped and frisked by the police because she appeared suspicious raises alarm bells for you, but not when it is a seventeen-year-old Black trans teen, you might need to consider who you have reserved agency for. You may have thought to yourself, *Well, I do not think either person should be treated as suspicious*, but that is not how any of us have been socialized to think or how our state operates.

From Latasha Harlins to Tamir Rice, countless Black children have been murdered because of racist notions that marked their bodies as inherently threatening. Black children are often adultified and treated as though they are much older than they actually are, stripping them of their innocence and forcing an agenda that says their bodies do not belong to them but to the narratives that leave white adults and children as perpetually innocent.

In 2018, Chrystul Kizer, a seventeen-year-old Black girl, shot and killed her sex trafficker, Randall Volar, a thirty-four-year-old white man in Kenosha, Wisconsin. Kizer documented that upon meeting Volar when she was sixteen years old, he sexually abused and trafficked her to other men in exchange for money and gifts. Four days before he died, Volar was arrested after the police received a call from a fifteen-year-old Black girl saying that Volar had drugged her and that she was going to die. She was found wandering the streets under the influence of LSD. Police arrested and searched Volar's home, finding footage of him sexually abusing Kizer and other Black children; he was released the same day without bail. In the state of Wisconsin, there are protections for victims of sex trafficking, but murder is not covered by those protections. Kizer was arrested and held on a million-dollar bail. The state made it clear that a seventeen-year-old sex-trafficked Black girl was a greater threat to their agenda than an adult white male abuser. Kizer's youth was stolen from her by a hebephile and the criminal injustice (justice is absent) system. I can't think of any instance in which a white child was trafficked, murdered their trafficker, but then was penalized for doing so.

Society conveniently drives Black people toward situations in which they have to fight to have their basic material needs met, making Black people, especially girls and women, susceptible to predators. In this situation, Kizer was seen as the perpetrator, not the victim—victimhood is rarely reserved for Black people, leading to increased harm without restitution. Systems of oppression (white supremacy, capitalism, ableism, fatphobia, homophobia, and others) continue to strip Black people and other marginalized groups of bodily autonomy to reinforce deviant sexuality created to justify white dominance. Controlling marginalized bodies and the narratives about them remains a lucrative form of currency that lines white pockets.

On October 7, 2023, a Palestinian resistance group called Hamas killed 1,400 Israelis and kidnapped 128 people as hostages at the Nova Music Festival. In the days following the attack, major US-based news outlets like the *New York Times* and CNN released reports from the Israeli government claiming that babies had been beheaded, women had been raped, and a baby had been cut out of a pregnant person's womb during the attack. Although firsthand accounts conflicted with allegations of sexual assault and beheading, Western press outlets continued to present Hamas as a critical threat to the Israeli people. *HuffPost* released an infomercial-style video filled with famous actors and well-known influencers speaking in support of Israel and urging Hamas to return the Israeli hostages. In what was allegedly a search to hold Hamas accountable for their actions, the Israeli government bombed hospitals and universities and ravaged homes, revealing a long history of Western power and greed, resulting in the murder of more than 35,000 Palestinians, most of whom were children.

For the past seventy-five years, Palestinians have been under siege by the apartheid state of Israel, backed by the United States and Great Britain. Zionists, people who believe in the creation of an Israeli ethno-state, have been working overtime to convince everyone that Palestinian suffering is necessary for Jewish safety. Many people believe that Zionism and Judaism are one and the same, but throughout history, there have been many Zionists who were not Jewish. Joe Biden, former president of the United States and career politician, has said multiple times that "you do not have to be Jewish to be a Zionist."

Theo Herzel created Zionism in 1896 in response to feeling as though anti-Semitism was too vast of an issue in Europe to have Jews assimilate and that in order to find a safe place to live, they would need Der Judenstaat, or The Jewish State. Herzel would shop this idea around, hoping that a Jewish state would be created in either East Africa, Uganda, or Armenia. When he visited Palestine in 1895, he wrote in his journal, "We must gently expropriate the private property on the estates assigned to us. We shall try to spirit the penniless population across the border by procuring employment for it in the transit countries while denying it employment in our country. The property owners will come over to our side. Both the process of expropriation and the removal of the poor must be carried out discreetly and circumspectly."

All of his proposals were declined, and he would die before he got to see his dream realized. Israel was established in 1948 by Great Britain following WWII, resulting in the genocide and dispossession of roughly 700,000 Palestinians. In 1917, Lord Balfour created the Balfour Declaration to establish a homeland for Jewish people in order to discourage Jewish people from migrating to Europe. Prior to WWII, a Jewish ethno-state was of interest to some Jewish people but took on more interest from Zionists who were not Jewish. Great Britain establishing a Jewish ethno-state allowed them to continue their colonial expansion. Post-WWII, the Israeli government used the pain and suffering from the Holocaust to justify the necessity of a Jewish ethno-state. After the October 7 attack, Israel started a war with the alleged intention of stopping Hamas. What so many people seemed to not understand is that in order to have an Israel, an ethno-state in an area where Jewish people are not the majority, it required dispossession and genocide.

As Joe Biden said in a 1986 speech, "If there were no Israel, the US would have to create one to protect its own interests in the region." The history of this region is oftentimes presented as "complex" as a very common white supremacist tactic to silence dissent. Or, as Hillary Clinton recently said in an interview on MSNBC, "Pro-Palestinian protestors do not know enough about the Middle East that led to the war in Gaza." The pro-Palestinian supporters she's referring to are the thousands of people who took to the streets in the US, Europe, South Africa, Canada, and many other countries around the world, created encampments on their college campuses urging their institutions to divest from Israel, and practiced social media political organizing on apps like Instagram and Tik Tok directly following the October 7 attack. Clinton's assertion that people are too stupid to understand discredits the many Palestinian Americans who have known firsthand what living under an apartheid regime has been like personally and for their families. It also employs paternalistic rhetoric that suggests a government run by a small group of people who do not represent the oppressed gets to decide the overall outcome of their lives with zero regard for their needs. Clinton is also working overtime to convince the masses that this is a complicated conflict between two willing parties that happen to be on the same land. As Rashid Khalidi's *The Hundred Years' War on Palestine: A History of Settler Colonialism and Resistance, 1917–2017* illuminates, "In 1899, Yusuf Diya al-Khalidi, former mayor of Jerusalem, alarmed by the Zionist call to create a Jewish national home in Palestine, wrote a letter aimed at Theodore Herzl: 'the country had an Indigenous people that would not accept displacement.'"

In 2021, after facilitating a two-and-a-half-hour racial and social justice workshop for Yale School of Law, I opened the workshop up for questions, and a student asked, "You mentioned every group except for Jews, although the FBI just released statistics that they are the most targeted group." I responded by explaining that when speaking about white, Black, and non-Black communities of color, Jewish people are included, as Jewish people phenotypically look many ways. I also did not speak about Islam or Christianity, so I was a bit caught off guard by the question, but I continued with an explanation. I mentioned the fact that Hitler learned how to subjugate anyone who was not seen as white from the US's disenfranchisement of Black people during Jim Crow. Someone who attended the workshop leaked my response and sent it to right-wing racist publications that claim to care about Jewish people, but only if it means they can demean a Black person. I received death threats via email for weeks, and someone figured out my home address and sent threats there as well. They claimed that I was making the Jewish plight about anti-Blackness, and that was wrong. They also claimed that I diminished the statistics from the FBI; but why would I believe anything the FBI says when they have been responsible for the murder of prominent Black activists and have intentionally curtailed every Black radical movement?

The dominant culture seeks to control how oppressions are viewed. If the oppressed recognize their struggles as interconnected, they might unite—putting marginalized groups in the majority. By controlling this narrative, the dominant culture determines who is considered a threat and who deserves safety and life.

It's no coincidence that I discussed Palestine at the start of this very workshop, as colonialism operates globally. Were they truly upset by my response to their whataboutism (a common tactic used to derail conversations by bringing up unmentioned groups or issues), or were they disturbed that I spoke about a people we're expected to forget?

How does this connect to consent? People often limit their understanding of bodily autonomy to sexual contexts, overlooking its role in mass disabling events like war, the suppression of radical thought, organizing, and genocide. Yet, these are typically the final stages of consent being systematically violated. We must ask: Who can make decisions about your body? Who can say no? Who can ensure their harm is acknowledged?

It's telling that the Israel Defense Forces (IDF) train United States police departments. The violent denial of Palestinians' bodily autonomy mirrors how the US inflicts violence on Black, Palestinian, and other non-Black people of color. Police in the US justify murdering children by claiming they appeared threatening—the same excuse used when Palestinian children are killed by the IDF. The Black community's fight for bodily autonomy, particularly our demand for self-determination, is inextricably linked to the Palestinian struggle for autonomy. Creating a culture of consent requires unlearning the racist ideologies that deny bodily autonomy to Black people globally and non-Black people of color within and beyond the borders of the US. In order to have a culture of consent, our relationship to other people's bodies needs to shift; collectively we would need to see and honor everyone as deserving autonomy, not just theoretically but in reality.

When I am grocery shopping, I find that white people will brush past me without saying "excuse me." I have actually wondered whether white people even say "excuse me" to each other, or perhaps this a Black expression? I have held the door open for white people, and they have walked through it without saying "thank you," as if the door opened by itself. Even in digital spaces, as someone with a large social media following, I have found that when I post mundane things about my life rather than current political events, people tend to message me wondering why I haven't talked about [insert any traumatic event] that is happening around the world. The lack of consideration that I have likely already heard about the event, how it's directly impacting me and my community, and that I may not be in the mental space to discuss it at all, none of these things matter—I and other creators who share similar identities are just supposed to be a source of constant labor. I have had to set parameters and boundaries around my social media as people think that they just should have access to my every thought and life experience. As I shared my breast cancer journey on social media, people would send unsolicited advice, and I had to tell people to stop. So many people understood, but there were many people who thought that I should have just been grateful for the advice. I felt weird asserting this boundary; when you have lived in a world that is constantly expecting you to do labor, your muscle to express your needs is severely weakened.

Parasocial relationships in essence have no consent: There is no discussion of how the relationship will be mutually beneficial; rather it is largely built on one person sharing information about their life and the viewer feeling an attachment to them. I have had to remind people time and time again that they do not in fact know me, that what I share on social media is one small aspect of my life. I do this to level-set, to reclaim autonomy, but when you have been pedestalized, your humanity has already been removed. I learned quickly how people will knock you off of the pedestal they put you on the second that you say or do something that they do not like. I think social media is so popular because it relies on the removal of consent, commenting on people's bodies, trying to decode where people live based on the photos they share, asking invasive questions, and in many instances demanding explanations about breakups, family dynamics, children, and health—people feel protected behind a keyboard to say the boldest things to complete strangers, because they have been taught to disregard autonomy in real life. We begin to learn that autonomy is not valued as children.

Children are one of the most subjugated groups of people in the world; they are particularly vulnerable because society doesn't recognize their right to bodily autonomy—instead, this control is given to parents or guardians rather than acknowledged as the child's inherent right as a human being. Children's bodies are routinely touched and handled by adults without consideration. When a friend once told me that children couldn't consent, I explained that consent conversations can happen at every age. While she's right that children can't verbally consent before they develop language, adults can still model consent behaviors.

From diaper changes to affection, children need to understand why their bodies are being touched so they can later recognize the difference between safe and unsafe touch. Sexual abuse affects one in five girls and one in twenty boys—and these are just the reported cases. The actual numbers are likely much higher. Children receive both explicit and implicit messages that they must respect and obey adults. They're often pressured to kiss or hug relatives, facing correction or punishment if they refuse. This treatment as passive participants in their adult-directed lives teaches children to defer to all adults. These notions are what ground the ongoing debate whether trans children should have access to gender-affirming care. As gender scholar Jules Gill-Peterson writes in her first book, *Histories of the Transgender Child*, "The ostensible concern is that the effects of these 'new' hormonal technologies are in some important way unknown or that children are too young to undergo hormonal therapy or even make the decision to alter their bodies as if sex and gender were otherwise natural unmodified forms in cisgender bodies. This narrative also grants immense authority to medicine in making the trans child an ontological possibility as if trans children were unthinkable, non-existent prior to puberty suppression therapy." Trans children are made real by how other people grant them access (or not) to what they already know about their bodies, due in large part to the belief that being cisgender is innate and must be constantly maintained.

The way trans children are regarded speaks to the dominance and control that divides us by race and gender, concurrently revealing its demonstrably violent hand in parent and child relationships. Moreover, anti-trans legislation or any governmental regime's panic around transness is more than likely a reaction to a loss of power over children's bodies. This panic is rooted in a fear that resistance to being told who they are might lead to *greater* resistance to the state's plans for both their bodies and minds. A similar manner of control is wielded over children of all genders, the thinking being that if children have any decision-making power, how will they continue to replicate our roles under capitalism: a zombielike, resigned workforce, zombielike unquestioning parenting, a comprador in their own exploitation, a willing participant in an empire who is unable to strike back. Trans youth, especially Black trans youth, are a reminder that a zombielike life is the choice; not being trans. A desire to control someone else's body is a choice and—unlike being queer or trans—no one is born that way.

Honoring children's bodily autonomy looks like explaining diaper changes and bath time—walking through each step and acknowledging completion, affirming and listening to what young people need—from a cookie to gender-affirming care and respecting their bodies as their own. In fourteen years of teaching sex education, the only time I receive pushback from parents is when I teach bodily autonomy lessons. Letting children know they don't have to hug or kiss anyone including parents if they don't want to. The children's immediate embrace of this choice reveals their inherent desire for autonomy. Yes, parents—your children shouldn't have to kiss you if they say no. Honor their refusal. Many of us become adults who struggle to say no, like my students, who felt uncomfortable even hearing the word during the handshake activity. Priming for a white supremacist society that demands you obey authority rather than resist begins at home. While children need to know the importance of necessary safety measures like holding hands to cross streets, or of taking baths, it's crucial to explain the reasons rather than simply demanding compliance. Building autonomy starts with modeling—explaining what's happening to their bodies rather than just showing obedience to authority figures. This not only helps them recognize unsafe touch but prepares them to resist. Cultural differences also affect how bodily autonomy is expressed. Some cultures greet each other with cheek kisses or handholding across genders. Regardless of these cultural variations, children must understand that their bodies belong to themselves.

At a predominantly Black elementary school where I worked, children were repeating lyrics about "eating the booty like groceries" and showing each other their genitals during bathroom breaks. While teachers worried this indicated abuse, I recognized this as normal childhood exploration—though it was important to teach them they didn't have to show their bodies to others. The lyrics came from a popular song, and when asked, the children had no understanding of its meaning—they were simply singing a song they enjoyed. While the school's caution was appropriate, at a predominantly Black school, this concern might have stemmed from assumptions about the hypersexualization of Black children. Black children aren't inherently sexual or predisposed to sexual behavior—they're often sexualized because of their Blackness.

Consent isn't just about sex—it is fundamental to all daily interactions. As mentioned, white people will casually bump into me in grocery store aisles, which might seem innocent, but this is a common experience for Black people. Black and non-Black people of color are treated like objects to be touched at will. I've had white people touch my hair as if inspecting it, followed by a compliment as though that justifies the invasion. While "consent is sexy" stickers serve as useful reminders and can start important conversations, they don't address the deep historical legacy of how certain bodies have been viewed and treated.

As of May 2025, over 62,000 Palestinians have been murdered; the majority of them were children. Sudan has seen over five million people displaced. In the Congo, millions of children have endured sexual assault and kidnapping. Across the United States, cop cities—police training bases—are emerging near every major city. Whiteness will pursue any means to control others' bodies in service of white supremacy. We must reject everything settler colonialism imposes. We must resist the inherited beliefs that deny communities their bodily autonomy. No one will truly have agency over their body until we all do.

Palestine, Puerto Rico, Sudan, Congo, Hawaii, Tigray, Haiti, Black people across the diaspora, and all colonized peoples will and must be free for any of us to also be free.

- What privileges allow you to move through the world without constantly negotiating consent? When have you wielded those privileges over others?
- How will you heal your inner child who was likely denied bodily autonomy?
- In what ways do you benefit from systems that deny others' bodily autonomy? What would it mean to truly divest from those benefits?

- When has your commitment to consent been tested by social pressure or personal convenience? What did you choose and why?
- Where do you see yourself unconsciously participating in nonconsensual culture? What would it take to unlearn those behaviors?

# 8

# Take the State Out of Your Relationships

"No one is healed in isolation."

—bell hooks

"Therefore, a man shall leave his father and his mother and hold fast to his wife, and they shall become one flesh."

—Genesis 2:24

"The oppressors do not favor promoting the community as a whole, but rather selected leaders."

—Paulo Freire, *Pedagogy of the Oppressed*

In the fall of 2014, I walked down a cement path in Brooklyn's Prospect Park holding my dad's arm, surrounded by eighty tearful smiling faces overlooking an algae-covered lake dotted with white swans. This was our wedding venue—$500 for a piece of cement beside a walking path where guests had to stand, as chairs weren't allowed. Friends and family formed a makeshift aisle, careful not to block passersby unaware of the ceremony unfolding. Music from cyclists' portable speakers, runners kicking up leaves, honking cars on Flatbush Avenue, and children's laughter colored the scene as two friends performed "We Found Love" by Rihanna on violin and acoustic bass.

The song was meant to commemorate how we met in the Peace Corps, though as the marital bliss wore thin, I'd realize its xenophobic portrayal of Ethiopia as "hopeless" foreshadowed the hopelessness that would define the marriage. The irony that we chose this song—with a music video that depicts Rihanna's turbulent, abusive relationship with Chris Brown—wasn't lost on me. As I shared in Chapter 3, I was diagnosed in May 2014, had my double mastectomy in July 2014, and got married in September 2014. The ceremony itself is a blur: I was two months post–double mastectomy and on the highest dose of chemotherapy, having just started treatment that month. Getting diagnosed with breast cancer wasn't exactly in the plans two months before we were supposed to say "I do." (Is cancer ever in the plans?)

My wedding dress had to be completely altered to fit the boxy tissue expanders that replaced my breasts. Each fitting now required warning the swanky Chelsea seamstress I could barely afford about potential bleeding, while we found creative ways to position my drains to envision how the dress would look without them.

As the ceremony closed, we read our vows and turned to face our guests at the officiant's direction. She asked everyone to hold us accountable for our commitment, and after a count of three, a unanimous "we will" erupted in applause and cheers. Ten years later, that day feels like a distant memory with an ending no newlyweds want to imagine. I recently asked my brother, Austin, who stood beside my dad, if he remembered being asked to hold us accountable. He laughed and replied, "No." After a year and a half of marriage, we divorced.

We didn't divorce because the guests failed to hold us accountable; they never stood a chance of influencing our marriage in the first place. Though thoughtful, that ceremonial gesture was symbolic at best. As Esther Perel, a Belgian American psychotherapist, observes: "Today, we turn to one person to provide what an entire village once did: a sense of grounding, meaning, and continuity. At the same time, we expect our committed relationships to be romantic as well as emotionally and sexually fulfilling. Is it any wonder that so many relationships crumble under the weight of it all?"

What may be even more elusive but equally challenging are the state-sanctioned capitalistic pressures embedded in long-term romantic relationships—bills, homes, children—and with these enhanced needs comes increased dependence on one's betrothed, actively encouraged by the state. The institution of marriage as an expression of love and romance emerged in the wake of chattel slavery, as a replacement for the Indigenous valuing of the community, and views about property, gender, and anti-Blackness didn't magically disappear—they became embedded into the institution itself.

The state's push for one person to fulfill all our needs was another attempt to deradicalize communities through romance propaganda—an intentional distancing from the cultural diasporic practices of Black people, particularly Black femmes. As discussed previously, enslaved Black women and those gendered as women were deliberately de-gendered, a process of dehumanization meant to justify white violence. Yet while whiteness degendered Black women, it was these same women who fulfilled domestic and child-rearing roles during slavery. White women did not breastfeed their own children; enslaved Black people were forced into this role exclusively.

So how did these domestic attributes, which white women had no skill in due to chattel slavery, come to be associated with white womanhood? The Reconstruction Era marked a period when white people could no longer rely on Black people's unfree labor outright. After decades of depending on Black labor, they continued to rely on degrading Black people—especially Black women—to maintain the myth of the white family as the ultimate symbol of domesticity, civility, and love.

From Black femme labor being advertised as a "Slave in a Box" in the 1880s to the Moynihan Report in the 1960s blaming Black women for the supposed downfall of the Black family, Black women have been made into vitriolic scapegoats for white America's lack of intimacy—an intimacy defined by domination and control. Black women and those gendered as women sit at multiple intersections of oppression under white supremacist patriarchal capitalist transmisogyny. Poor Black trans women especially have been relegated to society's margins, rendered invisible and reviled.

Despite this systemic devaluation and marginalization, Black women have transformed their collective pain into revolutionary power. This practice gives new meaning to Audre Lorde's famous words, "The personal is political." Black women and those gendered similarly have intentionally created spaces for safety, refuge, and political resistance. From Harriet Tubman to the Combahee River Collective, from the Black Panthers to SisterSong, from Black Lives Matter to Ballroom culture, Black women and femmes have taught us to value collective over individual action—to be a threat rather than complicit in a state committed to domination. This legacy of collective resistance offers profound insights into how we might reimagine love beyond the confines of individualistic, capitalistic frameworks.

A major part of love and intimacy is accepting the reality of grief—a reality Black women know intimately. Black women are supposed to save everyone from everything, while no one asks about their needs. People resist being in partnership or community for fear of or in reaction to losing people, but Black women are expected to shoulder the loss and especially to not have it all. As Cedric Robinson defines it, racial capitalism is "the idea that capitalism is built on racial lines, and that the accumulation of capital depends on the exploitation of racialized groups." Marriage and capitalism work hand in hand; if love and romance were truly valued, why would celebrating love be cost-prohibitive? The message from racial capitalism is clear: The working class and poor people are unlovable; class status determines value.

Racial capitalism intentionally stratifies identities, creating obstacles that cause subjugation while selling the belief that this hierarchy results from individual choices. This Tetris game of organizing people manifests in how we view our relationships with others and the world. The pressure to make nurturing a romantic relationship our purpose in life has us focusing on one individual at the expense of everything else: our relationships with friends, community, ourselves, and the earth.

Our collective disregard for the earth stems from how we organize which relationships matter and which don't. The uberwealthy continue to pillage the earth for profit, regardless of the horrible conditions they subject workers to or the environmental devastation—pollution, lead in water and soil, wildfires, deforestation, animal extinction, and toxic air quality—that their greed creates. We're taught that private ownership of land for individual benefit matters more than what Indigenous communities have long practiced: collective stewardship of land for the common good.

This hierarchy of relationships appears even in children's media. Although Disney movies have only recently begun shifting away from romantic relationships as their main arc, countless "classics" center on this premise. In *The Little Mermaid*, Ariel gives up her voice to be human and be with Prince Eric, a fisherman. The film never addresses how unusual this match is beyond Ariel being a mermaid—a mermaid should have never agreed to be with someone who kills sea life. We're taught from a very young age that our main focus should be finding a forever partner, not nurturing the planet for future generations—to be married so you can own land.

The success of long-term romantic relationships is measured by how couples navigate challenging times together, even if they're unhappy or unfulfilled. We celebrate the length of time people have been together, not how their union supports community efforts. What's most valued is how people have learned to navigate this world just a few people short of alone.

"Self-made millionaire" and "self-care" are trending buzzwords that speak to our obsession with individualism, binding our notions of class and upward mobility to the illusion of doing it alone. But it's impossible to amass great wealth without the unpaid or inequitable labor of many others. Similarly, self-care relies on more than just one person—since consumerism is the main outlet for relaxation, someone else's labor is required for your self-care. We frame self-care as an act of loving yourself, but what does loving oneself look like to someone who is poor or working class? Do they not love themselves if work has to come before a candlelit bubble bath, face mask, and chocolate-covered strawberries? Or is capitalism forcing us to work to prove our value, leaving no time for ease?

Our definitions of love must represent an actual departure from the ways the state has replicated domination and subjugation through racial capitalism, convincing us that love is only present alongside capitalism. Said another way: We cannot relate to love, romantic relationships, or marriage as if they exist outside the systems and structures that built the United States and the Western world. These systems are deeply embedded in how we've been taught who and what to love, how we pedestalize romantic relationships, and how we discard community as another way to discredit Black people, particularly Black women and those gendered to be.

Why would the US, one of the most racist and violent countries on earth, have any genuine interest in romance and love? And how do we move past these overtures of social status, exceptionalism, and stature toward revolution and liberation? The state discourages community, investing instead in keeping us longing for romantic relationships as the ultimate class achievement—a chance to be adored by family and friends at an overpriced ceremony, to have children, a house, and live happily ever after.

Many historians claim marriage shifted course in the nineteenth century, focusing more on love than economics, but I argue the economic focus never disappeared—it was simply masked with sweeping generalizations about love. The nineteenth century wasn't just marked by a shift in viewing marriages as more than economically advantageous arrangements due to Jane Austen's *Pride and Prejudice* (a book alt-right groups now use to perpetuate racial purity and marriage)—slavery was also abolished in the nineteenth century. White people, particularly white cisgender men, had to find new ways to own people to justify their sense of power.

White people's legacy of dominance has shaped their views of love and romance, and in turn their sociopolitical predominance and power in the global marketplace has pervaded much of society's conception of love and relation. In the West, love has been transformed into a product, opportunities emerging alongside it to capitalize on its commodification by any means, from the boom in "romantasy"-themed books, run-of-the-mill dating shows on streaming services, and other romance-centric media, but more insidiously, through the exaltation of those who are married versus those who are unmarried, because of the inherently legal and contractual nature of such a union.

Insomuch as marriage is foundational to the white cishet American middle-class imagination, Black poor and working-class trans people, particularly women and femmes, have always remained on the fringes of and an affront to that ideal. For example, at the Christopher Street Liberation Day Rally (which would later spawn the global LGBTQ+ Pride events following the first Stonewall riots in New York City), famed activists and founders of STAR (Street Transvestite Action Revolutionaries) Marsha P. Johnson and Sylvia Rivera were booed offstage by a largely white cisgender gay and lesbian audience who felt that Black and Puerto Rican sex workers would be a roadblock to acceptance in wider mainstream white society, a requisite of which is to be seen as "normal," part of the status quo. This would be some powerful foreshadowing to the fight for marriage equality among gay and lesbian activists that would happen just a few decades later that would end up being waged along heavily racialized and gendered lines.

Black cis and trans women's treatment has profoundly informed the institution of marriage itself, while the elevation of romantic relationships above all others has acted as another way to denigrate how Black women have demonstrated commitment to community. Consider how sex workers have been treated in this country, viewed as an assault to "traditional values," and connect that to the hypersexualization of Black women—even though in many ways cis-heterosexual marriage wherein the man is the breadwinner mimics sex work. On a viral episode of their podcast, British TV personality Zeze Millz and author and Black scholar Chidera Eggerue (also known as The Slumflower) debated whether marriage is different from sex work. Cisgender heterosexual marriage is an agreement hinged on one person, typically a man, taking care of the finances in exchange for childcare, meals, and sex. This arrangement isn't always how marriage functions. However, has marriage been deliberately presented as an alternative to sex work—a path for white women to avoid being labeled sexually deviant and instead maintain acceptance within whiteness? Was marriage intentionally elevated to discourage sex work while further dehumanizing Black women who are often forced into survival sex work?

The answer may lie in the fact that marriages are connected to the state and informed by Christianity, which not coincidentally was also used to maintain slavery. Married couples pay lower taxes, can share one spouse's employer health insurance, and typically own property together through marriage contracts. The belief in owning someone as property is a direct relic of Indigenous displacement and chattel slavery.

A common part of Christian wedding vows is to "forsake all others"—a promise rooted not just in monogamy and fidelity, but explicitly in leaving one's parents. The bride(s) or groom(s) are often "given away" by their parents, signifying a transfer of ownership to the spouse. While there have been shifts in the "giving away" tradition as people work to dismantle gender roles, the practice remains deeply rooted in the gender binary. In heterosexual marriages, a father "gives away" their daughter to her husband, typically after walking her down the aisle—the officiant asks, "Who gives this woman to be married to this man?" and the father responds, "I do." It's also common for a partner to ask a father for their daughter's hand in marriage before proposing.

Twentieth-century feminist thought has extensively analyzed patriarchy's role in marriage, but what's less apparent is how the very concept of owning enslaved Black people informed the institution of marriage itself. The idea that you could own someone as property has transformed into a $70 billion-plus industry. It wasn't until the 1970s—with some states waiting until the 1990s—that those laws shifted to acknowledge marital rape as real. This idea that your body belongs to your partner in marriage is pervasive, trickling down to romantic relationships as well.

I've spoken with countless couples who feel guilty for having natural ebbs and flows in their libido. They think pushing themselves to have sex anyway will keep their marriage intact. American marriages tend to have all the hallmarks of carcerality—we enter romantic relationships under this system knowing the foundation began with punishment, control, and domination. Before (white) women's suffrage, white cisgender women had no rights as single people, making marriage a transaction of survival. The practice of women changing their last names to their husbands' was a direct way for husbands to claim their wives as property. The wife loses herself and her identity to become one with her husband.

Although rooted in cis-heteropatriarchy, these practices of control still reveal themselves in queer relationships and marriages. Patriarchy, capitalism, and anti-Blackness have played leading roles in how we view romantic relationships and marriage, situating any other relationship below our romantic relationships or our quest to maintain them, forsaking ourselves and others to be seen as devoted.

In order for white people to maintain their position of superiority after slavery, they had to change the goalposts, creating value around the family connected to the "American dream"—the perfect mask for continued racial oppression, cementing the gender binary, all in service of white supremacy. But although marriage in the 1930s wasn't reserved for white people only, Black families didn't benefit from marriage granting access to the capitalistic circle of homeownership. When Black families moved across the country to live in suburban neighborhoods or even within major cities, white people did everything to keep their neighborhoods all white. Racial covenants still exist in many cities, and gentrification is simply redlining's cousin. Although many families moving into these areas were Black married couples, their marriages were never viewed the same way as white people's marriages.

Without marriage or a blooming romantic relationship, we're convinced that to fill our void of belonging and ease loneliness we must feed the capitalist machine with purchases from places like Amazon—where our needs can be met immediately with a shiny new package at the door, while completely disregarding employees forced to urinate in cups at their workstations or abandon packages in the woods from exhaustion, all while further enriching a white supremacist capitalist system. The state knows relying on one person to fulfill all our needs isn't sustainable and will lead back to depending on it further.

Romantic relationships are viewed as private—while boundaries and access are important considerations, what people in relationships share about their dynamics is often reserved for a select few or discussed only within the partnership. This secrecy in relationships mirrors familial dynamics where families keep secrets about harmful people or traumatic incidents to "protect" the family unit from scrutiny. But the felt need to keep relationships' challenging aspects secret speaks volumes about how we've internalized the idea that no one should be involved in our relationships.

Couples therapists often encourage keeping relationship issues private, worked out only between partners, warning that outside advice-givers might have ill intentions. Secrecy goes hand in hand with control, a major tenet of all relationships deeply informed by and connected to chattel slavery and racism. When a secret is kept, the person keeping it controls how a situation or person is viewed. If I love my friends who've been together five years, but one is being abused and forced to keep it secret, my view of their relationship is controlled by that secrecy. I'm unable to support my friend or intervene because I'm kept from the truth.

Forcing a child, family member, or spouse into secrecy creates conditions where people can't access needed support and may internalize harm that they could otherwise get help processing. Secrecy and control are inextricably linked to ownership—this idea is that once in a family dynamic or romantic relationship, autonomy becomes null and void. This happens especially to children, who have few rights and remain incredibly vulnerable, often viewed as under their parents' and guardians' control rather than as autonomous human beings.

According to the LGBTQ+ nonprofit that focuses on suicide prevention, The Trevor Project, "nearly 40% of transgender and nonbinary youth have experienced homelessness or housing instability at some point in their lifetimes." Children are told they can no longer live at home with their families or have shelter—a human right—all because someone believed that a young person wasn't an autonomous human being capable of knowing who they are and how they want to live and love.

The Western impulse to control others' bodies by revoking access to life-affirming support when they don't submit directly mirrors chattel slavery. These themes of control appear in romantic relationships but have been recharacterized as romantic. The socio-religious messaging that a union between two people must exclude all others, the normalization of secrecy, ownership, and control—these are embedded in the fabric of the wedding ceremony itself. This is why the guests stood little chance of influencing my relationship's success. What created and held the United States together was the flesh of Indigenous Africans who were intentionally separated from their families, subjected to sustained sexual violence and coercion all due to white people's relationship with and desire for power.

As Hortense Spillers posits in her speech "Shades of Intimacy: What the Eighteenth Century Teaches Us," "unless one is free, love cannot and will not matter." It's impossible to understand over two hundred fifty years of chattel slavery and not consider how it colors our views of relationships and love. There is no way for any of us to compartmentalize the impacts of a chattel slavery which has not been abolished in the US but only has changed shape, and not consider how its ongoing presence impacts our relationships today. Dominance, abuse, and ownership are seen as necessary components of a lasting relationship, making the line between an abusive relationship and a healthy one very thin.

Our first interactions with love often come from our parents or guardians. I learned very quickly how to receive love from my parents, listening to what they say, getting good grades, wearing the dresses I never wanted to wear. My compliance was currency for their affection and love. If I did the opposite, I would be met with upset and frustration. My dad would raise his voice if I didn't understand my multiplication homework; not grasping concepts at his acceptable pace resulted in disappointment. I would work hard to understand, not because I enjoyed learning math, but to avoid his upset.

Most of my romantic relationships centered around fear that I would mess up or had done something wrong and would lose my partner's affection or desire to be with me. I went to a Christian elementary school where we were sent to the principal's office and spanked with a wooden tennis paddle for breaking rules. When I got home, I would be spanked with a belt from my mother and then my father. My mother would say she loved me and just wanted me to listen in school directly following a spanking.

I grew up believing that expressions of love included yelling, being submissive and obedient. Even in households where spanking or yelling didn't occur, did your parents bury their feelings or avoid hard conversations and arguments with the silent treatment, attempting to keep the peace? None of these behaviors began with our parents—they inherited these ways of being from a long lineage of people who thought they were expressing love and care.

These abusive tactics disguised as love are also gendered, upheld by the gender binary to convince us that men and women have different connections to love. There's an expectation that human beings understand love innately. Pregnant people are often criticized by themselves or others for not feeling an immediate connection of love for their child during pregnancy or after birth. People struggle to separate the belief that a pregnant person, especially those identifying and gendered as women, should have an innate experience of maternity which implies immediate love for the child.

Meanwhile, the non-carrying parent, especially cisgender men, isn't expected to have any connection to their child or even raise their children—they're somehow granted the space to build that relationship and connectedness, or not. Although my mom also spanked me, I knew she was the person I could lean on for emotional connection. My dad, on the other hand, wasn't reliable for expressing a wide range of emotions—not that he didn't have them, but he felt his status as a father or a man naturally made him deficient in this area, often saying that mothers are the ones who will always have a soft spot for their children.

Children become a site for cisgender men's authority, their power as caregivers completely informed by a desire to be seen as a "man" rather than a parent, to the extent that care and tenderness are reserved for the "gentler sex." Just as maternal or caring instincts aren't innate to women and femmes, patriarchy, too, can be upheld by any gender and often conflates lack of feeling with authority, allowing my dad and other cisgender men to act with abandon regarding the emotional well-being that humans require—even their own.

What is the impact on the psyche of cisgender men who uphold patriarchy at the expense of expressing love for their children? I was in my late twenties, deep in countless therapy sessions, before I realized that while I had everything I wanted as a kid—toys, shelter, and food—and my dad clearly fulfilled the gender binary expectation to be a provider, I still longed for affection and connection from him. I'm fairly certain if I asked my dad today if he felt he was affectionate toward his kids, his response would be, "Absolutely, none of you wanted for anything."

My dad did express love to my mom and stepmom, "mi amor" being what he affectionately calls my stepmom. When he remarried, his focus became his wife—my brother and I often felt we were in the way of the new life they intended to create. Undoubtedly, some will object and say that they themselves are cisgender men who show love and affection to their children, like the social media–savvy "girl dads" capturing picture-perfect moments fixing their daughter's hair, painting her nails, and performing tasks falsely associated as "girly" rather than simply part of being a parent to a child of any gender. If you are doing these things for your children, being an anomaly is the issue.

As bell hooks posits in *All About Love*, there is no general consensus on love—we all have varying definitions of an arbitrary term that carries great pressure and weight to express. Without a universal definition, we fall back on notions of love provided by the state, which are strategically aligned with propping up white cis-heteropatriarchal relationships and families as ideal examples of love that will further ingratiate us with capitalism.

In 2013, Gabriel Fernandez, an eight-year-old boy from California, was tortured and murdered by his mother and her boyfriend because he said he was gay. Gabriel should absolutely still be here—his death was completely preventable. But due to the disregard for children and community intervention, his life was ended tragically by the people who claimed to love him.

At her trial's sentencing, Fernandez's mother stated: "I want to say I'm sorry for what happened. I wish Gabriel was alive. Every day I wish that I'd made better choices. I'm sorry to my children, and I want them to know that I love them." Even if Fernandez's mother can say she loved her children, how can violence, murder, and love coexist? Her love was a prison for her children, a coffin for one. It was not love that allowed her children to feel safe or protected but rather made them vulnerable to fatal harm.

How are we relating to each other and the notion of love when it can look like that? In a country founded on people killing and brutally harming other people, we might see what Gabriel's mother did as an extreme departure from love, but her actions only mimic a murderous country where people still claim they love it despite that history. In *All About Love*, hooks writes extensively about love and abuse being antithetical to each other. We've been taught that because parents are authority figures who essentially own their children, they are free to express love and care however they see fit.

Queer and trans people are often met with the conundrum of accepting that their parents and families had to "learn how to love them." We are expected to forgive the people closest to us who refuse to use our pronouns, honor our identities and self-expression, simply because they claim they love us, even when we're not getting what we need. The deep-seated belief that queer, trans, and nonbinary people are hard to love or shouldn't be loved reveals itself in staggering intimate partner violence statistics. According to the LGBTQ+ advocacy and political lobbying group Human Rights Campaign (HRC), "44% of lesbians and 61% of bisexual women experience rape, physical violence, or stalking by an intimate partner, compared to 35% of straight women." The 2015 U.S. Transgender Survey found that "more than half (54%) of transgender and nonbinary respondents experienced intimate partner violence in their lifetimes."

This doesn't mean that queer, lesbian, trans, nonbinary, and gay people are more violent or have a propensity toward violence. Rather, it reveals how queer and trans folks have inherited the belief that we are undeserving of love free from harm. We are not only taught by our first relationships that loving us is optional, but these relationships also have the complete backing and support of a queerphobic and transphobic (particularly transmisogynist) world.

The belief that love can be expressed in many diverse ways often comes at the expense of the most vulnerable being forced to accept whatever way someone claims they love, even when that includes harm. Children, queer and trans folks, people living with disabilities, Black and other non-Black people of color are discarded in the name of abuse thinly veiled as love.

As a queer person exploring my identity, I was willing and open to be with nearly anyone who showed me attention. R&B superstar Luther Vandross shared on *The Oprah Winfrey Show* that, among his many love songs, "Any Love" felt particularly personal, as it expressed his desire for romantic love that he felt he had never experienced:

"Everyone needs a love no doubt / Any love, any love / Everybody feels alone without / Any love, any love."

I was seeking someone to love me in the only way I had learned to receive love: through submission and compliance. I dated folks who were only interested in me for as long as they could orgasm—I was merely their vehicle for sexual desires. Although I wanted something more, I was perfectly content never having that need fulfilled as long as they didn't leave me. My ex-wife used to say R&B was "slow talking," and if you know anything about me, you know I love R&B. This should have been my sign that we weren't compatible, but instead I spent most of our relationship trying to be convinced that the Beatles were worth listening to.

Can you have different music tastes in a romantic relationship? Absolutely. The issue arose when I was willing to have one of my favorite forms of expression diminished by someone who loved a group that stole from Black artists. Comments like these that seemed casual were actually foreshadowing.

Before we wed, I recall watching CNN from the kitchen island in our gentrified Bed-Stuy apartment as my fiancée made dinner. The murder of Tamir Rice flashed across the screen: "Police officers thought Rice (eleven years old) was a suspect and that he had a weapon as he played at the nearby playground." I could feel my body seething with rage—a feeling that never goes away but gets suppressed just to function or to be in a relationship with a white person.

My partner didn't budge. Maybe the sound of onions sizzling in oil was too loud, or perhaps she had spent a lifetime being able to ignore state violence against Black people as background noise to her cooking. "I think we should go to Ohio," I stated without a question mark, ready to jump on the next plane and do whatever needed to be done. Since she was from Ohio where Rice was murdered, I thought this would be an immediate yes.

"Well . . ." she began, not with a yes, "work is really busy." She responded as if the onions' sizzle hadn't interrupted her hearing the headline—she was waiting for my reaction, a common dance white people do around racism. I got upset, frustrated by her lackluster response and reluctance to act, to which she replied, "Why are you so angry?"

How could someone claim they love me, a Black queer person, but have no urgency around state-sanctioned murders of Black people? What was it about being with this white lesbian that I was wrapped up in? I had been sold the lie that a Black person being in a romantic relationship with a white person marked the end of racial inequality.

In the *Loving v. Virginia* case, Richard and Mildred Loving were legally married in Washington, DC, but when they traveled to Virginia, their marriage violated the state's anti-miscegenation laws. They were arrested and sentenced to a year in prison, though due to Richard being a white man, they were able to fight and dismiss this ruling.

Richard Loving met his Black future wife, Mildred Jeter, when he was seventeen and she was eleven, a detail conveniently left out in the usual retelling of this case. Although the legislation cites this landmark case as between a Black woman and white man, according to her grandchildren, Mildred identified as Indigenous, despite her phenotypical appearance. While there are Black Indigenous people, I can't help but wonder if being courted by a white man almost twice her age influenced her desire to deny her Blackness.

*Loving v. Virginia* and gay marriage directly inform each other, as they are both based in white cisgender men getting what they want, using their privilege to pass legislation that maintains their access to power. A relationship being marked as revolutionary simply because it includes a white person is more of the same anti-Blackness positioning us to still see white relationships as superior. My white partner was the focal point of our relationship, who I was served solely as a complement to her whiteness.

The impetus for anti-miscegenation laws was fear that white people wouldn't maintain racial purity. But with shifts toward racial equality and desegregation in the nineteenth and twentieth centuries, liberal white people wanted to be seen as antiracist. Being friends with and even dating Black people became the litmus test for being a "good" white person—a designation bound up in class status, a way for white people to separate themselves from the image of the poor redneck hillbilly of the South.

After the MTV Video Music Awards in 2016, *Vogue* released an image of Jay Z, Beyoncé, P. Diddy, Cassie, Swizz Beatz, Alicia Keys, Steve Stoute, and Lauren Branche, with the women standing behind the men as they held up glasses of wine over pizza. They titled the article "The Ultimate Post-VMA Power Couple Dinner: Pizza and Wine with Bey and Jay, Kimye, and More." This image strikingly reveals the concluding lyric of Kanye West's "Gold Digger," a song that describes being with a Black woman until the final line: "And when he get on, he'll leave yo' ass for a white girl."

While Kim Kardashian was the only white woman in the photo, all the other women were light-skinned with European features. *Vogue* marking them as power couples wasn't solely connected to their mass wealth, but also their choice in partners. When Black cisgender men achieve higher class status, they often date white or light-skinned women who benefit from anti-Black desirability politics—as if to prove they're abiding by racial capitalism's rules by actively rejecting their Blackness to maintain their new status.

Kanye West's song disparages Black women, perpetuating tropes of Black women as nagging poor people who just want to depend on men for money—a seemingly cultural mainstay of rap music, which all the men in the photo are associated with. In 2020, during one of his first appearances as a potential presidential candidate, West stated, "Harriet Tubman never actually freed the slaves, she just had them work for other white people." This ahistorical statement would only be shocking if you failed to see the lengths to which people will go to climb racial capitalism's ladder, using the same playbook everyone with such power and capital has utilized: targeting Black women.

The former outposts of colonization in the Caribbean and

Latin America used the term "blanqueamiento" to depict their internalized desire to "whiten the race"; marrying people of lighter skin or white people was seen as improving the race. In the US, these notions are viewed differently—love and preference are cited as reasons. But this is only said without any investigation into how systems have convinced all of us that Blackness is better when mixed with or in proximity to whiteness. Black men with white or light-skinned partners are viewed as achieving positive cultural trajectory and upward mobility. People fetishize their kids, doting on how beautiful they'll be based on a long legacy of colorism and featurism. On the other hand, Black women who date white men are viewed differently. There's more criticism, their Blackness questioned—they're seen as having fallen prey to white supremacy, as self-hating Black women who must think they're better than other Black people.

While these assertions may be true in some instances (read: *Candace Owens*), they're rarely made about Black cisgender men in relationships with white women, who are seen as standing in their purpose, their Blackness, with desirability politics unquestioned. Since that *Vogue* photo was taken, Kanye West has firmly aligned himself with nazis—going as far as to sell swastika T-shirts; Sean Combs would be arrested for sex trafficking and have to pay Cassie a thirty-million-dollar settlement for physically abusing her throughout their relationship. Jay Z would accept a partnership with the NFL while actively discrediting Colin Kaepernick's protest. Swizz Beatz would smile with a martini in one hand while wrapping his other arm around Elon Musk, one of the most well-known white supremacists, to celebrate a business partnership that was once solely Black-owned.

As discussed earlier about desire, our choice in partners is wrapped up in colonial four-hundred-year-old ideals of beauty, and who we wish to be in a relationship with follows these same standards. A desire to be seen as wealthy or elite often means discrediting the very people who make up some of the largest numbers of the working class—dark-skinned Black women. While most of the women in the photo are Black women, colorism has informed who we believe is poor or rich, and it is wrapped up in desirability.

Dr. Sarah L. Webb, researcher and historian of colorism, reminds us that research shows "individuals with lighter skin tones tend to have better job opportunities, higher salaries, and more opportunities for promotion compared to those with darker skin tones." Contrary to popular belief, beyond the rainbow capitalist slogans that "love is love," queer and trans people don't differ much from cis-hetero people in this regard, also demonstrating anti-Black and colorist dating patterns. Although homophobia is a creation of white supremacy, as previously mentioned, Black people are marked as more homophobic than the people who created homophobia. If that wasn't made clear enough earlier on: Black people are not more homophobic than anyone else. The belief that only a white person can validate one's queerness plays directly into this fallacy.

White queer people benefit from proximity to Blackness, as Blackness is inherently queer and many white people have based their entire queer identities on mannerisms and expressions inherent to Black women. It is seen as beneficial to marry or date a white person regardless of that white person's anti-racist lens or lack thereof. It doesn't matter how they view the world; by virtue of a Black person being with a white person, they have supposedly evaded the racial order.

When Black people are explaining their experiences with racism and are righteously angry, like I was after Tamir Rice was murdered, love is misused as a way to silence and tone police our expression. Love is often used to pacify—Black people are just supposed to accept the racism they experience and still show love to those who harm us, regardless of whether our vulnerability, let alone our complexity, is honored.

I am not asserting that interracial relationships are invalid or unloving, but I am suggesting that, considering these power structures exist, folks must be more intentional in their partnerships. White people need to be working to constantly undo their anti-racist views of Black people, especially Black women, when they are in any relationship with Black people. White people will use their Black partners, friends, and even children as a shield for their racism rather than doing their own work to undo their proclivity toward racism. Overall, we must not fall prey to the idea that romantic relationships with white people are a revolutionary act that will end racism—fake notions of revolution to keep us from revolting.

My friends would lament after we divorced that they never liked her, candidly speaking about our relationship for the first time. When I asked why they didn't say something sooner, they would tell me, "You wouldn't have listened to us." Our unwillingness to postpone our wedding in the midst of a major transition spoke volumes about how hardheaded we were but also about the significance that marriage held—significant not necessarily in honoring love and commitment, but in mimicking what we thought was love and commitment.

For me, white people held the goalpost for who and what was queer—the US soccer players, Tegan and Sara, Melissa Etheridge, Shane from the *L Word*, and Ellen DeGeneres were the real lesbians; I didn't fit the mold of desirability for how a lesbian looked. Being in proximity to white queer people had me segregate my identity according to how whiteness has always situated identity—pedestalizing one identity over another. For so many white people, white is not an identity—it just is—so queer and transness becomes another pathway to deny their whiteness. White queer people want their relationship to their queerness or transness to erase their privilege as white people. I never stopped seeing their whiteness, and that was what I was interested in being in proximity to. Black people were (and are) constantly questioned, second-guessed, or removed entirely from queer discourse. I wanted desperately to just be seen as queer; as a relatively newly out queer person, my Blackness seemed like a barrier for white people to affirm me as such. White people want proximity to oppression while not realizing that gender and sexuality difference have been hinged on reaffirming differences between Black and white people.

I thought a romantic relationship with a white queer person would make my queerness real and well protected. Our relationship began as a transaction, a notion not unique to us but underlying many romantic relationships. We have all been taught to desire romantic relationships, and in order to make them real, sex, procreation, and marriage must be the defining factors. I couldn't just be friends with the only other lesbian in my Peace Corps cohort—I needed to be with her romantically and thus sexually. We probably would have been better off as friends, but societally we've been taught that friends are simply placeholders before the "real" relationship comes.

Compulsory sexuality, defined by Sherronda J. Brown in her book *Refusing Compulsory Sexuality*, is "the idea that sex is universally desired as a feature of human nature, that we are essentially obligated to participate in sex at some point in life, and that there is something fundamentally wrong with anyone who does not want to—whether it be perceived as a defect of morality, psychology or physiology." A country built on the premise of compulsory sexuality leaves no room for those who are asexual or aromantic—and marks everyone who has even the slightest shift in libido for whatever reason as defective. We are all just supposed to want a romantic relationship, have sex constantly, have kids, a house, and live happily ever after; in a word, marriage.

Marriage is one of the main institutions that uphold compulsory (hetero)sexuality. In *Queering the Color Line*, Siobhan B. Somerville offers this as a possible explanation for the potency and popularity of that long-standing, nearly unconscious social expectation: "compulsory heterosexuality has been not simply parallel to discourses of racial segregation but integral to its logic. To disrupt naturalized constructions of racial difference, involves simultaneously unsettling one's relationship to normative constructions of gender and sexuality as well." Marriage becomes a normative institution that people can use to normalize themselves, to distance themselves from those deemed abnormal or in an effort to identify with the dominant class, which can help explain why marriage is so vehemently gatekept by the dominant class, with many legal loopholes and punishments for those who are marginalized. For example, in the US, people living with disabilities who receive state or federal benefits such as DAC (Disabled Adult Child payments), or SSI (Supplemental Security Income) can be penalized and have their benefits rescinded if they were to marry.

If marriage is about love and connectedness, then everyone who wishes to be married should be able to take part, but as long as the state has control, those of us who hold identities that are a threat to the state will have more obstacles to participating on our terms. Alt-right racist groups have a long-standing vested interest in the "traditional family values," which is an ethno-religious dog whistle for conservative social and economic leanings. This is another iteration of white cisgender men being unwilling to enter into relationships without being at the helm or the head of them. Given this, the institution itself became an extension of colonial conquests and enslavement, except it replaced or supplemented subservience from Black and Indigenous unfree labor with their romantic and sexual partners in private life.

Enslaved Indigenous Africans were often kept from congregating even for religious purposes, for fear they would discuss their conditions and organize revolt. Legal marriage for the enslaved was also illegal—enslavers were well aware that marriage would complicate ownership and thus their ability to profit. Even though there were many instances where enslaved Africans were forced to be together for procreation, enslaved romantic relationships were often separated. Enslaved men were removed from their wives and children, causing enslaved people to find creative ways to congregate, often in spaces where domestic labor was occurring and white eyes and ears were not present.

As Angela Davis posits in her essay "Reflections on the Black Woman's Role in the Community of Slaves,"

> "In the area of production, the slaves pressed into the mold of beasts of burden were forcibly deprived of their humanity. (And a human being thoroughly dehumanized, has no desire for freedom.) But the community gravitating around the domestic quarters might possibly permit a retrieval of the man and the woman in their fundamental humanity. We can assume that in a very real material sense; it was only in domestic life—away from the eyes and whip of the overseer—that the slaves could attempt to assert the modicum of freedom they still retained. It was only

there that they might be inspired to project techniques of expanding it further by leveling what few weapons they had against the slaveholding class whose unmitigated drive for profit was the source of their misery."

Davis was writing in critique of the Moynihan Report; she pushed back against the idea that a matriarchy—a structure where women hold the majority of control and power—was possible under captivity. Moynihan explains why Black people's supposed proclivity for matriarchal societies impacts Black communities and white America:

> There is, presumably, no special reason why a society in which males are dominant in family relationships is to be preferred to a matriarchal arrangement. However, it is clearly a disadvantage for a minority group to be operating on one principle, while the great majority of the population, and the one with the most advantages to begin with, is operating on another. This is the present situation of the Negro. Ours is a society which presumes male leadership in private and public affairs. The arrangements of society facilitate such leadership and reward it. A subculture, such as that of the Negro American, in which this is not the pattern, is placed at a distinct disadvantage.

I see Moynihan's misogynoiristic take as a direct assault not only on Black people, especially Black women, but also on friendships and community building. His focus is not on how single-parent households, which are not endemic to any particular racial or ethnic group, could be supported through legislative means in his capacity as a lawmaker. Instead, Moynihan problematizes matriarchal societies as a departure from white supremacist notions of respectability and patriarchy camouflaged as the comparative normalcy and strength of white cis male–led family units. Precisely because of their communal nature, wherein a nuclear family structure or biological relationship is not a requisite for love or care, where the material survival of the family unit is hinged upon an interdependence with the entire group and far ranging in its diasporic Black ontological roots than could ever be understood by white social scientists, including the cadre that preceded Moynihan and his successors, the Black community's distinct diversity in familial structure and relationship configuration must be defective, he reasoned. Rather than engaging in an inquiry about how society at large can ensure single-parent homes are supported by community, Moynihan's report failed to offer any long-lasting or viable policy measures to end poverty but instead delved into racist tropes and stereotyping passed off as anthropological drivel. However, its indelible failure may also have been part of the state's success in vilifying the very existence of community, situating white families as the model for real or therefore functional families and discouraging any potential for community care, especially that practiced by poor and working-class Black families, as a standard or source for ending the systemic oppression that drives poverty.

To that end, the erosion of community could be seen as a strategic ploy by the state and those in power to quell dissent among the most vulnerable or marginalized. If a community forms and people can depend on each other through a community garden, what happens to the big-box grocery stores where the ultra-wealthy own stock? Having multiple people to rely on beyond a romantic partner to provide support through illness or medical changes, friends who will hold a baby so the parent can rest because it's not sustainable to rely on one person for all the ways life shifts—how will that upset or interrupt the notions of bootstrap individualism in our fictive meritocracy that repressive governmental authorities depend on to keep us from depending on one another?

As the African proverb states, "It takes a village to raise a child," but at what point does the child no longer need the village? We all need community, and I think the discarding of community happens so often because we exalt our romantic relationships by virtue of the state deeming them superior, while devaluing our friendships.

Society, at least in the Western context, has intentionally disconnected Black people from our ancestry—descendants of chattel slavery often do not know the geographical locations we're from, and as a result, we have lost our cultural memory around what love is and have been forced to define it under incredibly arduous circumstances. How do we get to the point where we decide what love is separate from what the state has told us it is?

The state has a vested interest in discarding people, unless it would result in increasing divorce-rate statistics. Staying in your marriage regardless of circumstances is upheld by the state—many divorce laws actually encourage people to stay in their dynamics and make divorce difficult, whether through financial constraints or requirements in some states to be separated for six months to a year before filing. People state their needs, saying they don't want to be with their romantic partner anymore, and the state—which easily discards people who fall out of bounds with white supremacy—suddenly emphasizes not discarding your romantic relationship. The state could care less if people are houseless or stripped of their humanity in a prison cell, but romantic relationships take precedence, as they uphold the state.

If we valued community and divorced ourselves from the

state's influence in our dynamics, there would be less anxiety or fear around belonging and loneliness. The presence of a romantic relationship doesn't correlate to no longer feeling lonely; people will be completely unhappy in romantic relationships and stay in them to avoid being alone.

People are referred to as dysfunctional if they are not in a romantic relationship. When people express being asexual or aromantic, they're questioned and believed to be going through a phase. Many sex ed books claim we are sexual from birth to death, completely excluding those who don't engage in sex. Expressing interest in going to movies, bars, or restaurants alone often prompts concern from others. These acts have been commodified as what you do in romantic relationships, so when done outside that context, people worry—even though being alone doesn't mean someone is lonely.

Belonging in this country seems limited to romantic relationships; so, often, people would rather settle for that paradigm of ownership or submitting to one person rather than a commitment to community.

The Black Panthers were an excellent example, albeit not perfect, of community building. They created intentional space to ensure Black people had not only protection from the state but also food, economic, and health care resources. The Black Panther party was completely destroyed by the US government and arguably by the cisgender men who chose toxic masculinity over the people they claimed they wanted to support. Most of the community programs were created by women and femmes. Elaine Brown, the former Black Panther, wrote extensively about how Huey P. Newton, founder of the Black Panthers, was physically abusive. Even while leading efforts to create community and depart from systems that devalue it, we remain so deeply indoctrinated in white supremacy that being seen as a man as defined by whiteness became, in Newton's case, more important than Black liberation.

Again, friendships and community building are linked with womanhood, and further grounded by Black womanhood. Misogynoir is one of the most common threads in community bonding. MOVE was a Black liberation organization founded in Philadelphia by John Africa, working to end racism, police brutality, and other injustices. In 1985, for the first time in history, the US government bombed its own citizens, launching two bombs over the home and neighborhood where the MOVE organization lived. This extreme measure came in response to the organization refusing to leave their home due to complaints. Eleven people were murdered, five of them children. The MOVE community existed like a commune—they lived together, had children and animals. To this day, the remains of Delisha Africa, a Black girl who was one of six Black children who were murdered in the MOVE bombing, are still in the possession of Penn State Museum.

So many forms of violence by white supremacists happen in places where Black people convene—Black churches have been constant sites of violence. Why are Black people living in community with each other such a threat to the state? It's not just about romantic relationships; our interests are wrapped up in evading the state for fear that we won't be protected by a system that only cares about its bottom line.

Black Lives Matter was created by Black women, a mostly youth-led movement that galvanized Black communities across the diaspora. Their fight against state-sanctioned violence rose under Barack Obama, who offered lukewarm support while president. It was under Obama that the National Guard was called on Black activists protesting George Floyd's murder in multiple cities across the country. White people and institutions did everything to discredit Black Lives Matter, pushing back with "all lives matter" and, worse, "blue lives matter"—a direct nod to police to keep operating as designed.

In a country where only one group has been centered, a whole country built for their domination, asserting that Black lives mattered was entirely too much community building for the white lives that wished to maintain their position of power. Not only was there resistance to honoring Black people at the core of this debate, but yet another beautiful display of community organized by Black women was being discredited, under a Black president, no less. If Obama had actually stood, as the young people say, "ten toes down" for the Black Lives Matter movement, his presidency would have ended abruptly. To remain in office, run for a second term, and win, he had to nurture his relationship with white people—a relationship that Black people are forced to participate in to survive.

How is it that people who brought their children to be spectators of lynchings, threw rocks at young Ruby Bridges as she entered school, justified the brutal murders of Black people by police, still hold the remains of the MOVE bombing victims including children, and voted for a sexual abuser to be president for a second term could also be dictating a standard for love?

Harriet Tubman escaped slavery in Maryland in 1849 after marrying John Tubman, a free Black man. She feared that she could be sold into slavery farther south, so she fled and promised to return for him. Two years later, she returned as promised, and he had remarried. The love that Black women have for humanity is so painfully rarely returned. Do you ever imagine or hold the grief that Black women experience or just expect them to be resilient and move on?

When I was diagnosed with breast cancer, my needs changed, but this wasn't a conversation that either of us knew how to have or felt necessary. Having spent the majority of our relationship not expressing our needs, how was cancer going to upend that? I certainly wasn't accustomed to telling any of my other relationships my needs. It was as if we were hoping to just bury our heads in the sand until enough time passed to move on. I asked that we go to couples therapy, which she refused. We were supposed to just know how to do a relationship; we would eventually make it to the other side without outside help. No one else suggested therapy either.

Our family and friends showed up for us, but at the end of the day we were expected to figure out how to work through cancer on our own. We live in a country where conflict is met with violence, where communication is discouraged. Instead of getting the tools to express my needs, a community that could support me in having them met, I turned to shopping and alcohol to numb my pain.

I was still in a romantic relationship where people thought we were doing well based on the pictures we posted, but it was all a façade. Since I didn't have access to expressing my needs, I suppressed them through consumerism. This is what the state wants—insecure, miserable people who think they only have one person they can truly rely on, when in reality they've never expressed their needs, as they don't even know what they are, beyond being in a committed relationship.

It's necessary for all of us to look at how the state takes up residency within our relationships. Do you rely on the silent treatment when upset, or yell and withhold your love, instead of expressing exactly how you feel? Many of us fear that even if we express what we need, what we want won't be on the other side;

yet it's still important to say what you need. Look to get what you need well beyond your romantic partnerships; it's not sustainable to rely on one person. What structures can be created where you can speak candidly with friends, family, and community about what you really need?

We all have needs, and many of us have not been granted the space to express them. We must support each other as a community in that—not by victim blaming with clichés about loving yourself, but rather with open and honest dialogue. You can rebel against the state in your relationships, but it must begin with removing the state from your relationship. When we have people, community care, and mutual aid, the state's role in our lives becomes reduced. Our tolerance of the state's violence is oftentimes an indication of how we think about abuse, authority, and connection. Because the state has taught us that certain abuses are the necessary means to justifiable ends (e.g., "Don't resist arrest in a police state"; "Have a full-time job in order to have health care"; "That country is full of terrorists, and that's why we bombed the hospital and the school"). We must untether ourselves from a violent state that will discard any of us in a heartbeat and must recommit ourselves to the collective, which will inevitably include conflict. If we can't handle a hard conversation with a friend or family member, do we even stand a chance in our resistance movements against an imperialist police state?

### QUESTIONS TO CONSIDER:

- How do you see carceral logic manifesting in your own relationships—romantic, familial, and platonic? What would it mean to actively work to remove these patterns?

- In what ways have your relationships (of all kinds) been shaped by capitalism's emphasis on ownership and control? How might they look different if they are freed from these influences?
- How can we practice transformative justice in our intimate relationships while still maintaining healthy boundaries? What's the difference between boundaries and control?
- How has the state's definition of love and relationships influenced your own understanding of intimacy? What would it mean to divorce your relationships from state validation?

# 9
# What About Your Friends?

> "Love is a contraband in hell, cause love is acid that eats away bars. But you, me and tomorrow hold hands and make vows that struggle will multiply. The hacksaw has two blades. The shotgun has two barrels. We are pregnant with freedom. We are conspiracy"
>
> —Assata Shakur,
> *The Autobiography of Assata Shakur*

Most sex ed curricula reserve lessons about relationships for the romantic and sexual. Friendships may have a short blurb on the margins of a sex ed textbook but rarely receive dedicated lectures. We are lectured about how to love yourself in order to love someone else, or how to sustain a relationship by working on yourself, but none of this messaging is directed toward friendships. We are taught that even having flourishing, thoughtful, loving friendships means very little if you don't also have a romantic relationship.

Friendships are often neglected, held together by an assumption they will last forever with very little investment, maintained simply by proximity or history. How we regard and have been taught to view friendships directly informs us of our unrealistically high standards for romantic relationships. The expectation that one person can and will be our main priority, best friend, whole community, and sole family member is an extension of individualism.

Individualism is a tenet of white supremacy culture; the Western world gives accolades to those who can do things on their own. Friendships exist in this weird landscape of relationships that are disregarded, considered optional in the grand scheme of the faux ideal of the American dream—two kids, a picket-fenced home adorned with framed wedding photos and baby pictures. Unless I am in a college dorm room or an apartment with roommates, rarely do I see photos of friends framed prominently. Social media is now the place to showcase your friends on trips, partying, or simply taking a walk, a broadcast for the world to see. The origins of social media began with the CEO of Facebook, Mark Zuckerberg, creating a website that rated college women based on their looks by other cisgender men college students. Although no longer a beauty contest organized by white cisgender men's proclivities to put women on display, organizing their value based on their appearance, this still plays a role in who we follow and who has the most followers on social media.

Our friend groups and who we wish to be friends with can be smaller versions of the same exclusionary racist, classist, and ableist practices that inform who we taught to see as desirable. Although and perhaps ironically, calls to follow marginalized creators are not rare on apps that make use of embedded racist algorithms, filtering who we see and do not see, but in comparison to their white counterparts, there is still a severe lack of parity in who receives the lion's share of parasocial support. Being able to see that people liked the photo you posted three hours ago or reading the comments on newly announced life events provides the dopamine rush that is harder to quickly attain off the internet. Social media allows people to take on any persona or life that they wish to portray. Before posting a photo or video, a filter to distort reality can be added, an app can remove your "ums," or you can edit your face out entirely and just use the soundbite. Social media provides anonymity, an antithesis to vulnerability.

Don't get me wrong, social media has its pros: the increased ability to organize in accessible ways, create mutual-aid funds, and stay connected with real-life friends and family has been largely due to social media. And still, no one who has strangers following them knows all the myriad reasons why they chose to do so, and I am not sure it matters to most. On white supremacist uber-capitalist apps, we exchange our data for algorithms that prioritize those who uphold the state in desirability and politics. Desirability politics often earn creators a like, share, or comment. How you look is sufficient enough in a consumer capitalist state that has convinced us that the perception we create for the world to consume is more important than intentional vulnerable connection. We see this reflected in movies depicting secondary schools where the popular kids are seen as conventionally attractive, which garners them many friends, while the unpopular kids are oftentimes alone. Social media has only mirrored society's belief that being conventionally attractive grants you access to friends—and that if you are not conventionally attractive, you should just accept your fate of being alone.

When I was in secondary school, I would cry to my mom that no one wanted to be my friend. When she would ask why, I'd tell her because people think I am ugly. She would reassure me that I was not ugly, although her argument didn't hold much weight to the incessant noise I endured about my looks daily. She'd go on to tell me, everyone is not and will not be your friend, a lesson a hardheaded Sagittarius would not learn until she got much older. I had friends, but I did not have a lot of friends. The popular kids stood with their cliques and teased everyone who was more vulnerable. I wanted to be insulated from bullying like the popular girls; I was learning the value of quantity over quality. Rappers gloat about their cliques or possessions, as if their friends make them or their music more valuable.

Without much guidance on how to be or what I needed in a friend, I have stumbled through many friendships, often blurring the line between lover and friend. I have been accused of flirting with my friends, treating them like lovers, and making their partners jealous of my presence. Some of my friendships have ended because we had sex. Some of my greatest lovers have been friends first. Friendships can play an important role in a couple's origin story, but once in a romantic relationship, other friends are expected to take a back seat. The roles that friends may have had in a person's life begin to dwindle since, as any R&B song from the 1990s and 2000s will tell you, a romantic partner is supposed to complete us, very Mary J. Blige "you are everything and everything is you": lover, secretary working every day of the week, therapist, and friend.

Even our definitions of love center romantic relationships, not friendships. In English you can love anything—vodka, shopping, soccer, getting in bed with clean sheets after a shower and a long day. According to definitions from Oxford Languages, in English, "love is translated to an intense feeling of deep affection or a great interest in pleasure of something." When you look at love as a verb, "to feel deep affection or attachment to someone," even the examples provided are of a sister to a brother or a romantic partner expressing love. In the dictionary, love is a verb to feel, not to do. Even the synonyms for love as a verb replicate this: "be in love with, be infatuated with, be besotted with, dote on, worship, idolize, treasure and prize." Do any of these encompass popular ways that society talks about friendships? While people speak of "romantic friendships," why do we need that qualifier if the role of friend is valued, if love can occur and flourish between friends?

When I turned thirty, I looked around the dinner table at the people who had supported me through college transitions, moving to New York City with a thousand dollars to my name and Broadway dreams, navigating my breast cancer diagnosis and surgeries—and didn't feel connected to many of them anymore. I had told them I loved them, spent quality time with them, but something snapped for me at that moment when those feelings started to slip away. As the young people say, my Saturn return was Saturn-returning! It was as if a switch had turned on a light bulb for me, illuminating that we didn't have much in common aside from knowing each other for many years or trauma bonding over being broke in New York City.

Many of my friends were white, and so was my partner at the time. I began to realize that I was their token "Black friend," a diversity and inclusion quota fulfilled for their mostly white friendship groups; but what was in it for me? Had we even discussed expectations of the friendship, like I had done with romantic partners? Was it just assumed how we were supposed to be in each other's life? I spent most of my twenties collecting people rather than actually figuring out what worked best for me in relationships. The quality didn't matter; I just wanted to have a lot of friendships so I never felt alone. I was coming to terms with the fact that I had never been asked what I needed in friendship, and now I was staring at a table full of people who felt unfamiliar to me. It was important for me to be friends with people who looked like me, who experienced the world in a similar way to how I did. And that wasn't this table. I wanted my friendships to be a soft place for me to land, but instead I was the one doing the most labor.

Like the Moynihan Report problematizes "matriarchal societies," our resistance to building meaningful friendships stems from how they're gendered and often associated with women. When cisgender men connect with other men and build relationships, society has named those relationships "bromances." The term "bromance" is rooted in homophobia, while also making it abnormal that cisgender heterosexual men could have emotional connections outside family.

When a cisgender heterosexual man has many relationships with cisgender women, this is seen as a threat to current or potential partners. Their sexuality comes into question if they cultivate relationships with cisgender women. If a cisgender woman is friends with cisgender men, she is seen as a "pick me" or "antagonistic to women." I think that these assumptions miss the mark on what is to blame for the apparent strangeness of friendship without shared gender identity. Friendships are largely seen as something women do, which plays into the fallacy that women can have many loves because they are innately more emotional than men. Once again, the impacts of colonialism and the gender binary are impeding our ability to develop quality relationships. Sweeping statements about the gender dynamics of friendship groups are a distraction from what could be possible if we kept our focus on how we can support each other.

I have had friends end their relationship with me because I did not tell them exactly where I was going the first time they asked—they believed I was lying to them, thus violating their trust. I have had friends get mad at me because they thought I did not respond to their text messages in the time they deemed suitable. I have had friends create carefully crafted lies about my other friends to fulfill their possessive desires to be my only friend. I have stayed in friendships where I noticed they might be jealous of me, but I gaslit myself into believing that could never be the case, because they were my friends. A recurring theme in many of my friendships is me expressing my needs in the relationship. When are we taught to express our boundaries and needs in any relationship, let alone a friendship? In most of the examples I shared, those relationships ended abruptly, with very little discourse or hopes for reconciliation—we just stopped talking to each other. The swift discard of a friend, without any tools for moving forward, illuminates how we've been taught to avoid community and prioritize romantic relationships.

In all of these examples are themes of carceral logic, possessiveness, control, and dominance. Barring instances of abuse, bullying, and violent harm in which cutting off contact with a person is not only valid but necessary, how do we have conflict in our relationships that does not include carcerality? What are the tools that are available to manage friendship conflicts? I have had friends I've known for two and three decades, yet even in my long-term friendships, we've never discussed a friendship anniversary, gone to dinner to commemorate how long we've known each other, or found a therapist to help us sort through our conflict—but this is all very common in romantic relationships.

I don't think we all need to be best friends to be in a community; even the notion of a "best" friend asserts hierarchy. I think we have to collectively develop the tools for expressing our needs in all of our relationships, but especially our friendships, to decenter romantic relationships, and to be willing participants in conflict. We are taught to view conflict as a sign that a relationship isn't working, but conflict is a sign that needs aren't being met, and it's an opportunity to figure out what works for all parties involved.

The very popular Disney film *The Lion King* has a scene where the main character Simba is reunited with their childhood best friend Nala. Instead of this being a scene where they connect and talk about what has happened to their hometown since Simba was chased away, they chase each other in flirtatious humanlike ways insinuating they are having sex. "Can You Feel the Love Tonight" plays in the background, the last lyric being sung by Simba's friends Timon and Pumbaa as they shed many tears at the lions' reunion and budding romantic relationship. Timon and Pumbaa fall to the background as the focus becomes about Nala and Simba's love that will reunite Pride Rock and conquer the enemy. A film for children about lions prominently places a love story to convince young people that they, too, should value romantic relationships above all else.

A part of your needs may center on establishing boundaries. Boundaries begin and end with saying no, especially if you exist in a marginalized body. People of marginalized identities often believe they must be open to everything, that if they say no, they'll be met with aggression. People are so accustomed to us laboring for everyone; a no reminds them that you are human, not a machine.

Honor the diverse needs of all relationships—they're not one-size-fits-all. Boundaries are often scary to create, as they're usually met with frustration, but not allowing total access to your existence, taking breaks, not spreading yourself thin to please others is necessary preservation work, not just of yourself but also the community. There is no way to practice community care without boundaries. To have boundaries without using control, our main focus must be how this supports the collective, not just individual needs.

In 2022, there was a trending conversation on social media about how people pleasers are manipulative. Many folks were saying that although pleasing people may come from trauma, their tendencies are employed to disarm people so that there is no conflict, or so they are not abandoned. The people pleaser has no boundaries and makes no demands, and this is often in service of keeping people around them rather than developing authentic relationships with people who can hear the word "no" or are capable of navigating conflict. As a recovering people pleaser, I found this conversation resonated with me deeply. I thought that my lack of boundaries was a way to make space for other people, dropping everything for them regardless of what I had going on; always saying yes when I really wanted to say maybe or no; and eventually I would become resentful because I had never stated my needs.

I was friends with someone who always texted me about what they were going through and never concerned themselves with what I was doing in the moment. When they texted me, I would drop everything to get back to them. I could be sitting at dinner with my partner, and I would stop mid-bite to text them back. Responding to their texts felt urgent for me. What pulled us apart was that when I had things going on and needed support, I'd wait days for a response; or if the response came right away, we'd quickly end up circling back to their stuff again. Boundaries are hard to set, especially as Black femmes: We have been regarded by society as people who should give and never receive care. I find that people often expect Black femmes to have no boundaries at all; we should just be thankful that we have anyone in our lives. But boundaries are necessary. They allow us to honor our needs, see who really wants to be in our lives in a reciprocal way and to ensure a level of care and tenderness throughout the relationship. This relationship crashed and burned; we ended up blocking each other, and there are times when I wish we would have talked about the boundaries that were lacking in our friendship. I believe that we are still in community with each other, and although the relationship has ended and there is lingering resentment and upset, their liberation as a Black person is still bound up with mine.

The impulse to cut people off, block or unfollow their social media accounts, stop speaking entirely, or resort to physical violence are all normalized ways to deal with conflict. (Note: This is not to say that blocking, unfollowing, or ending communication are not valid ways to deal with conflict—especially as it relates to abusive/harmful dynamics. I am asserting that this is the way we deal with conflict consistently.) We have learned a great deal from the oppressive structures we have been indoctrinated with on how not to deal with conflict. Racial capitalism determines who should be discarded, and we mimic these dynamics in conflict. Conflict should be addressed, rather than ignored or resolved by discarding people simply because that relationship or person is devalued under white supremacist capitalist patriarchy.

The most painful breakups I have ever experienced were with friends. Conflict in friendship has kept me up at night, kept my therapist in business, and made my other friends tired of hearing about it. There is a presumption that conflict in a friendship is a sign that the friendship is not working. I've heard people brag that they've never had any conflict or friction with their friends of ten or twenty-plus years, but I have found that if you are not having any conflict with your friends, you must ask yourself: What are you not saying or not doing to remain in that friendship? Conflict is not a sign that a relationship is not working; it could be an indication that there are needs not being met and presents a prime opportunity to address them.

While there are absolutely situations where cutting people off is completely understandable, I think we lean too heavily on discarding folks instead of working through the challenges. We owe it to ourselves and each other to work through conflict, not necessarily to preserve a relationship, but to honor all parties involved.

I don't think there's a one-size-fits-all equation to resolve conflict, as there is harm that is unbearable to confront. It's important to honor complexity rather than hit people over the head with how-tos that are often laced with abuser apologist rhetoric and decentering of the harmed. Although there are instances where everyone may feel like the harmed party, how can we work toward restorative and transformative justice practices that rely on the collective to support conflict, to be unbiased in their approach, ensuring all parties are heard and feel restoration has occurred?

My relationship with love is complex. I have to be honest: Writing the last two chapters was absolutely challenging for me. As I called out previous ways of being, I felt physically unwell. But what I am most present to is that even in my darkest times, the people who have always pulled me off the floor and been a soft place to land have been Black queer and trans women. Some of the most intimate, life-altering moments I have ever experienced have been with Black women. I was sharing frustrations with one of my friends about what I was navigating personally and they looked at me and said, "it's okay to cry, Ericka." Being invited to cry and be vulnerable made me feel held, safe, and deeply loved. They were not trying to fix or change how I was feeling, they were instead hyperaware that I was likely fighting back tears to remain strong when I really just needed to fall apart. How love has been shaped for me has not only allowed me to discredit and devalue these expressions of love, but, as a Black femme, to resist love being expressed in my direction.

Community spaces committed to addressing conflict, being vulnerable, and decentering romantic relationships and imperialistic desirability politics have been where I feel most at home. Relationships where the state's presence is actively removed are not easy, often come with lots of heartbreak and aspects we'd rather forget than confront, but these spaces are necessary for our survival. Love resistant to systems is at the heart of—and should be credited to—the unwavering commitment to the collective that Black women have demonstrated.

My journey through cancer, divorce, and the unlearning of state-sanctioned notions of love has taught me that true intimacy isn't found in the perfectly curated family photos or the sanitized versions of relationships we're sold. It exists in the messy, challenging spaces where we dare to be fully human with each other—where we can express rage at injustice, share our deepest fears, and still be held. It lives in the friends who show up not just for celebrations but for hard conversations, in the communities that make space for all our complexities rather than forcing us into prescribed roles.

The state would have us believe that love is scarce, that it must be earned through compliance, proven through consumption, or validated by legal recognition. But Black women have long demonstrated otherwise. Through centuries of resistance, they've shown us that love is abundant when we refuse to accept the terms of white supremacist capitalism—when we choose instead to build networks of care that honor our full humanity. This love doesn't ask us to shrink ourselves or sacrifice our dignity. It doesn't require us to choose between romantic partnership and community, between individual needs and collective well-being.

Love as a refusal of systems isn't just about who we love or how we love—it's about dismantling the very structures that have twisted love into a tool of control and conformity. It's about recognizing that our liberation is bound together, that we are worthy of love not because of what we produce or consume or who validates us, but simply because we exist. This is the love Black women have modeled, have fought for, have preserved against all odds. And it is this love—revolutionary, abundant, uncontainable—that points the way forward.

QUESTIONS TO PONDER:

- When do you find yourself treating friendships as less important than romantic relationships? How can you actively work to decenter romance as the primary form of meaningful connection?
- What concrete practices could help build true community care that exists outside of state-sanctioned relationship structures?
- How do you parse the connections between personal relationship patterns and larger systems of oppression? What role do intimate relationships play in either maintaining or dismantling these systems?

# 10

# What's Better Than an Orgy?

"All that you touch, you change. All that you change, changes you. The only lasting truth is Change. God is Change."

—Octavia Butler

I used to think that sexual liberation looked like orgies on the weekends, having every type of condom in my bag, wearing a short skirt that blessed everyone with my thigh meat, having a play party where people didn't "yuck" anyone's "yum," making out with friends, explaining every sex toy and its function, having a class full of students yell "penis" and "vagina," listening to and giving advice about everyone's deepest, darkest secrets about sex and polyamory, and being open to having sex with anyone who expressed interest. I used to say things like, "Starting a revolution one orgasm at a time." I cringe at the thought that I likely wrote this on the internet and it will live forever. While everything I listed could be seen as sexual freedom, it is completely devoid of the things that keep people from having orgasms and the fact that not everyone wants to have sexual encounters or romantic partners. Without racial, gender, class, disability, and body-image analysis, sexual liberation becomes another landscape where white supremacy runs amok, completely coloring who and what we view as sexually free.

A sexually liberatory framework requires a commitment to dismantling the barriers to pleasure, bodily autonomy, and gender expansiveness that often make an example out of marginalized bodies to be used as a talking point rather than a breakdown for everyone's access to pleasure. The quote "no one is free until all of us are free," attributed to Martin Luther King Jr., Audre Lorde, and Keeanga-Yamahtta Taylor (who actually made it more specific to gender and race), is ubiquitous to the point of banality, almost clichéd at this point, quick to be brought out after state-sanctioned violence has taken another Black or non-Black person of color's life. Using this quote when someone has died is too late; if the principle of this stance is not integrated into our everyday lives, what difference does it make beyond being able to use for likes and views on the internet?

Sex is a subject matter people consider private and salacious—where we ultimately get to focus on ourselves and derive our own individual idea of what feels sexually liberating and gratifying. You may be reading this and saying to yourself, "I have it 'all': car, job, money, health insurance, and a fulfilling sex life" (speaking nothing of your partner or partners' experience—you might be having a fulfilling sex life, they might not be). While there is nothing wrong with being grateful for what you have materially, none of that is freedom. It's the illusion of comfort under a capitalistic system that is constantly narrowing and shifting our concept of what's worth accumulating, producing, consuming—demanding more, and exploiting the masses in the process so that only very few can have it "all."

What happens to the person who thinks they have it all and then is diagnosed with a chronic illness? What if they experience houselessness? Most of us are one paycheck away from that reality. Does that mean experiences of having it "all" are now completely thwarted? Having it "all" and being sexually free are oftentimes hinged upon being seen as desirable to the state. When your existence is seen in opposition to or as a threat to the state, sexual freedom becomes a carrot that's dangled in front of our faces, another aspect of life that should be earned rather than a human right.

Many social justice movements throughout history have demonstrated that organizing can occur, and often be seen as effective, but are not devoid of or free from replicating the same misogynistic, colorist, abusive, fatphobic, and transphobic values that they ostensibly seek to disrupt. For example, white women dominated early suffrage movements (Black women led—hat tip to Ida B. Wells, Sojourner Truth, and many others); white women have consistently used their race privilege to make advancements while actively discarding Black, Latinx, and Indigenous women. The Gay Marriage movement centered the needs of white, cisgender gay men who wished to utilize their white privilege to still reap the benefits of white supremacy. Birth control and abortion became legal in the US after rampant exploitation and experimentation on Black women and disabled folks. The Civil Rights Movement and Black Panther Party centered Black cisgender men, although they were built and maintained by the organizing principles of Black women. The Black Lives Matter movement centered Black cisgender men, even though it was started by Black women; the names of Black women, especially Black trans women, were rarely a focal point.

Sexual liberation is viewed in the same regard: If the dominant group is free, then change must be afoot. Meanwhile, that "freedom" is built at the express disenfranchisement of someone else. The sexual revolution was marked in the US during the 1960s when birth control became widely available. Black people had access to birth control but were often kept from accessing it due to cost inaccessibility and fears that birth control was another way for the state to further genocide in the Black community. So why is this time marked as the sexual revolution if only white people could access it? How is it that white people control the narrative around what is sexually free, when historically they have had a propensity toward sexual violence?

White people's sexual freedom is hinged upon the continued repression of Black life and autonomy. Post-enslavement, the 1960s marked some of the most egregious examples of racial terror in this country's history: White people burned crosses on the lawns of Black people's homes, enforced segregated water fountains and restaurants, used water hoses and dogs to halt protests; and on the weekends, they had circle jerks? White people must delve into the reasons behind racial injustice, as the ability to control others is a cultural value that requires examination and dismantling.

The many industries that are dependent on us hating our bodies would go out of business due to no longer having purpose if we actually saw fatphobia as a systemic issue that supports eugenics. If we decentered our romantic relationships, stopped supporting toxic romanticism and the wedding industrial complex, and poured that money into our communities, how many people would have access to pleasure? Sex education has the ability to shift lives, to uproot systems of oppression, but instead the focus is on orgasms void of any politicization. There is not a single topic under the sex and sexuality sun that Black people have not been a part of consensually or nonconsensually, whose contributions are immense throughout the field, and yet we are often pushed out of institutions entirely for what we believe will make a difference toward sexual liberation.

The first Black woman Surgeon General of the United States, Dr. Jocelyn Elders, was fired from her job for advocating that students have the tools to talk about masturbation. When she was asked at a United Nations conference on AIDS her thoughts on teaching masturbation to children and if it might shift patterns of unsafe sex, she said, "I think that is something that is a part of human sexuality, and it's a part of something that perhaps should be taught. But we've not even taught our children the very basics." After her statements were shared publicly, conservatives started campaigns to have her resign. Although Dr. Elders also believed that condoms should be handed out in schools, she received nothing but pushback and went on to say that "our country does not want to talk about sex; we will have it but not talk about it." Ironically, a year later, a forty-nine-year-old President Bill Clinton would cheat on his wife with his twenty-two-year-old intern, Monica Lewinsky, which would make him appear to be the victim of Lewinsky's seduction, rather than a predator relative to someone over whom he had power and a significant age gap. Dr. Elders not only lost her position for affirming young people's bodily autonomy and telling the truth about how pleasure works, but because so much of sexuality education is about agency, and agency is about autonomy, and at the core of autonomy is freedom. Freedom which has held, time and again throughout history, the promise for upending power, including antiquated yet powerful messaging about sexual deviance passed down through generations of white cisgender heterosexual men as the arbiters of who and what is real, normal, natural, nasty, objectionable, abominable—all so they can be free to act out their sexual perversions or proclivities with discretion while the rest of us are given little room outside of the roles we play in their fantasies, sexual and political.

Dr. Elders became the issue that needed to be removed, not Clinton or the system that would further attempt to convince young people that touching their own bodies was wrong. Elders was not only the country's first Black woman Surgeon General, but also the country's first sex educator to serve as Surgeon General. As a former sharecropper in the state of Arkansas, which Clinton also calls home, Elders's labor—picking cotton with her family as a child—created the conditions for Clinton to become president. So, it is not lost on me that exploitation operates like a cycle, working herself up to one of the highest offices in US government only to be discarded by the same people who run that system. So how is it that he, that the state, has moral authority on what is sexually deviant, wrong, or violent?

The groundwork has been laid for centuries to relate to Black people as subhuman; when chattel slavery was abolished, that association did not end. The ways in which we relate to our and others' bodies are informed by being brought up in a white supremacist, capitalist, patriarchal police state, a state that is the intentional product of colonization. Land and bodies alike have been colonized, and that control is built on the binary of desired and ugly, civilized and savage, white and Black.

Colonialism has completely destroyed our relationship to nature, teaching us that humans are at the top of some imaginary hierarchy created by none other than white cisgender men who have a vested interest in creating categories for everything. Humans are not in some separate class from nature. We are also not at the top. We exist within and are a part of nature. The same white cisgender men and their descendants destroyed plant and animal life in order for white people to hoard mass wealth through the burning of fossil fuels, overconsumption, construction of industrial machinery, deforestation to build highways and buildings, AI technologies, and on, and on. Colonialism is not natural or normal; it is an assault on how life is intended to be.

As a kid, my mother, Gran Gran, and grandmother all had houseplants in every room of their homes. My great-grandmother had a golden pothos that sat above her refrigerator, a permanent fixture in many of our family photos. When my mother passed away, our neighbor, a Black woman, took care of all her houseplants for over twenty years. When I visited her home to retrieve some of the plants, they were so tall that I had to cut some down to fit them into the car. I continue this tradition with over forty-five houseplants in my own home, one of which was my mother's, and which now has my first child's placenta planted in its pot.

I don't think it is a coincidence that Black people often have houseplants and gardens. I think we understand, albeit are forced to understand through violent means, how to honor the natural and discard the unnatural—the most unnatural of which is white supremacy. Being surrounded by nature in our homes is a reminder that we not only share a planet with nature but that every living and breathing thing should be respected. I visited a house owned by a Black woman who was eighty and needed to move. She had the most beautiful plants in a solarium. When I asked her what she would be doing with the plants when she moved, she said they were going with her.

Before the white liberal with a house full of plants shouts at the pages in defense, I know white people have houseplants too. I am positing that the system of whiteness has uniquely interrupted Black people's ability to really see ourselves as part of nature on our terms, not solely as animals, beasts of burden, uncivilized "savages." The enduring sentiment that "white is right" suggests our deviance, our being "unnatural." Black people find refuge in nature. I have a beautiful magnolia tree in my backyard, and every year it goes dormant from June to April. When I look in the backyard and see a bare tree, none of the trees around it are upset about its appearance, the wind doesn't stop blowing in its direction because it hasn't sprouted its flowers yet, the sun doesn't stop shining on its bare branches. The other plant and animal life does not cower in fear of its appearance. They also do not halt their growth as a result. The birds and squirrels still perch on their branches for a moment of rest. It doesn't matter that I may look back there in July and wish I could see its pretty flowers. The magnolia tree is doing exactly what it needs to do, and no amount of force, control, or upset is going to change its trajectory.

It doesn't matter how much fertilizer, humidity, perfect sunlight conditions, watering, and a pot that drains, I cannot control how any plant grows. Leaving my plants alone, letting them be, paying attention when they need pruning, water, adjusted sunlight or need to be isolated from other plants when they have an infestation has been the greatest lesson in caring—not only for my plants but for myself, humanity, and the planet. Nature is resilient. Have you ever tried to kill a weed growing out of the cracks of a sidewalk? Impossible. I think of both the sidewalk and the Weedwacker as oppression. Oppressed people reach for the sun anyway; it doesn't matter how many times we are forced out, pushed to the side, or even lose our lives. We continue to rise.

Plants function much better with other plants. bell hooks writes in *All About Love* that "healing does not happen in isolation." Even plants are a reminder that we need each other. It's rare that I see a tree standing alone and not in close proximity to other plant and animal life. Humans are no different than the nature around them; it is all a reflection. What is not natural is anti-Blackness, fatphobia, transphobia, misogynoir, ageism, adultification. The next time you look at your body and your internalized fatphobia creeps up on you, consider that the trees never groan about the space they take up. If there is a young person in your life who is requesting to be on hormones to affirm their gender, meet their needs, because transphobia is unnatural, not trans youth. If you have been thinking you might be queer but have been in cis-heterosexual relationships your entire life, know that cis-heteronormativity is a made-up structure that has convinced you that gender and sexuality are fixed and will look exactly the same your entire life. That is unnatural. Displacing people, killing bloodlines, and silencing children are all unnatural. There are no binaries in nature. There are genderless fungi and queer penguins. Nature knows no bounds. Take up space, honor your bodies exactly as they are, confront the systems that we have been told over and over again are natural or normal that do nothing but distance us from the truth of who we are. Oh, and maybe get a houseplant too. 😊

A truly inclusive world of pleasure is not complicit in white supremacist systems and doesn't create conditions that actively push disabled and fat folks out of society. A world of true pleasure goes beyond hanging a nondescript sign about honoring all bodies—it interrogates and radically reorganizes itself around the bodies it has worked so hard to discard. A sexually free world is actively decolonizing and anti-racist. It means the end of wealth disparity, safe and affordable housing for all, disruption of cisgender heterosexual identity as *the* standard, restorative justice, safe and affirming abortions, reproductive justice, and the end of STI stigma. It means fat bodies exist without contest, it means accessibility for all bodies, abilities, and ages. It is very Black, queer, and Indigenous. It prioritizes the safety, dignity, and rights of sex workers and sees the decriminalization of their labor. It celebrates asexuality and trans femmes thriving. It demands reparations from the state for Black people.

A sexually free world will require radical change.

To the folks who will inevitably ask, what do I do now? How do I make this happen? There is a human tendency to search for a solution, a neat, easily digestible resolution to a troubling problem, a satisfying ending to a movie as a commensurate payoff for the time spent watching it; an answer seems to lie in each of us as we search frantically for a fix while the systems and structures at the root of the problem are held harmless. The answer is in us; a critical consideration of the racialized and gendered nature of how we view ourselves and others would lead to stronger bonds, connections, and community that would deprioritize consumer capitalist culture and, in turn, weaken the power that corporations have over our lives. Power would look different—not power over or above, but a collective refusal of the systems that go against nature.

This honestly might be better than an orgy, or it might make your orgies better. 😊

# Bibliography

Adams, Char. "Black Lives Matter Leaders Condemn Allegations of Mismanaged Funds." *NBC News*. April 12, 2022. www.nbcnews.com/news/nbcblk/black-lives-matter-leaders-condemn-allegations-mismanaged-funds-rcna23882.

Adichie, Chimamanda Ngozi. *We Should All Be Feminists*. TED Talk, 2017. www.ted.com/talks/chimamanda_ngozi_adichie_we_should_all_be_feminists.

Alexanian, Tamar Anna. "Black Women & Women's Suffrage: Understanding the Perception of the Nineteenth Amendment through the Pages of the Chicago Defender." *Michigan Journal of Gender & Law* 29, no. 1 (n.d.). University of Michigan Law School Scholarship Repository. Accessed April 18, 2025. repository.law.umich.edu/mjgl/vol29/iss1/3/.

Amnesty International. "Africa: Barrage of Discriminatory Laws Stoking Hate against LGBTI Persons." *Amnesty International*. January 9, 2024. www.amnesty.org/en/latest/news/2024/01/africa-barrage-of-discriminatory-laws-stoking-hate-against-lgbti-persons/.

Austen, Jane. *Pride and Prejudice*. London: Thomas Egerton, 1918.

Babcock, Gregory. "Grace Jones Takes Shots at Kim Kardashian for Her 'Paper' Cover." *Complex*. September 30, 2015. www.complex.com/style/a/gregory-babcock/grace-jones-kim-kardashian-is-basic.

Baker, Brent, Mark Busk-Cowley, Tom Gould, and Joe Scarrat, creators. *Love Island UK*. ITV Studios, 2015.

Bayoumi, Moustafa. "They Are 'Civilised' and 'Look like Us': The Racist Coverage of Ukraine." *The Guardian*, March 2, 2022. www.theguardian.com/commentisfree/2022/mar/02/civilised-european-look-like-us-racist-coverage-ukraine.

Biala, Yewande. "'My Name Is Yewande': Mispronouncing or Changing People's Names Is Just Another Form of Racism." *The Independent*,

January 26, 2021. www.the-independent.com/voices/yewande-biala-love-island-lucie-donlan-b1792717.html.

BlackPast. "The Combahee River Collective Statement." BlackPast.org, 1977. www.blackpast.org/african-american-history/combahee-river-collective-statement-1977/.

Brewster, Joe, and Michèle Stephenson, directors. *Going to Mars: The Nikki Giovanni Project*. HBO Documentary Films, 2023.

Brown, Christopher Leslie. "Little Ships of Horror." *The Nation*, January 17, 2008. www.thenation.com/article/archive/little-ships-horror/.

Brown, Sherronda J. *Refusing Compulsory Sexuality: A Black Asexual Lens on Our Sex-Obsessed Culture*. Berkeley: North Atlantic Books, 2022.

Butt, Maira. "'Marriage Is a Form of Prostitution': Zeze Millz and Slumflower Divide Internet with Debate." *The Independent*, October 8, 2024. www.the-independent.com/life-style/zeze-millz-slumflower-marriage-prostitution-b2625615.html.

Camp, Stephanie M. H. *Closer to Freedom: Enslaved Women and Everyday Resistance in the Plantation South*. Chapel Hill: University of North Carolina Press, 2004.

Chotiner, Isaac. "A Penn Law Professor Wants to Make America White Again." *The New Yorker*, August 23, 2019. www.newyorker.com/news/q-and-a/a-penn-law-professor-wants-to-make-america-white-again.

Coates, Ta-Nehisi. "Prop 8 and Blaming the Blacks." *The Atlantic*, January 7, 2009. www.theatlantic.com/entertainment/archive/2009/01/prop-8-and-blaming-the-blacks/6548/.

Collins, Rory. "Podcast Duo Sorry for Jokes About Black Women." *BBC News*, September 17, 2024. www.bbc.com/news/articles/ce81yy7l39mo.

Contributors to Wikimedia Projects. "Ugly Law." Wikipedia. Last modified April 6, 2025. en.wikipedia.org/wiki/Ugly_law.

Cooper, Brittney. *Eloquent Rage: A Black Feminist Discovers Her Superpower.* New York: St. Martin's Press, 2018.

"Cops Bought Burger King for Dylann Roof Following His Arrest." 6abc Philadelphia, June 23, 2015. 6abc.com/dylann-roof-south-carolina-church-shooting-emanuel-african-methodist-episcopal/801013/.

Crenshaw, Kimberlé. *On Intersectionality: Essential Writings*. New York: The New Press, 2019.

Davis, Angela. "Reflections on the Black Woman's Role in the Community of Slaves." *The Black Scholar* 3, no. 4 (1971): 2–15. doi.org/10.1080/00064246.1971.11431201.

__________. *Are Prisons Obsolete?* New York: Seven Stories Press, 2011.

D'Oyley, Demetria Lucas. "The News Isn't #TeacherBae's Clothing—It's the

Exploitation of Her Body." *Essence*, September 16, 2016. www.essence.com/news/teacher-bae-patrice-brown-exploitation/.

Epstein, Rebecca, Jamilia J. Blake, and Thalia González. *Girlhood Interrupted: The Erasure of Black Girls' Childhood*. Center on Poverty and Inequality, Georgetown Law, 2017.

"Esther Perel: We Expect Too Much From Our Partners," posted August 22, 2021, by Bqurious, YouTube. www.youtube.com/watch?v=gVgVJonyAu8.

Fanon, Frantz. *The Wretched of the Earth*. New York: Grove/Atlantic, 2007.

Fitzsimons, Tim. "Drag Queen Story Hour Brings Pride and Glamor to Libraries across U.S." *NBC News*, June 19, 2018. www.nbcnews.com/feature/nbc-out/drag-queen-story-hour-brings-pride-glamor-libraries-across-u-n884671.

Free Speech Coalition. "Moe Johnson Says Dogfart Director Ordered Racial Slurs for Money Shot (XBIZ)." May 17, 2018. www.freespeechcoalition.com/blog/2018/05/17/moe-johnson-says-dogfart-director-ordered-racial-slurs-for-money-shot-xbiz.

Fritze, John. "How Justice Amy Coney Barrett Drove the Supreme Court's Debate on Abortion and Trump Immunity." *CNN*, April 27, 2024. www.cnn.com/2024/04/27/politics/amy-coney-barrett-supreme-court-immunity-idaho-abortion/index.html.

Gabriel, Mike, and Eric Goldberg, directors. *Pocahontas*. Buena Vista Pictures Distribution, 1995.

Gallagher, Diane, Sara Smart, and Emma Tucker. "Woman Whose Accusation Led to the Lynching of Emmett Till Has Died at 88, Coroner Says." *CNN*, April 17, 2023. www.cnn.com/2023/04/27/us/carolyn-bryant-donham-emmett-till/index.html.

Gariano, Francesca. "24 Rules You Didn't Know 'Love Island' Contestants Have to Follow." *People*, July 12, 2024. people.com/love-island-rules-contestants-must-follow-8676427.

Gill-Peterson, Jules. *Histories of the Transgender Child*. Minneapolis: University of Minnesota Press, 2018.

———. *A Short History of Trans Misogyny*. London: Verso Books, 2024.

Grant, Melissa Gira. "Amy Coney Barrett's Gentle Deceptions." *The New Republic*, October 14, 2020. newrepublic.com/article/159779/amy-coney-barrett-femininity-roe-impartial.

Haley, Sarah. *No Mercy Here: Gender, Punishment, and the Making of Jim Crow Modernity*. Chapel Hill: University of North Carolina Press, 2019.

Harris-Perry, Melissa V. *Sister Citizen: Shame, Stereotypes, and Black Women in America*. New Haven: Yale University Press, 2011.

Held, Amy. "Controversial Serena Williams Cartoon Ruled 'Non-Racist' by Australia's Press Council." *NPR*, February 25, 2019. www.npr.org/2019/02/

25/697672690/controversial-serena-cartoon-ruled-non-racist-by-australia-s-governing-press-bod.

Hibler, Joan. "Henry Box Brown." *Encyclopedia Britannica*, May 19, 2013. www.britannica.com/biography/Henry-Box-Brown.

hooks, bell. *Ain't I a Woman: Black Women and Feminism*. New York: Routledge, 2014.

———. *All About Love: New Visions*. New York: HarperCollins, 2000.

Hurston, Zora Neale. *Their Eyes Were Watching God*. New York: HarperCollins, 1937.

Jabali, Malaika. "Black Women Want The Statue Of This Famed Gynecologist TO Come Down For Good Reason." *Essence*, December 6, 2020. www.essence.com/news/j-marion-sims-statue-protest-experiment-black-women-slaves/.

Jackson, Zakiyyah Iman. *Becoming Human: Matter and Meaning in an Antiblack World*. New York: NYU Press, 2020.

Jacobs, Harriet. *Incidents in the Life of a Slave Girl*. Oxford: Oxford University Press, 2016.

Jezer-Morton, Katherine. "Why You'll Never Really Know Ballerina Farm." *The Cut*, August 1, 2024. www.thecut.com/article/ballerina-farm-hannah-neeleman-culture-war-response.html.

Jordan, June. *Directed by Desire: The Collected Poems of June Jordan*. Port Townsend, WA: Copper Canyon Press, 2012.

Kestenbaum, Richard. "The Beauty Business Keeps Growing but It's Missing a Huge Opportunity." *Forbes*, June 27, 2024. www.forbes.com/sites/richardkestenbaum/2024/06/27/the-beauty-business-keeps-growing-but-its-missing-a-huge-opportunity/.

Khalidi, Rashid. *The Hundred Years' War on Palestine: A History of Settler Colonialism and Resistance, 1917–2017*. New York: Metropolitan Books, 2020.

Kochhar, Rakesh, and Mohamad Moslimani. "Wealth Gaps across Racial and Ethnic Groups." Pew Research Center, December 4, 2023. www.pewresearch.org/2023/12/04/wealth-gaps-across-racial-and-ethnic-groups/.

Kotliuk, Galyna. "Gender on Stage: Drag Queens and Performative Femininity." *International Journal of European Studies* 7, no. 1(2023): 8–14. 10.11648/j.ijes.20230701.12.

Lorde, Audre. *The Cancer Journals*. London: Penguin UK, 2020.

Mills, Charles W. *The Racial Contract*. Ithaca, NY: Cornell University Press, 2014.

"The More Up Campus—Anarcha, Lucy & Betsey." Anarcha Lucy Betsey. Accessed April 18, 2025. www.anarchalucybetsey.org/.

Moynihan, Daniel P. *The Negro Family: The Case for National Action*. U.S.

Department of Labor, 1965. www.dol.gov/general/aboutdol/history/webid-moynihan.

"Murdered & Missing Indigenous Women." Native Womens Wilderness. Accessed December 23, 2024. https://www.nativewomenswilderness.org/mmiw

"Museum Finds Remains from a Victim of a Notorious 1980s Philadelphia Police Bombing." *AP News*, November 14, 2024. apnews.com/article/move-bombing-philadelphia-human-remains-penn-museum-cc10e504fb620fc0903165e92ecfb2e0.

Narins, Elizabeth. "A Serious Health Scare Helped Me Love My Body More than Ever." *Cosmopolitan*, April 10, 2017. https://www.yahoo.com/lifestyle/serious-health-scare-helped-love-170803726.html.

"On the First National Coming Out Day in 1988, *The Oprah Winfrey Show* Spent the Whole Hour Letting Lesbians and Gay Men Come Out to Family and Friends via . . ." Facebook video. Posted by *By Alternate Channels—LGBTQ Images on Television—Steven Capsuto*. Accessed April 17, 2025. www.facebook.com/alternatechannels/videos/on-the-first-national-coming-out-day-in-1988-the-oprah-winfrey-show-spent-the-wh/679668459671196/.

Oyěwùmí, Oyèrónkẹ́. *The Invention of Women: Making an African Sense of Western Gender Discourses*. Minneapolis: University of Minnesota Press, 1997.

Philpott, Tom. "White People Own 98 Percent of Rural Land. Young Black Farmers Want to Reclaim Their Share." *Mother Jones*, June 27, 2020. www.motherjones.com/food/2020/06/black-farmers-soul-fire-farm-reparations-african-legacy-agriculture/.

Pilkington, Ed. "New York Governor Said Black Kids in the Bronx Do Not Know the Word 'Computer.'" *The Guardian*, May 7, 2024. www.theguardian.com/us-news/article/2024/may/07/kathy-hochul-bronx-computer-comment.

Puente, Maria. "Twitter Accuses 'Cosmopolitan' of Pushing 'Cancer as a Diet' Plan." *USA Today*, April 11, 2017. www.usatoday.com/story/life/people/2017/04/11/twitter-accuses-cosmopolitan-pushing-cancer-diet-plan/100340022/.

"Radical Thought: Cedric J. Robinson," posted November 6, 2008, by University of California Television, YouTube, Series: Voices 3/2005, ID: 9301. www.youtube.com/watch?v=IK16BExR1KU.

Roberts, Dorothy. *Killing the Black Body: Race, Reproduction, and the Meaning of Liberty*. New York: Vintage Books, 2017.

Robinson, Cedric J. *Black Marxism, Revised and Updated Third Edition: The Making of the Black Radical Tradition*. Chapel Hill: University of North Carolina Press, 2020.

Salt-N-Pepa. "Shoop." By Mark.Sparks, Cheryl "Salt" James, and Sandra "Pepa" Denton. Next Plateau Records, 1993.

Schonfeld, Zach. "Remember That Time Bill Clinton Fired His Surgeon General for Encouraging Masturbation Education?" *Newsweek*, February 5, 2016. www.newsweek.com/remember-time-bill-clinton-fired-his-surgeon-general-encouraging-masturbation-423302.

Shakur, Assata. *Assata: An Autobiography*. London: Zed Books, 2016.

Shane, Cari. "The First Self-Proclaimed Drag Queen Was a Formerly Enslaved Man." *Smithsonian Magazine*, June 9, 2023. www.smithsonianmag.com/history/the-first-self-proclaimed-drag-queen-was-a-formerly-enslaved-man-180982311/.

SisterSong. "Reproductive Justice." Accessed April 18, 2025. www.sistersong.net/reproductive-justice.

Snorton, C. Riley. *Black on Both Sides: A Racial History of Trans Identity*. Minneapolis: University of Minnesota Press, 2017.

Somerville, Siobhan B. *Queering the Color Line: Race and the Invention of Homosexuality in American Culture*. Durham, NC: Duke University Press, 2000.

Spillers, Hortense J. *Black, White, and in Color: Essays on American Literature and Culture*. Chicago: University of Chicago Press, 2003.

Spillers, Hortense J. "Shades of Intimacy: What the Eighteenth Century Teaches Us." YouTube. Posted May 26, 2016, by Yale University. www.youtube.com/watch?v=10haBLXN1r0.

"Stop-and-Frisk Data." New York Civil Liberties Union, March 14, 2019. www.nyclu.org/data/stop-and-frisk-data.

Strings, Sabrina. *Fearing the Black Body: The Racial Origins of Fat Phobia*. New York: NYU Press, 2019.

"The Trevor Project—Suicide Prevention for LGBTQ+ Young People." The Trevor Project. Accessed June 1, 2023. www.thetrevorproject.org.

"2025 Anti-Trans Bills Tracker." Trans Legislation Tracker. Accessed April 18, 2025. translegislation.com.

Walter-Warner, Holden. "Chimamanda Ngozi Adichie Launches Blistering Attack on Former Student Who Name-Dropped Her in Book." *Daily Mail*, June 16, 2021. www.dailymail.co.uk/news/article-9694527/Chimamanda-Ngozi-Adichie-launches-blistering-attack-former-student-dropped-book.html.

Washington, Harriet A. *Medical Apartheid: The Dark History of Medical Experimentation on Black Americans from Colonial Times to the Present*. New York: Vintage, 2008.

Webb, Sarah L. "Colorism Healing." Accessed April 22, 2025. colorismhealing.com/author/sarah/.

Whitaker, Forest, director. *Waiting to Exhale*. Twentieth Century Fox, 1995.

Wittig, Monique. *The Straight Mind and Other Essays*. Boston: Beacon Press, 1992.

Woodard, Vincent. *The Delectable Negro: Human Consumption and Homoeroticism within US Slave Culture*. New York: NYU Press, 2014.

# Acknowledgments

Writing a book has quite frankly been the hardest thing I have ever done next to childbirth. Nothing is possible without community, and writing a book is no different. I want to thank Michelle Rodriguez, who has since transitioned from this realm, for believing in my dreams of becoming a sex educator and hiring me for my first job. The sex educators who have molded me, just to name a few:

Cindy Lee Alves
Zuri Pryor Graves
Cherisse "Redz" Staten
Dr. Tracie Gilbert
Jenna Emerson
Dr. Lynn Roberts
Dr. Erika Evans
Racha Tahani Lawler Queen
Chanel Porchia Albert
Sevonna Brown
Sonalee Rashatwar
Hilary Rae
Marla Renee
Kenneth "SymbaMcQueen" Solerios

Kiki Ballroom community
Mercy Graves

To my students, from elementary school to collegiate level, all of you have been the ultimate teachers.

To my family (my brothers Diego and Austin, who became live-in babysitters), Aunt Net, Elle Moxley, and Nzinga Dotson-Newman.

To my friends who have checked on me, lifted me up, picked me off the floor. I love you with every fiber of my being.

To Lydia Wills for believing in my work and being the first to urge me to write this book.

To Jen Marshall, my book agent, thank you for rocking with me, crying with me, and pushing me to bring this into the world. Margaux Weisman, thank you for helping me organize my thoughts in the final hour! To my editor, Chelcee Johns, for your indispensable and keen feedback—you are a gift (thank you for not firing me!).

To all the people who have supported me online, it is impossible to overstate my gratitude.

To Ebony, my partner in love and life, words can truly not express my deepest gratitude for holding me in the darkest times throughout this process, your encouragement via Post-it note reminders on every surface of our Brooklyn apt, to late nights and solo weeks with East so I could write, I am forever indebted to you. You have made me a better writer and human. I love you.

# Index

# About the Author

ERICKA HART (SHE/THEY) has been teaching comprehensive, trauma informed, consent and pleasure–based sex ed from an anti-racist, queer lens at the elementary, high school, undergraduate, and graduate levels for the past fourteen years. Her work began as a Health Educator with a community-based organization in East Harlem NYC and to date she has taught in all five boroughs and several states across the country. Currently, she runs her own highly acclaimed sexuality education training program, Sex Ed as Resistance, in addition to being an adjunct professor teaching human sexuality at Widener University, where she earned her Masters of Education in Human Sexuality. Ericka is also the co-host of the long-running independent podcast *Hoodrat to Headwrap* and a bratty switchy Sagittarius service bottom who misses Whitney more than you.